4-12-65   (63-14541)

They'd Rather
Be Right

They'd Rather Be Right

YOUTH AND THE CONSERVATIVE MOVEMENT

by EDWARD CAIN

THE MACMILLAN COMPANY, NEW YORK
COLLIER-MACMILLAN LIMITED, LONDON

First Printing

The Macmillan Company, New York
Collier-Macmillan Canada, Ltd., Toronto, Ontario

Printed in the United States of America
Library of Congress catalog card number: 63-14541

DESIGNED BY CHRISTIAN OHSER

To Margaret and Albert

Contents

CHAPTER I

The *"Liberal Establishment"*

To BE in the cultural swim in America today, one is expected to see plays by Tennessee Williams and Jack Gelber and to read plays by Jean Anouilh and Bertolt Brecht. You may read any novel that cannot be profitably condensed by *Reader's Digest* and hang any print sure to stop a game of animal, vegetable, or mineral. Your schooling will have stressed experimentalism and the rigors of a conditioning environment. Hence your morality is likely to be skeptical of absolutes, and permissive, and so is your religion.

This stereotype is a product of what conservatives have come to call the Liberal Establishment. To the alienated conservative, American arts, education, communications media, and even morality are determined by liberal values. While undoubtedly true of the arts and education, liberal domination of communications media and morality is debatable, and religion has weathered liberalism's siege. But to many conservatives, an irritating liberal domination has been established in all these areas.

1

A frontal assault has been mounted by a group of New Conservatives against the debilitating effects of this alleged behemoth of liberalism. One regrettable effect of such an attack is that the conservatives are sometimes seen as repudiating cultural sophistication per se. This is unfortunate, since many conservatives obviously appreciate Picasso, *avant-guard* literature, and are sophisticated aesthetically.

But to start at the beginning, given equal levels of intellect and sophistication, what makes one person liberal and the other conservative? Partly it is a matter of temperament. The conservative is skeptical of human nature and of any misplaced trust in it. Personally he is more apt to be reserved, stoic, and concerned about preserving the forms of social relations. He has a strong sense of limit or measure, and boasts an instinctive feeling for the fitness of things. Civility might be a word for this. In avoiding excess in personal or social relations, he may place an unusual stress on etiquette. Formality helps to minimize the friction of society. The conservative has usually benefited from society, and would like to preserve it as he has known it.

Because of his fondness for society, the conservative likes it nicely ordered. He looks for neatness and dependability in dress, the arts, and deportment. There is a strong sense of responsibility for maintaining decorum. Dropping a piece of Kleenex in the park is almost as reprehensible as applying for public welfare. Both acts demonstrate a paucity of responsibility. There are restless forebodings about innovations that appear to undermine individual responsibility for preserving society as it has been experienced and loved. Tremendous emphasis is placed on individual responsibility before God, society, and the economy.

The moderate liberal is not so precipitous as his more extreme cousin the radical, whom Chesterton once defined as a man who glows with the memory of tomorrow afternoon. However, the liberal is optimistic, and treats the risks of change lightly. His plans for society as it might be conflict with the conservative's sentiment for society as it is.

There is a restlessness about the liberal. Even if he is well situated in the present, he has a compulsion to rearrange it and an incurable curiosity about the possibilities of the future. A liberal is like a woman who can't decide where the furniture of earth looks best because she spends so much time trying to outguess the choirs of heaven.

Captivated by theories of environmentalism, the modern liberal is likely to become intoxicated with the idea that virtually any transformation can be brought about by manipulating and remolding society's institutions. The liberal's conceit in reason matches the conservative's conceit in society. Because of the liberal's penchant for change, he has less veneration for the forms of society but an immense respect for what he considers its substance: freedom.

In every area except the economic, and to a limited extent the political, the liberal wants a thoroughgoing laissez-faire policy. Only in economic terms can the conservative match the liberal's faith in the naturally curative effect of liberty, that in the long run the excesses of freedom will be overcome by its benefits.

There is a common meeting ground of the moderate conservative and liberal formed by a triangle of belief in freedom, individualism, and due process. But although these values are held in common, neither camp can usually agree how to define each of them or how they should be applied.

Most of the conservatives spell out freedom as a defense of the natural right of property. As Locke explained it, private property arises when a person mixes his individual capacity with something material. "Whatsoever then he removes out of the state that nature hath provided and left it in, he hath mixed his labor with, and joined to it something that is his own, and thereby makes it his property." According to Locke, civil society was brought into being primarily to protect these rights of property.

Liberals like to point out that Locke qualified his view of property by adding that it applied ". . . at least where there is enough and as good left in common for others." This would depend upon the evidence of time and circumstance. Rousseau's warning that property is the greatest source of inequality bothers the liberal and explains his fears of monopoly and economic privilege.

Many liberals are likely to go along with Hobbes's contention that "rights" of private property could not exist until the state came along and made them possible through law. If private property rights are dependent upon the state, then property rights may be redefined at the convenience of majority rule.

Thus private property emerges as a highly relative concept for the liberal, while the conservative considers it an absolute right, and probably the single most effective force to check ambitious political power.

The innovating potential of freedom is stressed by the liberal. He defines individualism primarily in terms of the intellectuals' freedoms of belief and expression. These are his absolutes, and he may pursue them to extremes that horrify the conservative. In economic terms, the conservative does see individualism as *the* innovating force. Otherwise, the conservative speaks of the "moral responsibility" of the individual, stressing his duties toward certain authorities: his religion, country, social institutions, and family.

Why does an American conservative feel such strong obligations to save for a rainy day and to come to the aid of his country, while he remains indifferent to censorship and sit-ins? The liberal might reply that this is because the conservative is preoccupied with form over substance. In defending censorship, the conservative is trying to protect the static forms of political orthodoxy, or perhaps sexual propriety, against the amorphous exuberance of free speculation. Sit-ins are resisted by conservatives who allow the formal rights of business law to obscure the substance of Christian love. If idolatry can be defined as elevating contingent forms into ultimate values, perhaps the conservative is limited by an idolatrous social ethic, while the liberal tends to underplay the necessity and utility of forms.

Both camps are firm champions of constitutionalism and the rule of law. But when the liberals use the Supreme Court to compel states to reapportion election districts, and the conservatives use the courts to enjoin Federal intervention in a steel strike, both sides yell foul. Liberals want more due process in civil liberties; the conservatives are looking for less arbitrariness in the administration of economic laws.

Part of the difficulty of moderate conservatives and liberals to come to more understanding is due to pressure from the extremes. The cool liberal, so proud of his rationalism, frequently gives in to the passionate embrace of the radical democrat to his left. The aphrodisiac is equality, and it easily turns the head of the liberal.

A native tradition stemming from Jacksonian democracy and Populism nourishes this radicalism. By insisting that a willing sentient human being is the basis of God's concern, the radical democrat ridiculed the necessity for any additional qualities for membership in American democracy. He worked for complete majority rule and a suffrage not shackled to any property or literacy test. The radical believed any honest red-blooded American was good enough to hold down public office, and campaigned for frequent rotation in office by means of the spoils system.

The liberal, on the other hand, favored a literacy test, longer tenure in office, and merit civil service. Use of the long "jungle ballot" exasperated the liberal, who preferred the rational efficiency of a short ballot and more executive appointments. When the radical democrats insisted on more direct democracy with even more referenda, recall, and initiative petitions, the liberals held out for representative democracy with more delegated powers.

The radicals were also more willing to experiment in the economic sphere, and some were easily tempted by the false equalitarian promises of Communism.

To the radical democrat, the liberal looks like an aristocrat in disguise. It's a case of La Follette, Norris, and perhaps Henry Wallace versus Wilson, Franklin Roosevelt, and Stevenson.

Each of these liberal positions regarding the political process could be endorsed by moderate conservatives, but fear of alienating radical democrats and being unfaithful to the ideal of equality obscures the liberal stand. They appear more radical than they are.

The liberals themselves find this a problem in foreign-policy determinations. Frequently they have to drag along their reluctant radical brothers who have never been enthusiastic internationalists (for example, La Follette) or who allowed their egalitarian passion to obscure their reason (Henry Wallace). Dean Acheson represented the cool liberal position. His anti-Communism was unquestionable, and he maintained his perspective. In temperament and policy, he should have attracted the moderate conservatives. Instead there were antagonism and misunderstanding. Why? Pressure from the far Right, perhaps.

If equality is the disruptive force from the Left, inequality is the problem on the Right. Here the emphasis is on what separates people. Inequality depends upon the recognition of order and authority, of the subordination of inferior to superior. There are several of these authorities vocalizing on the Right. Foremost is the voice of Racialism, whose invective is directed not only against nonwhites but also against those who are neither Anglo-Saxons nor Nordics. Whether violence or innuendo is employed, the message of privileged peoples is clear.

Religious fundamentalism is another force active on the Right. While all racialists are merchants of dissension, only some of the fundamentalists are. Suspicion of the techniques and motives of modern scholarship increases fundamentalists' isolation. Fundamentalists fear that they are losing strength within Protestantism and that Catholics may soon outnumber Protestants. This heightens their sense of heresy and apocalypse, which reinforces their parochialism and makes them especially receptive to a third major pressure from the Right: Americanism. People must be saved politically as well as religiously.

Americanism is also distrustful of the motives and techniques of modern scholarship, and is conceived in parochialism. A national is a citizen by birth or legal process. Nationalists say Americanism is the affirmation of "My country right or wrong." Americanism maintains that only certain citizens are qualified nationalists. Traditional nationalism tried to include all nationals. Americanism is exclusive. Nothing is taken for granted. The initiates must take an additional pledge to cultural and political orthodoxy. Not only must you be anti-Communist; you must also abstain from socialism, welfarism, centralism, deficit spending, legalized integration, radical agitation, and too much cultural sophistication.

Americanism is like adding a pair of faded, inelastic, tricolored galluses to the American's constitutional belt. They may make a folksy prop for patriotic orations, but they are superfluous, offer no support, and should make you feel a bit silly.

As defined by the American Legion and the House Committee on Un-American Activities, Americanism is incompatible with liberalism. Moderate conservatives should have trouble keeping a straight face, but far too many take it seriously. Americanism arbitrarily draws lines sharp enough to delineate patriot from subverter by indiscriminately invoking the plausible cry of national security. There is no shorter road to acceptance for the socially uncertain than to take the Americanist pledge and silence the complaints of the only people who were criticizing you in the first place, the Americanists.

Champions of the privileges of great economic inequality make another voice from the Right. These are the people F.D.R. used to call economic royalists, the heirs of 1936's Liberal League which did battle royal against the New Deal. They may represent old wealth (which is frequently liberal) longing for lost status or new wealth that exploits the technology of modern capitalism while ignoring its social consequences. Opposition to the income tax, to social security, foreign aid, and other contemporary necessities would be characteristic of this group. Their economic power makes them a pressure difficult for the moderates to ignore.

Because these voices of the far Right are louder than those of the moderates, conservatives are likely to be unfairly pictured in the far Right's image. Moderate conservatives are not escapist reactionaries longing for the past. They are content to borrow from the past in order to treat the present more realistically, and are convinced that more of the present could be salvaged for the future if the liberals would stop wearing it out by unnecessary experimentation.

"Conservatism," said Emerson, "makes no poetry, breathes no prayer, has no invention, it is all memory. Reform has no gratitude, no prudence, no husbandry. . . . each is a good half but an impossible whole."

This is to be a book dealing with the "impossible whole" of conservatism. It should be affirmed at the outset that few people are wholly conservative or liberal. Not very many people have worked out a world view of conservatism or liberalism comprehensive enough to cover their views on religion, economics, politics, and culture in general. Most of us exist in combination. Certainly we are all familiar with liberals having conservative personalities (Stevenson) and vice versa (Goody Knight).

Perhaps the only way to weather the conservative liberal controversy is to apply Charles Renouvier's advice on socialism: "Having laid down socialism as a principle, you must deny it in practice." Dogmatists may deplore this sentiment, but victories usually go to the camp with the greater powers of accommodation. At present a group called the New Conservatives (discussed in Chapter 2) claims that there have already been too many accommodations to the Liberal Establishment and that as a result our economy is dragging, our foreign policy is at an impasse, and our moral fiber is limp.

Cultural liberalism is as strong as ever. More reservations are heard about New Deal economics, but the real trouble is political. There is no denying that many Americans are disenchanted with liberalism in politics. When you stand on the beach it is difficult to tell whether the tide is coming in or going out, but if there is any wind you are certainly aware of plenty of commotion.

That's about where we are politically—in an impressive surf. Political labels now have about as much accuracy as Hollywood adjectives. Leaders and movements calling themselves conservative demand a foreign policy that ridicules diplomacy, scoffs at prudence as pusillanimity, and scorns compromise as retreat. Demands for moderation, measure, and sense of proportion in foreign affairs come from liberals who speak eloquently of a sense of history.

Some of the most imposing breakers have been stirred up by conservative criticism of the liberal's attitude toward Communism. But anti-Communism is not the "phony issue" some liberals make it out to be. It is a misleading one, and for the conservative it includes both fear of Russian power and dread of Fabian infiltrations. Failure of some conservatives to admit the double nature of their anti-Communism exasperates liberals and confuses the public, which can't understand why anyone would oppose anti-Communism. On the other hand, liberal failures to admit past transgressions and omissions exasperate conservatives.

Domestically moderate social reform falters because of a failure of liberalism to sell its case. Whether this is due to prosperity or a failure of liberal ideology is not clear and is frustrating. Politicians who merely ride tides are more confused than ever. All they seem certain of is that they are being wet by the spray of this surf created by the impact of conservatism's challenges against the Establishment.

New and popular conservative figures have appeared to storm the Establishment. They range from fierce casuists like Robert Welch and Billy James Hargis to amiable persuaders like Peter Viereck and Clinton Rossiter. More articles and books are being written about conservatism than ever before, and more people are reading them.

The American Library Association reported in 1961 that 27 percent of the librarians recorded a growing interest in conservatism. More than 50 percent of those reporting from the South and West commented on this interest. Slightly less than the national average was recorded in the Midwest.

Less than 10 percent in the East mentioned a conservative trend of reading. Indeed, much of this renewed interest is regional. The Birch Society is more popular in Santa Barbara, California, than in Welch's home town of Belmont, Massachusetts. One difficulty is that Belmont claims more resident professors than any town in America, but the East has generally been a poor recruiting ground for extreme Rightists. The Americanist territory of the Southwest oil wells has been especially rewarding. Besides producing tax-privileged oil wealth, this area has been a reservoir of brash frontiersmanship that has been interventionist in the past and is quick on the draw when sensing an affront.

The telling question is going to be, How many young people are disenchanted enough with liberalism to rebel? It is safe to say in advance that the cultural aspects of the Liberal Establishment are almost universally accepted by students. In the arts, education, and morality, it would be difficult to deny that the students are liberal (some qualifications will be made in Chapter 10). The conservative hope is that the young may be persuaded to the Right politically. However, the attack is on all fronts.

This book is an attempt to examine the origins and nature of the conservative response among young people. We are cutting off youth at Jack Benny's age, which is also the limit for Young Republicans. Since most of the ferment centers upon the campus, where the potential opinion formers are in training, much of this book will deal with student activities and interests.

Conservatism and the American Right

THE political terms Left and Right have been altered in translation from their European usage. These are essentially Continental terms conceived in the wake of the French Revolution. The Left stems from the radical second phase of the revolution. When Robespierre and the Jacobins in 1793 came out against the nobility of money as well as of birth, and Babeuf called for a second social revolution, middle-class supporters who had joined up for political reform saw the handwriting on the wall. The Republic was not to be merely "Freemasonry in the open."

Along with these rumblings of the proletariat and the class war soon urged by Louis Blanc, in the next generation there emerged a variety of utopian socialists like Saint-Simon and Fourier who hoped to achieve miracles of social reorganization through nonviolent persuasion. The speculative idealism of the utopians combined with the utilitarian realism of the Jacobins'

11

descendants to form the social-democratic movement, most of which was later to be captivated by revisionist Marxism.

Neither the workers' class consciousness nor a virulent anti-clerical secularism also characteristic of the Continental "Left" survived the North Atlantic crossing. When Americans adopted the radicalism of the French Revolution, they were more interested in the Rousseau that went into it than in the Louis Blanc that came out of it. Jefferson, Paine, and most American radicals were interested in applying Rousseau's theories of popular sovereignty and universal education. Privilege must be destroyed to make the suffrage universal and to ensure that political power never avoids popular control.

It turned out that the wealth of our economic resources postponed class conflict indefinitely and frustrated more than one economic dogmatist. Our religious heritage was English, and an amicable Lockean tolerance finally carried the day in that area. There was genteel freethinking and astounding religious improvisations but almost no harsh secularism. This helped raise the general level of tolerance in society.

The American Left is really a response to the first, or political, phase of the French Revolution, which called for reaffirmation and extension of political equality. This became institutionalized as radical direct democracy in the manner described in Chapter 1. The extension of social equality was more the prompting of our frontier than of Rousseau. Jacksonian democracy brought the partial marriage of political and social equality.

The watershed of Left-wing economic protest came in the presidential election of 1912 when Populism, Progressivism, the New Nationalism, and the New Freedom conspired against President Taft. All these movements were influenced by pressure from the Left. Rivulets from the watershed eventually reached their level in the New Deal, which in part strove for economic justice by providing for an equality of minimum needs. The Progressive's readiness to use Federal power to tackle the problems of the hour became a fixed part of twentieth century liberalism. Popular sovereignty was no longer measured by the radical standards of direct democracy. Limiting Congress to one-year terms was no longer so important as getting Congress to act.

When radical democrats felt the support of the Democratic Party, they listened more seriously to the liberalist center talk of executive responsibility and bureaucratic necessity.

The contemporary liberal may be described as a rationalist, generally optimistic about human nature, with an appreciative eye for innovation. The revolutionary tradition of the Left alerts him to tolerance of heterodoxy and a stewardship in civil liberties and civil rights. He means by economic equality, says J. S. Schapiro, not equal division of wealth, but the abolition of extremes of poverty through the "welfare state," which accepts social reform as a permanent responsibility and attempts to realize greater security and well-being for all its people and ultimately for the world.

The political Right in modern politics arose from a reaction to both phases of the French Revolution. As a counterrevolutionary force, it stressed the order and authorities uprooted by the revolution. De Maistre attacked the liberal presumption of the eighteenth century which "distrusted itself in nothing, hesitated at nothing," and he believed that man can not change for the better institutions already established. De Bonald contributed the idea that constitutions are born, not made, and that everything is from God; man has discovered or invented nothing.

Order centered around divinely appointed monarchs. "When God wanted to punish France," said De Bonald, "he took away the Bourbon from her gouvernance." They really meant business about vested interest. A king was God's lieutenant on earth, and was seen precisely as James I had pictured himself two hundred years before in England. "I am the Husband and the whole isle is my lawful wife, I am the Head and it is my body." James addressed these remarks to Parliament, and nobody laughed. Neither did nineteenth century French monarchists.

These counterrevolutionists especially feared that the impudent individualism unleashed by the revolution would shatter the organic bonds of society. Since the institutions of society were divinely appointed, only an irreverent hand would raise itself against them. To accept one's station in life and to fulfill the responsibilities and prerogatives of one's class were merely to accept destiny. Social dislocations and conflicts were accepted as natural rhythms of society. People were expected to sigh with Pope, "All discord [is] harmony not understood."

As a constitutional monarchist, Edmund Burke was not so alarmed over the beheading of a divinely appointed monarch as he was appalled at the prospect of knifing organic society. Behind the hierarchies of this privileged organic society lay the principle of inequality, the main target of the revolution, and an absolute necessity to Burke's social theory:

> Believe me, Sir, those who attempt to level, never equalize. In all societies . . . some description must be upper-most. The levelers therefore only change and pervert the natural order of things; they load the edifice of society, by setting up in the air what the solidity of the structure requires to be on the ground. . . .[1]

The nature of man is too intricate and the complexity of society too vast to attempt any radical or simple abstract rearrangement. "One sure symptom of an ill-conducted state," said Burke, "is the propensity of the people to resort to theories." One of the most demonic abstractions to plague society, Burke felt, was the principle of equality uncaged in the French Revolution. Egalitarianism threatened to disturb beyond repair "the intricate equilibrium of countless ages."

Although Burke did favor "reform with equity," any doubt was to be decided in favor of what had survived the alchemy of time. Whatever can not be presently understood should be venerated, said Burke. The traditions of society, including the tradition of property, have been "prescribed" by the practical wisdom of usage and convention and do not require the services of philosophical apologetics.

The distance between the privileges of aristocracy and the inelegance of commoners could be bridged only by an essentially romantic conception of society. "Burke," commented John Morley, "could cry about the plight of Marie Antoinette, but did not the protracted agony of the nation deserve the tribute of a tear?" Not if the agonies are necessary for the continuance of the

---

1. *Reflections on the Revolution in France*, Harvard Classics, Vol. 24, p. 197.

privileges. One man's agony may be another's harmony not understood.

Clericalism and authoritarianism, which pestered Continental politics, were not part of Burke's conservatism. A society engendered by religion, steeped in prudential traditions, and tried by history was arterial to his beliefs. Such a society was felt to be organic in the sense that an organism is composed of parts that have function and significance only in relation to other organs and in subservience to the life of the whole. Destroy an organ's relation to the whole and you kill its essential nature. Burke did not anticipate Hegel in applying this theory to the state, but it was an integral part of his theory of society. Essentially medieval in origin, this theory emphasizes the interdependence of estates, classes, stations, and individuals. If the responsibilities of privilege are honored, everybody's significance is appreciated. The object is to minimize alienation from community.

To be moral, said F. H. Bradley, I must will my station and its duties. A man, he continues, who does his work in the world is good, despite his faults, if his faults do not prevent him from fulfilling his station. This may be a stronger ethical consequence than Burke intended, but it is a consequent of the organic conception of society.

The political Right lost even more in American translation than the Left. Clericalism became a dead issue with the First Amendment. Even John Adams, the first American translator of conservatism, said, "I hope that Congress will never meddle with religion further than to say their own prayers. . . ." Not until the advent of twentieth century fundamentalism do we find a native version of clericalism on the Right.

All teeth were withdrawn from Right-wing authoritarianism. Except for a brief lapse with the Alien and Sedition Acts, the conservative Federalists showed no taste for authoritarianism. The sociological defense of the slave economy offered by George Fitzhugh might have led to a thoroughgoing regional authoritarianism. Instead the controversy produced Calhoun's elaborate theory of minority rights.

Antidemocratic thought in America never took political root. Most of the complaints about the debasing effects of democracy came from poets or professors. James Russell Lowell and Irving Babbitt were as much alarmed about plutocracy as they were about mobocracy. The social criticism of the latter-day Brothers Adams stressed the same twin themes.

When there was a brutal application of the Right's commitment to inequality, it erupted in the black freemasonry of the Know-Nothing movement or the Ku Klux Klan, which survive as social prejudices rather than political forces. As long as conservatives remain loyal to constitutionalism, which they boast of fathering, there can be no political authoritarianism on the American Right.

Except for a New England elite too austere to enjoy its prerogatives and a southern oligarchy too cavalier to husband its privileges, America has had no aristocracy. This has made it difficult for an organic theory of society to survive. In America, one's only duty to station is to improve it as rapidly as possible. With a few exceptions, class is determined by income rather than tradition, and most of the exceptions are made merely to honor the difference between income and wealth. With an open-ended society exalting individualism, self-reliance, experimentation, and change, there was not much of an audience for the "misunderstood harmonies" of privilege or the reciprocity of duties. Roman Catholic circles pay deference to the organic society, but they are joined by only a small group of academicians and Platonic intellectuals.

When you neutralize organic society, take away aristocracy and an established church, about all that remains of the British Right is a tradition of Hobbesian realism and strong state action, neither of which especially interested the Americans. The present Marquess of Salisbury must have completely baffled American conservatives when he said that the conservative ideal is neither capitalist nor socialist; it is precapitalist. The phrase "Tory socialism" connotes a pragmatic, nondoctrinaire readiness of conservatives to accept new social measures if they are really inevitable.

With virtually no European conservative legacy to build upon except a vague preference for tradition over change, American conservatives had to improvise. The Constitution had established a liberal-conservative compromise on the political process. Except for a conservative rearguard action defending property qualifications for suffrage, political questions were usually resolved by the ins and outs of political office.

Variations on the Burkean theme of organic society were attempted by John Adams, Calhoun, Irving Babbitt, Ralph Cram, and others. But Burke's social style was based upon the existence of an aristocracy that had doggedly nurtured a paternalism, hauteur, and unique accommodation to the upper middle class almost impossible to imitate. Burkean transplants to America were dissolved into a philosophy of humanistic discipline or puritanical order. As Arthur Schlesinger, Jr., put it: "An odd and often contradictory collection of figures has to be pressed somewhat desperately into service: John C. Calhoun, great theorist of slavery and states' rights, and John Q. Adams, apostle of abolition and nationalism . . . Irving Babbitt, the Archbishop of the Genteel Tradition, and George Santayana, its urbane and devastating critic. . . ."[2]

A theory of strong central government was propagated by Hamilton and Madison, only to go into eclipse when the Federalists went out of power. Webster revived it again to defend the superiority of federal prerogative against the claims of states' rights of another conservative, John Calhoun. In each case, circumstance rather than theory determined policy.

At least five prominent conservatives—John Adams, Hamilton, Madison, Webster, and Calhoun—agreed on one thing: the reality of class conflict. If there was to be no aristocracy, social or natural, conservatives were at least determined to defend middle-class privileges. A stout defense was improvised by drawing upon theories of economic liberalism.

Out went Burke's idea of community solidarity and in came Bentham's utilitarian society of individuals each pursuing his own interest. This atomistic society that seeks to maximize pleasure and minimize pain could do only the opposite for the traditionalist conservative. All of the classical economists, including Smith, Ricardo, Malthus, and James Mill, were taken into the conservative lodge. By 1867 Edwin Godkin was writing in the *Nation* that

2. A. Schlesinger, "The New Conservatism in America," *Confluence*, December, 1953.

laissez-faire was the only economic theory fit for a free society and that there was no adequate ethical case against it. Sociologist William Sumner, importing Spencer's "survival of the fittest" doctrine, agreed. To favor the survival of the unfittest, said Sumner, is to destroy liberty.

No heed was paid to John Stuart Mill's conversion to "qualified socialism" in his autobiography published in 1873. There was no further laissez-faire in liberalism after J. S. Mill except for Herbert Spencer. The 1870's saw the advent of T. H. Green and the Oxford Idealists who added a religious element to utilitarianism, defined the self as a social self, and spoke of a continuous reciprocity between law and morals. Legal coercion, said Green, may offset and neutralize other forms of coercion that are less tolerable. The rights of property, wrote Hobhouse, cannot be considered as axiomatic. Latter-day liberals were continually correcting and enlarging the meaning of liberalism.

With its emphasis on social responsibility, mutuality, the accommodation of all interests, religious sensitivity, and the necessity of state action, the new liberalism was closer to the traditionalist organic conservative position than were the conservatives who had embraced the laissez-faire philosophy.

Those who refuse to admit that liberalism could outgrow its laissez-faire stage we today call conservatives. A few agrarians and traditionalists are an exception to this. The far Right in America represents those who are irreconcilably opposed to compromising on the principle of economic laissez faire. Since inequality is the talisman of the Right and laissez faire is the ultimate in economic inequality, this is understandable.

The conservative is not defending laissez faire merely for economic self-interest. He applies to economics what Jefferson said to Du Pont de Nemours about political democracy: "We both love the people, but you love them as infants, whom you are afraid to trust without nurses; and I as adults whom I freely leave to self-government." If they are paying attention to their traditionalist mentors, conservatives know how fallible and perverse human beings are. They do not expect miracles from the uninhibited entrepreneur, but they do feel that over the distance of time, less damage will be done if you trust the economy to the trained instinct and quick reflexes of private individuals.

For one thing, individuals are in a position to be more flexible if wrong. Even if you turn off the bureaucratic machine, it inflicts unnecessary damage just slowing down. This tragicomic prospect would never occur if entrepreneurs were treated as adults. There is danger of failure either way, but the damage is less universal and can be more readily contained if it is privately administered. Profit and loss are balanced quicker and sooner than election returns. A few corporate bankruptcies here and there are better than paralyzing an industry by cutting a wrong nerve in Washington, however nobly inspired the surgery.

Only a doctrinaire liberal overpressured from the Left could dismiss this argument. It must be seriously considered as each economic issue is deliberated, otherwise we shall have relinquished our claim to capitalism or common sense. But the far Right insists on resolving each issue dogmatically rather than empirically, and thus matches the far-Left's reflex reaction.

The outstanding problem of authoritarianism on the contemporary far Right is Americanism, which alleges a veneration of the Constitution but not its Amendments (except the Tenth). Believing order is always more important than freedom, it comes to quick conclusions about national security by means of erratic logic. Essentially an anti-intellectual force, Americanism especially distrusts the social scientist. Jingoism is equated with patriotism. Varying with region and class, you will find ethnic, racial, and religious prejudice added to the malaise.

Insofar as he successfully resists the pressures of the far Right, an American conservative may be defined as one who has a highly developed sense of limit and order in social and political life. Skeptical of human nature, and certain of man's presumptuousness, the conservative does not generate reform, but he can accommodate to it. Although more literal than the liberal, the conservative is prone to prefer comfortable instinct to unfamiliar logic. The vast majority of conservatives have merged with laissez-faire economic theory, and hence claim to be "true liberals."

To the traditionalist conservative "true liberalism" is a vice, not a virtue, and reflects the atomistic individualism and skepticism of Bentham and Co. Some recent American scholars, known as "New Conservatives," reflect this Burkean, or traditionalist, distaste for excessive individualism. Included in this group might be August Heckscher, Robert Nisbit, Thomas Cook, Milton Hindus, John Hallowell, Clinton Rossiter, Peter Viereck, Russell Kirk, and Chad Walsh. However, the term "New Conservative" must be used with caution. Since Peter Viereck suggested the above names in 1956, the New Conservative movement has assumed a more "libertarian" line. Those centering around William Buckley's *National Review* have acquired an un-Burkean reputation for imprudence, among other heresies.

High in the good regard of most New Conservatives is Russell Kirk who represents the latest and most popular attempt to breathe life into the forlorn myth of Burkean influence. Kirk makes it clear that he distrusts intellectuals (a Marxian term, he says).

According to Kirk, an intellectual, unlike a scholar, is too conceited about his own "notion" and not humble enough before the mystery of the universe. Given the invective Kirk reserves for liberals and the "confidence" of his own beliefs, this seems an ungracious beginning for his *Prospects for Conservatives*. Love, says Kirk, is the object of human life, and he closes Chapter One by saying that enlightened conservatives know with Burke that "they will never love where they ought to love, who do not hate where they ought to hate." This is the sentiment of Polemarchus in Plato's *Republic*, but hardly of Jesus in the New Testament.

At least Mr. Kirk puts his cards on the table. The penultimate paragraph of *Prospects* runs: "The grand question before us is really this: Is life worth living? Are men and women to live as human persons formed in God's image . . . , or are they to become creatures less than human herded by the masters of the total state, debauched by the indulgence of every appetite, deprived of the consolations of religion and tradition and learning and the sense of continuity, drenched in propaganda, aimless amusements and the flood of sensual triviality which is supplanting the private reason?"[3]

Essentially a social prophet, Kirk addresses himself primarily

3. R. Kirk, *Prospects for Conservatives*, Gateway edition, Regnery, 1956, p. 3.

to our cultural malaise: problems of the heart, boredom, wants, loyalty, tradition, lack of confidence in "qualified classes," and so on. In politics he questions the justice of universal suffrage, distrusts the executive and bureaucracy, condemns social security and school lunches, and appears to be oblivious to political parties and pressure groups.

Kirk's diatribe against the ideologue becomes amusing when you consider his preference for the economics of Wilhelm Röpke, whose distributionism calls for an agricultural way of life, decentralization of industry, smaller factories, preserving shopkeepers and a system of domestic economy in which workers supplement their incomes with vegetable gardens.[4]

Except for the faithful, Kirk's audience seems to reflect the inattention and disbelief rendered a Cassandra. Among the faithful young conservatives are the college-educated "gentlemen" upon whom Kirk places so much hope and for whom Kirk is such a hero.

To do Russell Kirk and his colleagues justice, it is only fair to spend more time examining specific concepts that most conservatives still agree upon as expressing their ideology.

Conservatism will be considered as an autonomous system of ideas, an ideology generally held to be valid for all time. Historically the word "conservative" came into use during the Restoration period after the French Revolution. Ironically, "conservative" is more recent in usage than the word "liberal." Chateaubriand has been credited with first using the word in its current meaning in his periodical *The Conservative*.[5]

Philip Chapman also speaks of the "relational" sense of the word: "Any ideology which is conservative in the relational sense of the word will cease to be such and will become radical [that is, reactionary] once the institutions it has supported pass from the historical stage. . . . In this relational sense, 'conservative' is an adjective. . . ."[6] If you get involved in this line-up game, Ken-

4. *Ibid.*, pp. 169, 153, 207, 190, 185. For a critique of Kirk, see M. Auerbach, *The Conservative Illusion*, Columbia, 1959.

5. Karl Mannheim, *Essays on Sociology and Social Psychology*, Oxford, 1953, p. 98.

6. "The New Conservatism," *Political Science Quarterly*, March, 1960.

nedy liberals become conservatives because they are defending the existing New Deal, and conservatives become radicals because they are challenging it. This may be true, but it's confusing.

Both liberalism and conservatism have defensive and aggressive postures. Far too much confusion is bred by defining either strictly in a "situational" or "relational" sense. Sometimes conservatives like the status quo and sometimes not. Few are out defending the existing New Deal tax structure. The only way to avoid this confusion of "Who's on first?" is to consider conservatism as an autonomous body of beliefs that are believed to be true regardless of who is in the White House and whose status is quo.

One of the keystones of conservative belief is its view of man. Virtually all conservatives accept the orthodox Christian view of man as a fallen creature. Socrates was dead wrong. Men do not commit evil actions only because they were not fully cognizant of the consequences. They can be evil and know full well what they are doing. Ever since Adam could not withstand the temptation to be *as* God and not merely to walk *with* God, man has been destined to a will not always responsive to reason and a presumptuous Adam's pride that is always his own undoing. Man's one hope to be made whole again is to have restored that element of grace lost in Eden. As man contains his pride and watches for God, his chances improve.

Given such limitations in man, conservatives feel it is bumptious and foolhardy for any variety of social engineer to think he can remold people into any neat plan of action. Marxian socialism has compounded the error by suggesting that no consideration of God is necessary. As Dostoevski put it, socialists turned the problem of God inside out. But liberals are just as bad in trying to spin elaborate social controls. The sensible thing to do is to benefit from human pride and aggressiveness in a free-enterprise system. If you can't beat it, join it. An awareness of man's natural limitations gives you an invaluable social and political realism.

Two reservations must be made about this view. First of all, the present major American expositor of the thoroughgoing Augustinian view of fallen man, free of any trace of Thomistic Pelagianism, is Reinhold Niebuhr, former socialist and co-founder of Americans for Democratic Action. Niebuhr and his neo-orthodox co-believers have produced some of the best liberal political criticism of our day. They believe the Christian Church must bear witness against every form of pride and vainglory. (Nor are Catholics less orthodox for being political and social liberals.)

Secondly, conservatives like Kirk imply that modern liberals are about as utopian as those of the eighteenth century. M. Morton Auerbach suggests that it has been a long time since liberals have believed in the "natural goodness of man."

Even more puzzling is conservative application of this belief to policy. Take price controls. We don't need them, said the conservatives. A free mechanism will automatically hold down prices. Nonsense, said the liberals; people are too weak and self-centered; you need a law. In almost every major piece of social and economic legislation, it has been the liberals who have been most skeptical of human nature. The conservatives have been the utopians.

Reason is venerated by most conservatives and generally offered as one of their virtues. Certainly the conservatives can claim distinguished men of intellect. Men such as Richard Weaver, Leo Strauss, Eric Voegelin, John Hallowell, F. A. von Hayek, Peter Viereck, and others prove that today's conservatives can be men of distinguished mind. But what do you do with someone like Russell Kirk when he says of the Kinsey Report, "This prurient inquisitiveness turns the hearts of a generation to stone"?[7] Or Frank S. Meyer when he condemns liberalism because it "prefers psychoanalysis to the dark night of the soul . . . admires experts and fears prophets. . . ."?[8]

Kirk likes to write eloquently about showing more deference to nonrational factors. He wants a society with "more heart." David Riesman is criticized for being "all head and no heart." Kirk allows himself to get sentimental about the nonrational but not scientific. Whether prudery or poetry soured Kirk on Kinsey, you are left with the impression that Montesquieu is the last word in sociologists.

7. *Op. cit.*, p. 15.
8. "Freedom, Tradition, Conservatism," Intercollegiate Society of Individualists pamphlet.

Meyer's preference for "dark nights" to psychoanalysis is disturbing evidence of how gun-shy some conservatives can be of new ideas. In this instance he appears to be repudiating one of the most exciting and profound modern adventures of the mind. The preference for prophets to experts shows a lamentable reluctance of some conservatives to apply reason to pratical problems and to honor the expert for seeking this application in all areas of life. A pronounced failure of most conservatives to enter or even exploit the behavioral sciences is a sign of their questionable utilization of reason for anything beyond deductive rhetoric. This, of course, is not true of moderate conservatives like Clinton Rossiter and John Hallowell, who are not suspicious of the scientific method and will deal with truths in lower case.

The conservatives use Reason in connection with a demand for more deductive absolutes. Truth and Virtue are being scorned. We need fixed standards. Liberalism is carrying us into a fatal quagmire of relativism. Fixed absolute standards give assurance and dependable guidance. Without them life is an undisciplined indulgence. Religion, morality, and art demand the certainty of absolute concepts. The task of conservatism is to remind people of these values and to explain them in contemporary terms, to demonstrate their continuity and universality.

Two dangers await the conservative in this endeavor. In dutifully etching his morality in ink drawings, the conservative is likely to become overliteral, given the clear choice of alternatives he has drawn. He is then tempted to make absolute judgments about his absolute values. This is indulging in original sin. Adam's unpardonable sin was to presume that he, like God, could partake of the Tree of Knowledge, that he, like God, could distinguish absolute right from absolute wrong. God made it quite clear that He was to have the last word and that all our judgments were to be contingent and relative. No definite decision could be absolute. The more dogmatic New Conservatives and Communists both share a confidence in their absolute judgments, and make politics—"the art of compromise"—more troublesome than ever.

This would not be true of a conservative like Peter Viereck who speaks of the art of the second best when the best is historically impossible, but Viereck's prudence is not in harmony with the current New Conservatism.

The other danger is that conservatives may stop moralizing too soon. Their absolutism might convice them that no judgment should be made unless one's own hands are clean. Judgment should be made only from a "pure" or untainted position. Such moral absolutism led Senator Taft to condemn the Nuremberg Trials, many Northern conservatives to condemn the Supreme Court decision on segregation, and New Conservatives to denounce the United Nations. In such ways, moral absolutism obscures and may prevent relative justice.

This absolutism runs counter to the Burkean principle of prudence. Looking at the present through the perspective of history and tradition, the conservative claims a detachment, sense of timing, and restraint denied the more impetuous liberal. In his Speech on American Taxation, Burke said it was important not to make the tax revisions too clear. He also cautioned against making the choice of American freedom versus Parliament's sovereignty too sharp. Reconciliation and compromise were urged for the American, Irish, and Indian crises.

Except for his attitude toward the French Revolution, where, as Auerbach puts it, his ideology went into a tailspin from which it never recovered, Burke's moderate conservatism continually urged policies of prudence. Peter Viereck has faithfully applied this concept, and speaks of politics as a gray rather than black or white area. But most of the New Conservatives have ignored prudence in domestic (where the New Deal is perhaps the essence of prudence) and especially foreign affairs. Today's conservatives appear to want to take on the Communists in an extralegal "rumble," avoiding responsible authorities.

Domestically their suggested economic "reforms" often range from the radical to the revolutionary. Silence in the face of abridgments of civil liberties can not be construed as prudence. Conservatives may exasperate liberals by calling for more intricate political timing, but they can not eviscerate their principles in the name of prudence.

Frequently conservatives will claim that liberals are too involved in "abstract" principles, that they carry these abstractions to an extreme and are stubbornly doctrinaire. They will cite as an example an excessive liberal attachment to equality and the consequent abuses of mediocrity and unlimited majority rule. Or conservatives will point to an undisciplined fondness for freedom and the license that results as an illustration of the liberal's unfortunate penchant for getting into trouble because he has carried theory too far.

The conservative likes to believe that he is better grounded in common sense and does not allow theory to obscure the facts. Pragmatism is extolled when the enemy's theory approaches, and repudiated when "eternal verities" appear to be jeopardized.

Conservative clichés are recklessly abstracted. No radicals or liberals are among the Founding Fathers. The Constitution is assumed to be in a literal vacuum immune to Court, congressional or presidential alterations. "Socialism" can be found creeping to your left or right, and "freedom" is seldom spelled out in lower case.

Unfortunately for the conservatives, the only theorist systematically to unite theory and practice, before Marx got his hands on it, was Hegel. And there is not a vocal Hegelian among practicing conservatives. Until conservatives master something equivalent to Hegel's "concrete universal," it is most unbecoming for them to cast stones at "liberal abstractions." The theoretical and the practical will have to continue in uneasy and obscure correspondence.

The major charges of irrationalism and obscurantism against the conservatives probably came because of the stress they give tradition. "Prescription, or tradition," says Kirk, "is the means by which this healthy society preserves the wisdom of our ancestors and applies that wisdom to the new problems which it faces."[9] What ancestors? Tom Paine, Andrew Jackson, Albert Brisbane, Edward Bellamy, Eugene Debs, Lester Ward, and Thorstein Veblen all have pieces of wisdom to offer our time. Faced with such ancestors, Kirk might claim to be a foundling.

In reciting the "Credo of an Old-Fashioned Conservative," George B. Cutten said, "Nature is not only his mother but his

9. *Op. cit.*, p. 264.

teacher—slow but sure—when she finally lets go of any vestigial organ, you can be sure it is outdated."[10]

The problem is that men have to assume the role of Mother Nature. Without the matriarch's fiat, there is violent disagreement over when something has become outdated. Then there is the question of competing traditions. The tradition of revolt is older than that of the state. Class warfare, equalitarianism, nonconformity, and disrespect for authority have deep roots and hoary traditions that must be reckoned with.

"Any tradition," says Gordon Lewis, "is a limited apprehension of a social truth that must be validated in terms of the social groups that they serve and the historical periods within which they flourish".[11] Tradition as such is merely an indication that something has survived. Conservatives tend to give too much credit to endurance per se, and refuse equal consideration to innovation.

A refreshing breeze was blown over the problem of tradition by W. H. Auden in "The Dyer's Hand," where he suggests that technological society, by putting at our immediate disposal the arts of all ages and cultures, has completely changed the meaning of the word "tradition." It now means a consciousness of the whole of the past of all societies—with their infinite ways and values—*as present.*[12] On a less sophisticated plane, the major distinction between liberals and conservatives on this issue is that conservatives will more often give the edge to tradition over innovation. Reactionaries will prefer tradition every time, with predictable nostalgia.

How does fallen man with his prudent eye on absolute verities and sustained by concrete traditions hope to change society? Well, confides the conservative, this isn't exactly the idea. The plan is to regenerate men. The conservative, says Kirk, is inclined to look for the real causes of our troubles in the heart of man. The liberals are putting the cart before the horse in trying

10. "Credo of an Old-Fashioned Conservative," *American Mercury,* November, 1942.

11. "The Metaphysics of Conservatism," *Western Political Quarterly,* December, 1953.

12. Cited in W. Carlton, "American Intellectuals and American Democracy," *Antioch Review,* Summer, 1959.

to reform society first. Clarence Darrow's arguments for the defense in the Leopold-Loeb case dramatized the conservative's fear that modern behavioral studies would suffocate individual responsibility. The trial focused on the problem of individual guilt but raised the whole issue of individual versus social responsibility.

The Protestant nonconformist base of American conservatism rallied against any theory that might explain away individual guilt or lessen the awesomeness of the individual's responsibility to God and country. This responsibility should be tangible and direct. Children must be disciplined in God and law in the home. Private charity is preferred to governmental action. The individual should never shirk duties. The voluntary way is always preferable to the compulsory resolution of a problem.

An intense individualism convinced the conservative that not only religious but social salvation must start in a person's heart. The only regeneration is personal. Any social scheme that promises reform through reorganizing society is vain boasting. "The Conservative," says Auerbach, "cannot accept the thesis that changes in individual morality are caused by changes in societal relations, without destroying his whole ideology. . . . Conservatives must, therefore, assert that, far from being an effect of history, inner moral change is the first cause of each historical change".[13]

Short of falling back upon chance or the intervention of God, conservatives, claims Auerbach, are without a rational explanation of change. A social-moral system can resist change or it can adjust to it, admits Auerbach, but there is no evidence that it initiates change. This is conservatism's greatest illusion. William Newman attacks at the same point in his *The Futilitarian Society*. "By using change at best as a means of killing change, conservatism aims to do away with it, [but] . . . freedom, change and innovation are all bound together: one does not exist without the other."[14] Samuel Huntington aims a *coup de grâce*. "Conservatism is not just the absence of change. It is the articulate, systematic and theoretical resistance to change."

Conservatives may be moved to claim that Huntington's in-

13. *The Conservative Illusion*, p. 289.
14. *The Futilitarian Society*, Braziller, 1961, p. 38.

dictment is too sweeping and that Auerbach's views are overly environmentalist, but they have to refute these charges in terms of political theory, and not merely of rhetoric. Failure to do this leaves American conservatism open to being called a futile illusion on the vulnerable question of change.

Emphasis on moral as opposed to social regeneration does not mean that conservatives are without a strong sense of community. On the contrary, Russell Kirk says enlightened conservatives have always stood for "true community, the union of men, through love and common interest for the common welfare." He wants to see the economy humanized; but don't look for help from the unions. (He has compared the UAW to a totalitarian state.) "The friends of industrial management, indeed, show more concern for the idea of community."[15]

Kirk does want to deemphasize the economic element and heighten the sense of association in family, profession, church, neighborhood, and local government. Local and prescriptive political methods are singled out as the essence of a free society, and we are warned against the state's consolidation of power. Of course, this sense of community is no conservative monopoly. Radical followers of Owen or Fourier had an even stronger sense of community; and as Gordon Lewis has pointed out, a "sense of local citizenship" is central to the creeds of both syndicalism and guild socialism.

This current conservative penchant for decentralized power has curious origins. Back in the running debate between Burke and Paine, Burke had maintained that the divine ordering of society could not be challenged by any claim of natural rights against it. It is easy to see the manifold problems of trying to package Burke for the American market. Kirk is trying to use Burke's theory of decentralized aristocracy (Burke was fighting the central government, too), currently marketed as "localism" or "states' rights," to fend off the claims of today's petitioners for natural rights—whether they be for economic security, civil rights, or civil liberties (speech, association, and so on).

The liberterian conservative's emphasis on moral regeneration leads him to a limited view of power. He is preoccupied with the

15. *Op. cit.,* pp. 129, 145.

origin of power. Does it come from me or some source outside? Outside sources of power are automatically suspect, regardless of what they might be trying to accomplish. For example, integration is bad because it is coercing me into acceptance of the Negro. This I must do on my own. All right. When? "It is not compulsion which is unjust," says Paul Tillich, "but a compulsion which destroys the object of compulsion [one's freedom] instead of working toward its fulfilment."[16]

The conservative's war against centralized government has erupted into the slogan "This is a republic, not a democracy. Let's keep it that way." Until the Post Office Department objected, this slogan was metered upon the mail of the John Birch Society. Mr. Day has since asked private meter manufacturers not to imprint any ideological slogans because the public might think it is government policy. This alleged distinction between democracy and republic has been a parlor game of the Right for some time.

In 1946 Drew Pearson received a letter from Attorney Adamson of the House Committee on Un-American Activities that said, "Several people have called to my attention the closing line of your Sunday night broadcast, 'make democracy work.' I should like very much to have your definition of the word 'democracy,' as you are using it over the radio. If you will be good enough to supply the information, I will give the matter further consideration to determine whether it should be called to the attention of the members of the committee for such action as they deem proper."[17] Pearson suggested warming up a padded cell for Attorney Ernie Adamson.

Robert Welch has a pamphlet, "Republics and Democracy," whose theme is how to make the world safe *from* democracies. William Kullgren in *Beacon Light Herald* insists that "democracy" characterizes our form of government, "a crazy demon. . . . Unfortunately in America we have a democracy since the communists are in power, but we have no use for it".[18]

16. *Love, Power and Justice*, Oxford, 1960, p. 67.
17. Cited in D. Wesley, "Hate Groups and the Un-American Activities Committee," Emergency Civil Liberties Committee.
18. *Beacon Light Herald*, August, 1951.

The idea is that a republic is a limited government of laws, whereas a democracy is an unlimited government of men where everything is fair game. Limited government is implicit in the etymology of the word only to the extent that *res publica* means public things as opposed to private things. Some affairs are to be private and others public, with an appropriate body of law for each area. This distinction was a great contribution of Roman law, since it did not exist for the Greeks. The denotation of the word gives us the realm of private versus public law. Within this public realm, the connotation of the word "republic" implies that representatives elected by, and responsible to, the people shall exercise power. The connotation of the word makes it clear that the people should have the last word, that is, be sovereign. This is democracy, which is merely a Greek word—*demos* (people) plus *kratos* (authority)—for the same thing.

The only conceivable difference is that the denotation of the Latin word does imply private versus public areas, but historically this has meant almost nothing. The Latin word for republic has been used (most of our political terms are from the Latin) to denote the absence of a king (but not always). It has described a motley collection of governments. Machiavelli was a republican. Perón, Hitler, and Stalin all ruled republics. Each South American dictator has one.

With the disappearance of kings, the antimonarchical term "republic" lost much of its impact. The question then became how much rational freedom does an ideal republic enjoy. This is measured by the Rule of Law: laws must be universal, equal, and rational. Here is what the conservative thinks he is talking about when he uses the word "republic." But the Rule of Law can work within any of the three basic forms of government: monarchy, oligarchy, or democracy.

Republic is a negative term telling you what the government is not. Democracy is a positive, more inclusive term, with social implications that the ultraconservative fears. When he speaks of democracy he caricatures it as direct mob rule, whereas virtually every responsible democrat today believes in indirect representative democracy, which is what we have in the United States Constitution. Liberals have no objection to the use of the negative term "republic," as long as it is not used to supplant the positive term "democracy" whose meaning is still kneaded in modern politics.

The conservative hopes to get less government by using the word "republic." It would be far less confusing if he would merely say so and drop the word game.

Real confusion erupts when you consider that there are two schools of conservatives contending for the title. The difficulty goes back to Burke who believed it was possible to include the emerging economic liberal (eighteenth century capitalists) within the traditional aristocratic ethic. But the liberal capitalist believed man and business were essentially good, and capable of infinite expansion. He preferred "imprudent" revolutionary changes to the tranquillity of tradition. Harmony has always been a pivotal value of conservatism. As Auerbach points out, this involves a minimization of desires, whereas capitalism maximizes desires, strives for a consumer-oriented utility, and encourages breaking away from one's station in life . . . all of which leads to the cacophony of the marketplace.

These entrepreneurs became the nineteenth century liberals, or Manchester liberals. Their liberalism specifically meant freedom of enterprise and property, and they were generally conservative in other directions. In America, where there was no traditionalist force to oppose them, these men were the conservatives. Today they prefer to call themselves "real" liberals, or libertarians. Since their use of the word "liberty" refers almost exclusively to property, it would be helpful if we had some other word, such as "propertarian," to describe them.

Traditional conservatives, those who endorse most of the dozen concepts discussed above, have carried on relentless warfare against the bumptious libertarians. Mostly men of letters, the traditionalists are primarily social critics who accuse the irreverent libertarians of dehumanizing society and of being vulgar materialists.

The Southern Agrarians, who roughly came in and went out with the 1930 depression, represent one form of traditionalist protest. Herbert Agar, Allen Tate, and Robert Penn Warren were leaders. Agar wrote that the United States had lost her moral purpose and become the victim of economic determinism. He felt the monopolist and exploiting element of capitalism had prevented a wide distribution of property, and quoted Chesterton: "'A pickpocket is obviously a champion of private enterprise. But it would perhaps be an exaggeration to say that a pickpocket is a champion of private property.'"[19] Agar feared we had become an unscrupulous plutocracy, and hoped that the New Deal would help remedy things by controlling credit.

Religious lapses, moral deterioration, educational adulteration, and cultural vulgarity are frequent themes of the traditionalists, who range from the moderate Peter Viereck to the quasi-reactionary Russell Kirk. Libertarians or propertarians are busy defending the economic flank, and have little time or interest for anything else. They are keeping a beady eye on creeping socialism, galloping debt, gamboling welfarism, and marauding statism of every description.

The traditionalist generally does not share the propertarian's enthusiasm for laissez-faire economics, huckstering, sloganeering, pressure-group activities, or bombastic foreign policy. While more alienated in a cultural sense from the mass of society and liberalism, they are frequently more adjusted politically: for example, the endorsement of Adlai Stevenson by Viereck, Rossiter, and Lippmann, and their support of the United Nations.

With the exception of the economists von Hayek and Ludwig Von Mises, virtually all of the conservatives heavyweights are traditionalists. The libertarians or propertarians abound in frisky lightweights. Most of them are publicists: David Lawrence, Eugene Lyons, James Burnham, William Buckley, and so on, and grand standing umpires like Westbrook Pegler and Fulton Lewis, Jr.

The "New Conservatives" centering around *National Review* have recruited only one recognized political theorist, Willmoore Kendall, and he has been around for some time. A few, such as Russell Kirk, Will Herberg, and Richard Weaver, are traditionalists. But most of the New Conservatives are libertarian or some comfortable composite. Uninhibited by traditionalist reservations, they are gleefully sailing full jib on a sea of controversy.

19. "The Task for Conservatism," *American Review*, April, 1934.

What sort of political theory does this leave them? Philip Chapman insists that the New Conservatives are not fundamentally interested in political theory, and seldom address its categories, which are discussed only fragmentarily if at all. The nature and responsibilities of political authority and the rights and obligations of citizens never get beyond the one-dimensional stage. Chapman finds their writings characterized by haste, unqualified generalizations, and an impatience with close reasoning.

The problem is even deeper to Samuel Huntington, who insists upon defining conservatism as a positional ideology. Since positional ideologies do not reflect the continuing interests and needs of a group, but only the external relations between groups, there is no permanent conservative group interest. Men are driven to conservatism by the shock of events. Consider the "states' rights" argument in the United States.

Furthermore, says Huntington, conservative thought does not evolve; consequently, the conservative thinkers of one age have little influence on those of the next. Hobbes left no school. Burke did not draw from Hooker but from the events around him. Lacking a substantive intellectual tradition, conservatism is rarely treated in political-theory textbooks (even when traditional conservatives like John Hallowell and Thomas Cook write them).

Gordon Lewis accuses the New Conservatives of ignoring social science in general. In "Metaphysics of Conservatism," Lewis zeroes in on Russell Kirk, charging that the disciplines of statistics, sociology, psychology, and psychoanalysis are alien to him. This, Lewis says, is "an unpardonable neglect of the established consensus of fact and analysis about the nature and behavior patterns of man in culture that these disciplines have put together since their inception." Then he proceeds to point out the specific studies Kirk has ignored in arriving at some of his "romantic generalizations".

Auerbach's *The Conservative Illusion*, which is a grandiose assault on conservatism's basic theory, concludes that the defeat of conservatism has been a constant of history all along and has become more decisive with each age. The real choice before the New Conservative, he says, is whether he wants to be irrelevant or unconservative.

This devastating theoretical onslaught doesn't especially disturb the New Conservatives. For one thing, they aren't talking to liberals. And they are too busy running a new enterprise: the Conservative Revival. History may be against them, but they have enjoyed a positional fillip. People are listening as never before, and dedicated New Conservatives have proved themselves superb hucksters. The important (and impressive) thing is that *they* believe everything they say.

They are primarily recruiting from America's vast reservoir of libertarian or propertarian conservatives who they hope will stand up and be counted as sort of American poujadists. Also drawn in is what Adorno has called the pseudoconservative, who in the name of upholding traditional American institutions against more or less fictitious dangers, consciously or unconsciously aims at their abolition. They are "more than ordinarily incoherent about politics."[20]

These are the chronic grousers and near psychopaths who have a phobia that some outside force is trying to poison their religion, Constitution, or water supply. They may range from opposition to fluoridation because you need natural water for baptism (Boston's Father Feeney) to blaming the income tax on the *Communist Manifesto* (Frank Chodorov). Such characters add considerable color and confusion to the Right.

The anti-Communist common front of the Right has made it difficult for the moderate conservatives to dissociate themselves from the pseudos and ultras, especially if they happen to be well heeled. Whether for reasons of conviction, indifference, or expediency, the Right honorables have become identified with the Right dishonorables. Until conservatives come up with some equivalent of the Communist disclaimer affidavit, they are going to have real problems of press.

In the profiles to follow, an attempt has been made to present half a dozen conservative figures who have created a stir among young people. They represent all shades of the Right. Professors Rossiter and Viereck represent the academic voice of the more

20. See R. Hofstadter, "The Pseudo-Conservative Revolt," *American Scholar*, Winter, 1944-1945.

moderate traditional conservatives. Senator Goldwater is sort of a Right Honorable libertarian conservative. William Buckley is the proud New Conservative trying to bridge traditional and libertarian conservatism.

Robert Welch is the libertarian conservative *ad absurdum*. Novelist Ayn Rand is not a conservative at all but claims to be very relevant. She is a radical capitalist, and is the closest to what I mean by a propertarian. This makes Miss Rand the most radical figure on the Right. Welch by comparison is a hopeless traditionalist. Ayn Rand is the most inventive of the Right-wing figures, as you will discover.

CHAPTER 3

Ayn Rand as Theorist

"*I* DECIDED to become a writer," says Ayn Rand, "not in order to save the world nor to serve my fellow men, but for the simple, personal, selfish, egotistical happiness of creating the kind of men and events I could like, respect, and admire. . . . I did not start by trying to describe the folks next door—but by inventing people who did things the folks next door would never do."[1]

Among the writers of the far Right, none has proposed a more earnest philosophical defense in depth than Ayn Rand. She has extended gratuitously an intellectual umbrella over political positions most ultraconservatives have not yet dared to occupy. In a paean to self-interest that would make any arch-Rotarian blush, Miss Rand announces through her architect hero in *The Fountainhead:* "I came here to say that I do not recognize anybody's right to one minute of my life. Nor to any part of my energy. Nor to any achievement of mine. No matter

1. *Twentieth Century Authors*, First Supplement, Wilson, 1955.

who makes the claim, how large their number or how great their need. . . . I wish to come here to say that I am a man who does not exist for others."[2]

How does she carry this off? It's done in stages through her four novels and a philosophical essay. First came *We the Living* (1936), a story about the evils of totalitarian society in the U.S.S.R. Kera speaks to Andrei, a commissar whom she has used but who is not her true love (only her comrade): "You came as a solemn army to bring a new life to me. You tore that life you knew nothing about out of their guts—and you told them what it had to be. . . . You came and you forbade life to the living."[3]

Anthem (1938) projects a totalitarian society of the future. Collectivism has poisoned society to its roots; everything is reduced to primitivism. The local science institute has just invented candles. The word "I" has vanished; only the plural is used, "we" and "they." It's very confusing during love scenes. People are identified by serial numbers, as in the telephone directory. Listen to the exchanges: Liberty, Solidarity, Equality, Collective, International, Similarity—and all the other political pejoratives. The collective spirit is grotesquely portrayed when "We," hoping for the job in science, gets a "Life Mandate" as a street sweeper. We reply: "The will of our brothers be done," and sing a "Hymn of Equality," or you could render the "Hymn of the Collective Spirit."

The drama concerns the frustrated street sweeper who escapes into the great uncharted forest and becomes an "I." The three holy words of the new life become "I will it!" Reflecting on his bondage, the hero decides that "to be free, a man must be free of his brothers. That is freedom. That and nothing else."[4] The fable closes with the new man cutting a new word over his portal: "EGO," a new anthem.

With *The Fountainhead* (1943) we return to the contemporary scene and turn to a more intellectual theme. In fact, twelve publishers thought the novel was too intellectual, and refused to publish it. A half-million sales proved that this was an

2. Bobbs-Merrill, 1943, p. 678.
3. Macmillan, 1936, p. 388.
4. Pamphleteers, Inc., 1946, p. 118.

error. Here among the skyscrapers, executives, and literati of New York City, Miss Rand probes at what she considers to be the ideological cancer leading us to the mindless society in *Anthem*.

Spokesman for this villainy is Ellsworth Toohey, liberal critic, architectural journalist, and general "do-gooder." (He's short and dumpy. You wouldn't like him.) Here is Ellsworth's trouble: "I don't believe in individualism, Peter. I don't believe that any one man is any one thing which everybody else can't be. I believe we are all equal and interchangeable."[5]

Preach selflessness, continues Ellsworth. Since the supreme ideal is beyond man's grasp, he will eventually give up all ideals and take comfort in effortless drifting. "Enshrine mediocrity— and all the shrines are razed." The quickest way to induce stagnation is to reassure men that they can't really go any higher. One of the quickest ways to breed mediocrity is to urge all men to sacrifice, and allow none to profit. Deny incentive to aspiration. Declare a moratorium on reason. Then if there is anything left standing, kill by laughter. Tell people that a sense of humor is an unlimited virtue. If you can kill reverence, you can kill the hero in man.

This giggling, unheroic mediocrity is the enemy, and the enemy is seen on all sides. Why so omnipresent? Because, Ellsworth confesses, "everything I have said is contained in a single word—collectivism." The new opiate, the "Great Bromide," the seductive siren of the hour is *collectivism*. The word is made to cover any cooperative venture.

Miss Rand's antipathy to collectivism approaches phobia. "I don't work with collectives," says hero Roark, "I don't consult. I don't cooperate." This was when he was asked to collaborate with several other architects in planning a world's fair. Enlightened self-interest is the only antidote, and "enlightenment" refers to the self, not to others. Independence is felt to be the sole measure of value: "What a man is and makes of himself; not what he has or hasn't done for others." Architect Roark makes it quite clear where others should stand and what they are after. "When the first creator invented the wheel, the first second-hander re-

5. P. 562.

sponded. He invented altruism. . . . The only good which man can do to one another and the only statement of their proper relationship is—'Hands Off!' "

Roark prefers reason and ideas to emotions and people. He is moralistic, and "internalizes" authority. Listen to him lay into the second-handers, the noncreators who are unreflective parasites. "They have no concern for facts, ideas, work. They're concerned only with people. They don't ask: 'Is this true?' They ask: 'Is this what others think is true?' Not to judge but to repeat. Not to do, but to give the impression of doing. Not creation but show. Not ability but friendship. Not merit but pull."[6]

Here is Ayn Rand's central theme: The splendid isolation of the individual. It's not misanthropy, but classical cynicism. *Cynos* is the Greek word for dog. Members of the school of Cynics were thought to be doglike in their boorish captiousness and indifference to the proprieties of life. Manners, customs, and the niceties of social intercourse, as well as the larger problems of political relationships, were thought to be without value, and therefore could be ignored.

The Fountainhead finally erupts in a climactic courtroom speech of Roark's in which he defends his action of dynamiting (without loss of life) a public housing project he had designed because some lesser bureaucrats altered his plans without his knowledge. And since you can't sue the government, what else could any self-respecting architect do? "I agreed to design Cortland for the purpose of seeing it constructed as I designed it and for no other reason." Furthermore, he couldn't find out which second-hander among the dozens in authority could be held to account. It is difficult to know which should infuriate us more: knowing that someone had presumed to alter Roark's design, or not being able to determine guilt in the bureaucratic maze. Anyway, this victory of the collective spirit over the creative will prove to be both short-lived and Pyrrhic. The architectural sacrilege is expiated by dynamite, and the jury acquits on the basis of justifiable immolation.

For those who didn't get the point of *The Fountainhead*, Miss Rand wrote *Atlas Shrugged* (1957). Here she wasn't taking

6. P. 599.

any chances. The plot is very definitely subordinated to the ideological line. Characters have little more substance than the symbols she used in *Anthem*. This is avowedly a philosophical novel. The forces of Good and Evil are clearly arranged on a simplified checkerboard. All battles are fought in the full light of day. Readers might be appalled or pleased, but they could never be confused, by the issues.

The setting is the near present. The slow poison of the welfare state is just taking hold. The initiative and drive of entrepreneurship have been systematically bred out of society and a strange lethargy bred in. The economy is gradually unwinding, but most people do not know why. A few key businessmen and other creative spirits do know. One of them speaks, giving us the title situation: If you saw Atlas, the giant who holds the world on his shoulders, standing with buckling knees and trembling arms but still trying to hold the world aloft with the last of his strength, and the greater his effort the heavier the world bore down on his shoulders—what would you tell him to do? The answer: To shrug.

So, led by the most resolute of individualists, John Galt, a few of the most select creative spirits decide to withdraw into a mountain retreat and go on strike against society. Let's see them make a go of it now! In a sixty-page justification of his move, Galt announces: "We are on strike, we the men of the mind. We are on strike against the creed of unearned rewards and unrewarded duties. . . . We are evil according to your morality. We have chosen not to harm you any longer. We are useless according to your economics. We have chosen not to exploit you any longer. . . . It's your moral code that's through this time."[7] The only redemption for those behind is not to return to morality —they have never known any—but to discover it.

The story concerns the attempt of Galt and his followers to persuade the creative souls remaining behind to give up the hapless fight against the second-handers and looters and join his strike. To give you an idea of what he is up against, the heroine, Dagny Taggart, of flawlessly tailored mind, body, and raiment, is doing a bang-up job of running her family's railroad in spite

7. (Random House), p. 937.

of incompetent help. She is John's prime target, in more ways than one. But she won't budge for over nine hundred pages. This is undoubtedly a reflection of Grandfather Taggart's steadfast independence. When this founder of the line was desperate for funds for his railroad, he threw down three flights of stairs a gentleman who offered him a government loan. Instead he pledged his wife against a loan for one million dollars. You can see John's problems.

As an index of how sick society had become, Miss Rand describes a prosperous automobile factory that falls into the hands of hapless idealistic heirs. Not content with implementing a fair-shares plan, they organize the plant on the basis of the Marxian formula "From each according to his ability, to each according to his need." Of course, everything and everybody goes to pot.

The remedy for the moral and economic malaise of the world is to admit bankruptcy and go into receivership under John Galt's New Morality: Face the fact that pride is man's highest value and that it must be earned. There will be no conflict among men who reject the unearned. These are the men who neither make sacrifices nor accept them. The symbol of respect for human beings is the Trader. Miss Rand insists that a trader earns what he gets, and does not give or take the undeserved. He never asks to be paid for his failures. And he never gives his love or esteem except in trade for his own pleasure, which he can receive only from men he can trust and respect.

Here is a Benthamite calculus of pleasures with a vengeance, minus, of course, the part about "the greatest happiness of the greatest number." Miss Rand does go on to say that man's one moral obligation to others is his rationality. What does this tell us? Let's turn to her latest work, *For the New Intellectual* (1961), to examine the larger context of her theory of egotism.

America, proclaims Miss Rand, is culturally bankrupt. We have been betrayed by our intellectual bodyguards, most of whom are frightened zombies preaching the importance of reason and contributing to the atmosphere of self-righteous depravity, guilt, panic, despair, boredom, and evasion. They present a "grotesque spectacle of militant uncertainty." Depravity is a result of not sufficiently exalting man. Guilt comes from either an irrational belief in original sin or the refusal to reject altruism. Despair is the product of the uncertainty of all norms and values. This refusal to accept absolute standards leads to evasion and ends in boredom.

After this warm-up, we are introduced to a new psycho-epistemology—a psychology of knowledge (or "The New Rand Atlas," as Donald Malcolm of the *New Yorker* has it). Intellectual history is portrayed as an endless contest between Attila (brute force), the Witch Doctor (faith and superstition), and the Thinker (creative reason). With the gusto of Spengler and the glibness of his *Decline and Fall of the West,* Miss Rand demonstrates that the intellectual climate of an age depends on how these three forces are in combination. Usually it is a case of a distrustful alliance of Attila and the Witch Doctor against the Thinker.

Things weren't too bad by the time of the Renaissance. The firm hold of the mystics had been broken. Then Descartes had to come along and start talking about "the prior certainty of consciousness" and innate ideas. This let the Witch Doctor in through the back door. Philosophers who chose to abandon reality joined the mystics and became known as Rationalists. Those who clung stubbornly to reality by abandoning their mind became Empiricists. The man who finally closed the door to reason and made possible an alliance of force and faith was Kant. He did this by turning the world over to Attila, but reserving the realm of morality to the Witch Doctor. *And* it was a morality of self-sacrifice, of altruism. Furthermore, Kant insisted that reality as seen by man's mind is a distortion; men can never really see things as they are. Unfortunately, laments Miss Rand, Kant is still the dominant intellectual influence today. Hence we believe that reality is mere appearance, that rational certainty is impossible, and that morality is altruism.

Pragmatism—"whatever one wishes to be true *is* true . . . provided it works or makes you feel better"—sold a bill of goods to science and left us without any absolute principles or standards. When you combine Kant's subjectivism with pragmatism, whatever the majority says is true. All of the post-Kantian idealists are dismissed. Hegel is pure Witch Doctory and Marx pure Attila-ism. What's left?

Apparently we left the track back with Aristotle. He is the sole survivor of Miss Rand's critique. It is his logic that is so highly esteemed. Aristotle's logic has two features: the Law of Identity insists that whatever you are talking about you must mean, and not something else; and the Law of Contradiction holds that a thing cannot both be and not be at the same time.

This gives us a method of logic, but how is reason related to reality? Ayn Rand suggests a new philosophy: objectivism. Things exist independently of our consciousness of them. No sort of perceiving consciousness is required to establish their validity. Form (the way we have of recognizing things, for example, "squareness" or "dryness") exists only *in* matter, not outside or apart from it. This, says Miss Rand, is Aristotle's metaphysical realism. But Aristotle went on to say that form has a universal substance to embody it. Such a substance is the unmoved mover, God. All change and motion depend upon this Mover. Even matter is ultimately merely potentiality or possibility. (Later Idealists say matter is the energy of God's mind.)

Since Miss Rand rejects God and all theistic explanations, she cannot base much of a metaphysical case on Aristotle. She is so nimbly eclectic, it is impossible to assign her to any of the recognized philosophical schools. Borrowing Aristotle's logic and the bottom half of his theory of knowledge (that is, the real exists), Miss Rand rejects the top half (God), his ethics and his political philosophy. Without admitting any debt, she seems to borrow Hegel's concept of the "concrete-universal," which asserts that thought and reality are identical and there are no things-in-themselves beyond experience. But she cannot bear the idealistic consequences. God is waiting around the corner there, too.

Does Miss Rand mean that everything is object? This would bring her into the materialist camp, where she appears to be more at home. Professor Ralph B. Perry has suggested the term "panobjectivism" for those believing that all reality is to be found in objects. This also would make her a monist, which means that she has given up the attempt to distinguish between idea and object. If idea and object are not two but one, which is the one? If you answer, object, what happens to the subject? Miss Rand's vaunted individualism would be sold short.

Perhaps what Miss Rand is really playing is axiology, the theory of value. Rather than giving us a new theory of knowledge in any terms we can recognize, isn't she really trying to give us a justification for a new standard of values? The primary question in such an inquiry is whether values are subjective or objective. Subjective value is wholly related to the private feelings of the individual, and social subjectivism means that environment and human conditions determine all value. The objectivist claims that there is more to the meaning of value than just the individual experience of it. He insists that a value judgment (the aurora borealis is beautiful) is just as objective a fact as our sense perception (I have seen the aurora borealis). Objectivism goes on to see that the aurora borealis is beautiful for the universe whether you saw it or not. Furthermore, the values of science cannot be subjective, or it would be meaningless. Reason itself demands objective norms.

In her campaign against subjectivism, Miss Rand is limited by her repudiation[8] of the coherence theory of truth. Hegel has a good statement of this: "The true is the whole." Your theory must not only be consistent; it must also be coherently connected with your whole picture of experience. The more connections, the better, and you are morally obligated to explore as many aspects of experience as you can.

For example, when Howard Roark decides to blow up the public housing project because of its bastardized architecture, he is being relentlessly consistent with all of his personal philosophy of egoist self-interest, but the coherence of his action is another matter. When you start balancing the aesthetic satisfaction of one man against the needs, interests, and rights of others, you are engaging in coherence theory. You may well decide that

8. "Objectivism rejects in its entirety the coherence theory of truth, with the corollary idea of 'degrees of truth,'" says her disciple Nathaniel Branden.

Roark's truth is not *as* true as that of others. You also must appraise his actions in terms of objective norms.

Miss Rand's objectivism seems to unravel at this point. The one major defense offered for the architect's action is that his sensibilities as a creative-producer were being outraged. The dynamiting was the product of individual subjectivism. If not the hedonistic "I enjoy it," then the egoistic voluntarism of "I desire it." Without any higher or truly objective reference, you are apt to end up in the anarchy of subjectivism where value is determined by dynamite caps. The difficulties of attempting to bind together egotistical self-interest with a theory of objectivism are endless.

The comparison with Nietzsche is obvious and tempting. All of the Rand heroes tell the truth and shoot straight. These, says Nietzsche, are the great Persian virtues. They are "the great despisers of things as they are" and the "great adorers and arrows of longing for the other shore," says Zarathustra. Certainly Roark and John Galt are Nietzsche's "free spirits," the bridges to the superman. Resentment of the noncreative looters is explicit in one of his apothegms: "It is not enough to possess a talent: one must also have your permission to possess it—eh, my friend." This supreme confidence in talent is matched by near eloquence in describing the untalented masses. Where Nietzsche speaks of "the superfluous ones," "the many too many," and (a real gem) "cobweb spinners of the spirit," Miss Rand complies with "human ballast" and those in a state of "unfocused stupor." Neither can abide the weak or the meek.

Yet Nietzsche is criticized in *For the New Intellectual* because he sacrifices others to the self. This violates John Galt's sacred oath: "I swear—by my life and my love of it—that I will never live for the sake of another man, nor ask another man to live for mine."

How does a heroic free spirit manage this? Above all, one must be a free trader: "A free mind and a free market are corollaries." Miss Rand insists that the intellectual's rebellion against "commercialism" is really a rebellion against "the open market of ideas . . . where no protector exists but objective reality." The finest expression of this free trade in ideas is capitalism, which "demands the best of every man—his rationality—and rewards him accordingly." While the intellectual is bankrupt, the businessman (who applies the science of the laboratory) has done "a superlative job."

Now Miss Rand has to prove that capitalism has not involved the sacrifice of men and their interests. To do this she would have to answer more than Marxist critics. The neat trick is to prevent free traders from treading on each other in a society where altruism has been eradicated. The Communist utopia appears simple by comparison. You can't even distill a social utilitarianism out of this, because the individual creator-thinker is the sole judge of utility.

We are almost reduced to Nietzsche's answer: anarchy. Zarathustra spoke of the state, that new idol, as "the coldest of all cold monsters." Miss Rand is willing to take us along as far as Adam Smith. We are allowed a police force, law courts, and the military—provided we accept implicitly Smith's story about an "Unseen Hand" that guides entrepreneurs down their separate paths of economic virtue. But since all transcendent referents are taboo, we are to be denied even this comfort.

A chaotic political theory results. The concept of equality has been caricatured beyond recognition in all four novels. Any attempt at government regulation is immediately Rousseau forcing people to be free. The suggestion that private power might have to be tamed is never seriously considered. Human nature is defined in hopelessly naïve terms. Property rights are to be absolute (to be guaranteed by a constitutional amendment). A mythical golden age of free trade is presumed to exist. Minority interests may be exerted over political consensus. And political parties seem to be in an absolute limbo. Not much democratic theory is left.

What is Ayn Rand's appeal? People we used to describe as economic royalists might take indiscriminate comfort in her unlimited defense of free enterprise. The general public ("human ballast"?) likes her absorbing storytelling. And she has a message that might well impress certain inquiring minds. Her philosophy, For the New Intellectual, has a beguiling plausibility about it at first glance. Young intellectuals who are looking for an earnest but nonreligious (Miss Rand's system is a triumph of her justice over love) defense of our capitalism with forceful, humorless, unashamed bravado might be quite willing to listen—especially if they shared her blind spots in the social sciences. She is standing up to the Communists, sounding the call for absolute standards, and willing to give unlimited recognition to merit.

Certainly Miss Rand has a bold, energetic, and alert mind. She boasts that she sold her first novel (*We the Living*), first movie (*The Red Pawn* to Universal), and first play (*The Night of January 16th*, 285 Broadway runs). Her books have now sold over two million copies. The "Class of '43" commemorates publication of *The Fountainhead*. It is a group of young people interested in her ideas who meet for weekly discussions. Nathaniel Branden, New York City psychologist, has organized the Nathaniel Branden Institute, and gives a series of lectures on Miss Rand's philosophy. These are given twice a year in New York City and Philadelphia and by means of tape recordings in a dozen other United States and Canadian cities. Los Angeles, for example, draws about a hundred at one of these taped sessions. Most of those attending are college students.

At a typical meeting at the Hotel Roosevelt in New York City, Mr. Branden drew about two hundred people. Very few present looked over forty years old. The median age for those signed up for the twenty weeks of lecture was 31.5 years. The group was very well dressed, looked sophisticated, and appeared to consist of white, Anglo-Germanic freethinkers. About 40 percent of those enrolled were students.

A young German exchange student present regretted that he would have to leave the country before the lectures were completed. Miss Rand is just being read in Germany, he said. He had first come across *The Fountainhead* in Switzerland. Is Miss Rand popular with students here, he asked?

The type of student to whom Miss Rand would appeal is very limited but qualitatively very important. He is very likely to picture himself as someone whom John Galt might call to his mountain retreat. Bright, alert, and conscious of his capacity, he would admire the boldness of heroic action. Having something to offer, he feels there should be appropriate reward for a job well done, and has probably long despised the "second-handers," or drones, who have had to crib from his chemistry reports or term papers.

Miss Rand does not appeal to those whom she labels "militantly uncertain." Her primary appeal is to those confident of their talent, especially those who feel that the talented, "the producers," are not being adequately recognized or rewarded. The young man who has no wealth except talent is suceptible, especially if he has avoided what he might refer to as sentimental egalitarianism.

No one has ever launched a more horrendous attack against the egalitarian implications of the welfare state than Ayn Rand. Young people bred in an era of prosperity who believe that their talents or times will never make them dependent upon the benevolences of a welfare state are apt to stress the malevolent consequences inferred by its critics. Moral autonomy must not disintegrate into obsequious dependence, and excellence must never give way to mediocrity.

Self-reliant young men going into the nonacademic professions and business careers are more likely to resent the drone implications of a welfare society. Miss Rand provides an ethical depth defense of this resentment.

Capitalism itself has enhanced its reputation since World War II. The remarkable success of the German free economy demonstrated what could be done with more verve. Prosperity and the greater participation of Americans in investments such as mutual funds identified more people with capitalism and helped wash away some of the old prejudices. Furthermore, capitalism was no longer identified with the enemy fascism. In being anti-Communist, one tried harder to be even more sympathetic with capitalism.

Young people don't joke about capitalism as they once did. For those young men whose families always took capitalism seriously and/or successfully, this new sympathetic mood allowed them to remain sophisticated and pretty much a la mode while they searched even further for rationalizations of their status or predispositions. Ayn Rand is an intoxicating discovery to such young people.

The only force that could definitively undermine Randian egotism is the Christian exposé of pride. But the species of religious "revival" experienced after World War II did not feature a prominent reaffirmation of original sin, with the exception of a few neo-orthodox intellectuals. The inevitable self-righteousness incident to prosperity and anti-Communism remained unmolested.

The religious defense of young people was not reinforced on this front. If anything, self-satisfaction has been heightened by a sense of economic security and crusading anti-Communism. This makes for a weak spiritual defense on the part of heroically disposed young men of capacity whose ethical guard has given in to Miss Rand's blandishments.

I think Ayn Rand will become an increasing favorite of those discomfited by democratic liberalism and looking for a new world view. In a new preface to her first novel, she says someone must restore a view of the forest to people who have been too busy looking at the trees. The new forest view is presented in contrasts made more absolute by constant recourse to the *non sequitur*. For example, the police state is always inferred from democratic socialism. (Actually, no democratic socialist state has ever gone Communist.) The momentum of the *non sequitur* allows one to affirm that a new proposal is just a "first step" toward something more disastrous—with a minimum of discussion about the nature of the proposed step.

For the conspiracy-conscious, for those who above all want to feel that they are not being "duped" by the next step, Ayn Rand's militant arguments are indeed persuasive. Foremost among her supporters will be those who have never accepted the counsel of James Harrington who wrote in the seventeenth century: "The wisdom of the few may be the light of mankind, but the interest of the few is not the profit of mankind."

CHAPTER 4

William F. Buckley, Jr., as Publicist

"WHO WILL nail the thesis on Communism's church door? Chester Bowles?"

Despite a mouthul of nails, Mr. Buckley hammers home his point with the clarity of Demosthenes. Don't expect any help from the liberals. Anyway, liberalism is on the way out. It "cannot *care* deeply, and so cannot be cared about deeply." Unrelenting, Mr. Buckley's *Up From Liberalism* goes on to claim that "the large majority of students, angled as they are toward Liberalism, are silent, reflecting the great emptiness of their faith. . . . There is growing up a generation that has not been too busy fighting for Liberalism to wonder whether Liberalism is worth fighting for."

William Buckley is effectively exploiting his "Jr." standing. He speaks from and to this generation. The mantle of conservatism he has assumed has been lovingly tailored to any "Ivy" cut.

For many conservatives, young or old, he presents a striking figure. On certain occasions the mantle resembles a cowl. You
wouldn't be too far off in describing Buckley as an Ayn Rand
with a Newman Club card. He attempts to fortify a theory of
rigorous economic individualism and Catholic philosophy with a
brilliantly polemic flare. A debater essentially out to score points,
Mr. Buckley uses scholastic logic, Latin phrases, and the metaphysical preserve of the Church to lay low opponents. As a
member of the Yale debating team that defeated Oxford on the
issue of Capitalism versus Socialism, Buckley tasted blood early
and has been in pursuit ever since.

Evidence of Buckley's skill is conceded by one of his favorite
antagonists, Editor James Wechsler of the *New York Post*.
"Buckley and I have achieved something of the relationship of
vaudeville performers. We are each other's straight man. . . . As
a debater Buckley is glib, erudite, alternately the perfect gentleman and the slugger, deferential and contemptuous, and rarely
dull."[1] Every quarter acknowledges his debater's talents.

Irving Kristol did a *Reporter* article called "On the Burning
Deck." Even this liberal journalist admits that ". . . personally
Buckley is gay, witty, candid, intelligent, and unassuming." He
then goes on to say that "Mr. Buckley is a man provoked," and
that ". . . this irritation, though genuine enough, is merely pyro-
technic and lends itself to no rational use." Or, to stack the cards
for the last time, Dwight MacDonald says, "Buckley is a debater—his mind is quick, clear, plausible, and shallow."

This argumentive talent has been irritating and unsettling to
liberals. The Headmaster of Brooks School, North Andover,
Massachusetts, described his fellow Yale alumnus as "Torque-
mada reincarnated in his early twenties. . . ." He proceeds to
depict Buckley as "a young advocate whose grip on accuracy is
less firm than his grasp of assumptions . . . a man who can arrange
his arguments so persuasively and support them so recklessly
seems certain to have a profitable polemic future."[2]

1. *Reflections of an Angry, Middle-Aged Editor*, Random House, 1960,
p. 200.
2. F. Ashburn, "Isms and the University," *Saturday Review*, Dec. 15,
1951.

Young debaters always make me uncomfortable. You know they are brushing their teeth twice a day, and their ties always look so tight. There is also the feeling that you are being "had." Their self-assurance, marshaled evidence, logic, and rhetoric send you into quick flight. The part I could never stand was when they got deferential—something like having Khrushchev unfold your napkin. The arguments are so immaculately polished that they slide through your skeptical defenses effortlessly. You know there is sophistry around here somewhere, but you are never sure just where. You frequently find them putting the Q.E.D. on a point before you realized that the argument had begun. If the debater is a wit to boot, you're finished.

It's the debater's highly selective use of facts and excessive use of stark logical constructs that offend. All points must be resolved in absolute terms. In this war of Right versus Wrong, nothing short of unconditional surrender is thinkable. The heat of battle is on. The blood pulsates in your earlobes, and your nose smarts from the last blow.

Now, this is one way of getting across your point, but it is not the only way. A speculative argument might begin inductively and consider the longer view through the telescope. An essay might appraise the fuller contexts of the arguments and moderate their claims. A forum or group discussion might try to discover the truth rather than win a point. Finally, an editorial presents a point of view, but it generally considers both sides first.

In challenging liberalism, Mr. Buckley has chosen his own weapon. It is beautifully fashioned and expertly employed. But it has tactical limitations. Mr. Buckley wants to debate the issue, not discuss it. Flexibility, experimentation, and free exchange are therefore compromised. Temperate discussion would foster more accurate thinking and offer more of a chance for overcoming misunderstanding. But Mr. Buckley has chosen a different course.

William Buckley's career as a polemicist started with the publication of his first book. *God and Man at Yale* (1951). He attacked Yale for its neglect of religion, its disparagment of economic individualism, and its liberal abuse of academic freedom. When religious courses are offered, they suffer from secular influences. The Bible is pictured as "a monument over the grave of Christianity" because it is taught as literature and history. Student Christian groups are dismissed as unimportant forces, since it is what they read in their books and hear in lectures that counts. If Yale were faithful to its Christian heritage, the university would actively promote the Christian message. Religious indoctrination (which Buckley equates with education) is in order. The faculty should be loyally Christian.[3]

Mr. Buckley has not distinguished between the Catholic and Protestant approach to education, though Yale's religious tradition is Protestant, and Protestantism has a quite different attitude toward secularism from the Roman Catholic attitude. Paul Tillich has an emphatic statement of this difference. In speaking of Continental theologians like the Blumhardts, Tillich says:

They understood that the church whose nature is to be a Gestalt of grace may lose its true nature and that a secular group or movement may be called to become a bearer grace, though latently. From this it follows that Protestantism bears a unique relationship to secularism: Protestantism, by its very nature, demands a secular reality. It demands a concrete protest against the sacred sphere and against ecclesiastical pride, a protest that is incorporated in secularism. . . . If Protestantism retires from secularism, it ceases to be Protestant. . . ."
Protestantism denies in principle the cleavage between a sacred and a profane sphere. Since to it God alone is holy in himself and since no church, no doctrine, no saint, no institution, and no rite is holy in itself, every man and everything and every group is profane in itself and is sacred only in so far as it becomes a symbol of the divine holiness. . . . Protestantism is always learning, without the claim of being itself the Kingdom of God.[4]

This might be deplorable Catholicism, but it is sound neo-orthodox Protestantism. It means that the Protestant does not mistrust secular learning the same way the Catholic does, hence the different attitude toward the public schools. Mr. Buckley's

3. Even Buckley could unearth only five professors out of 1,100 who were atheists or agnostics.
4. *The Protestant Era*, University of Chicago, 1957, pp. 213, 214, 229, 230.

suggested reforms are hardly necessary, if he is willing to concede Yale's Protestant heritage.

The next target is rampant collectivism. Nobody in Yale's Economics Department is sufficiently enamored of free enterprises to suit Mr. Buckley, who is an exacting paramour. He laments, "No tribute is paid to the support of the weak that is an automatic result of the free enterprise system because no one can bring prosperity to himself without bringing it to others. . . ."[5] With such faith, no wonder Mr. Buckley is sensitive about professors who advocate the "desirability" of government action and the "waning" of free enterprise.

A crucial part of Buckley's attack is directed against a text in economics by Professor Paul A. Samuelson of the Massachusetts Institute of Technology. This book (*Economics: An Introductory Analysis*) is used in basic economics courses in scores of colleges and universities, all of which are cited in an appendix to *God and Man at Yale*. In his textual analysis, Buckley finds the following quotation from Samuels on free enterprise especially disturbing: "A cynic might say of free competition what Bernard Shaw once said of Christianity: the only trouble with it is that it has never been tried. There never was a golden age of free competition, and competition is not now perfect in the economists' sense; probably it is becoming less so every day, in large part because of the fundamental nature of large scale production and technology, consumers' tastes, and business organization."[6] This text is offered as evidence that Samuelson is hopelessly committed to reliance upon state intervention and collectivism. (At least in his fourth and fifth editions, Mr. Samuelson does not say "probably" competition is becoming less. He says ". . . we don't even know whether competition is becoming more or less.")

Samuelson goes on to say, on the same page, "But in any case . . . the challenge is to work out laws and customs that help to improve the working of our less-than-perfect competitive system." He *denied* in a preceding paragraph that the price mechanism would work chaotically if not controlled by some-

5. *God and Man at Yale*, Regnery, p. 53.
6. *Economics: An Introductory Analysis*, McGraw-Hill, 4th Ed., p. 38.

one: "Hundreds of thousands of commodities are produced by millions of people more or less at their own volition without central direction or master plan. This alone is convincing proof that a competitive system of markets and prices—whatever else it may be, however imperfectly it might function—is not a system of chaos and anarchy. It works. It functions." Then Samuelson goes on to show the chaos that resulted from price fixing in Hitler's Germany.

In his parting message on the last page of his book, Samuelson says: "It is too easy to compare the obvious imperfections of our known system with the ideal perfections of an unknown planned order. And it is only too easy to gloss over the tremendous dynamic vitality of our mixed free enterprise system, which, with all its defects, has given the world a century of progress such as an actual socialized order might find it impossible to equal." The American economy has behind it "a long-term record of the most rapid advance of productivity and living standards ever achieved anywhere," and it has ". . . a great future before it."

Sounds pretty safe to me. None of the economics textbooks examined by Mr. Buckley could be labeled collectivist in any sense other than recognizing the inevitability and desirability of a mixed economy. If Buckley can show one period of our economic history when either government or monopoly did not interfere, he might have a case for his "golden age." It is difficult to condemn professors for recognizing the economic facts of life, as rough as these facts may be on romantic views of economics.

Another Yale alumnus, F. McGeorge Bundy, points out that not one of the authors criticized in Buckley's broadside supported a full leveling of income and that three of the four texts urged changes in tax laws to encourage venture capital.

Buckley's views on "The Superstitions of Academic Freedom" were more novel. The relations of faculty and alumni take up half the book. Buckley applies a rigid consumer theory to the problem of this relationship. Since parents and alumni pay the bills, they should be able to determine what is being taught, or at least the general policy of the curriculum. Alumni have "the power, right, and duty to interfere." A new twist is given to the meaning of academic freedom. "For in the last analysis, academic freedom must mean the freedom of men and women to supervise the educational activities and aims of the schools they oversee and support."[7]

Somehow Buckley doesn't show the same enthusiasm for citizens with ballots as he does for consumers with dollars. He prefers to restrict political mandates and expand economic sanctions. Unfortunately, the consumer does not always receive the solicitous concern that Buckley showers on Yale alumni.

In early Greece the Sophists emerged to service a ready market. *Nouveau riche* merchants wanted their sons educated as gentlemen. Peripatetic Sophists filled the bill. They made silk purses out of sow's ears to order. Worldly, skeptical, and clever, they were journeymen for hire. Plato's Academy and Aristotle's Lyceum were altogether different affairs. Here scholars and students congregated around great teachers preoccupied with the conscientious search for knowledge for its own sake. This was the beginning of the liberal-arts ideal. Can't you see some Athenian olive tycoon laying down the educational line to Plato? You come to an institution of learning to participate, not to buy. At most you partake of what is offered. Ideally, it's like church; you really have little to offer. You go to church as a sinner and to a university as an ignoramus. You are free to choose your church or school. But once the choice is made, you are expected to defer to the institution's authority. You are not a sovereign consumer; wisdom or grace cannot be bought. It is possible to shop for the best conditions that will allow you to grow in both, but you are in no position to dictate terms.

Academic freedom is the homage paid to the open mind in the open society. Most of us would profit from sitting still and listening. Even if we made education synonymous with indoctrination, as Mr. Buckley does, we would still insist that it is up to the faculty to decide what the educational line is to be. Mr. Buckley is a great one for giving privilege its due. If the alumni are really more knowledgeable than the faculty, aren't they wearing the wrong hats?

7. *God and Man at Yale*, p. 190.

After his onslaught against liberalism, Buckley forever secured his place among fellow Right-wingers by writing with his
brother-in-law, L. Brent Bozell, a high-powered defense of Senator McCarthy called *McCarthy and His Enemies* (Regnery,
1954). The book had so many earmarks of high-priced legal
talent that Dwight MacDonald suggested, "It gives the effect of
a brief by Cadwallader, Wickersham and Taft on behalf of a
pickpocket caught in the men's room of the subway." At least
MacDonald admitted that an eloquent defense had been mustered
in the senator's behalf. The major point the authors want to make
is that McCarthy did have a *prima facie* case against laxity in the
State Department's security program and that the Tydings Committee gave the State Department a whitewashing and Senator
McCarthy a shellacking. Every instance of the committee's irritating high-handedness and the senator's charitable forbearance
is quoted. Some of McCarthy's exaggerated statements are mentioned to demonstrate the authors' balance, but you are left with
the impression that McCarthy was definitely abused by the Tydings Committee.

As Elmer Davis pointed out, there is nothing in the book
about the exploits that took up most of McCarthy's time: the
long, futile, and devastating[8] investigations at Fort Monmouth,
the shattering attack on the Overseas Information Agency, or the
strange antics of underlings Cohn and Schine. Nor is anything said
of the censure hearings and Joseph Welch of Boston, or the campaign against the Voice of America.

The leapfrogging to conclusions is far from playful. A case
against Professor Philip Jessup of Columbia is made on the evidence of his change of attitude toward the Embargo Act. In
January, 1939, Jessup wrote a letter to the *New York Times*
favoring the repeal of the Embargo Act (which prevented ship-
ment of arms to belligerents). This was done, allege the authors,
to favor the Spanish Loyalists who were pro-Communists. In

8. No Communists were discovered, but key scientists were suspended,
fifteen of whom were section chiefs. At least twenty projects were curtailed, and one, on which $32 million had been spent, was seriously
crippled. Telford Taylor, *Grand Inquest*, Simon and Schuster, 1955, p. 265.
Who needs Communist saboteurs?

September of the same year, he reverses himself and comes out for maintaining the Embargo Act. Jessup wanted to maintain the Embargo Act in the fall, our authors claim, because of the Hitler-Stalin nonaggression pact; that is, Jessup wanted to help Germany's ally, Russia. But Professor Jessup was an isolationist at this time. Defending the embargo in the fall of 1939 might help keep the United States out of war. Dropping the embargo in the winter of 1939 held little prospect of involving the United States in war. This is a startling case of fact juggling and motive reading on the part of Buckley and Bozell.

Listen to their positions on the government's security program: "Where reconciliation of an individual's and the government's interests cannot be achieved, the interests of the government shall be given exclusive consideration." How's that for laissez faire? It is made clear that ". . . dismissals must be summary in nature without reference to the traditional jurisprudential safeguards. . . . The presumption of innocence will remain the major barrier in the way of an effective security program. . . ."[9]

Resolving every benefit of doubt in favor of the state is a peculiar position for an archindividualist to assume. Seldom has the line between Buckley's political and economic morality been clearer. Apparently, economic rights like property and contract are rooted in nature and are not to be molested, but political rights are up for grabs. Economic rights must not be subjected to the community's interests; political rights may be. It won't do to say that, after all, a government job is only a privilege, not a right, when the privilege is being withdrawn because of the violation of rights of conscience, speech, or association.

If Buckley is blind to this political tyranny, a jurist like Frede Castberg is not. "There is no reason to place the individual's right to a free expression of his opinion in a different class from that of other human rights which it would be very far-fetched to base on the grounds of social utility. That the individual should be protected against torture is a human right. . . . Even though an overwhelming majority would be served by the use of torture in order to elicit the truth, or for other reasons, this consideration

9. *McCarthy and His Enemies*, pp. 247, 248, 250.

can nevertheless at no time supersede the individual's right to freedom from treatment of this kind."[10]

Castberg sees no difference in principle between freedom of expression and protection against torture. Both rights are rooted in respect for individual dignity. Meanwhile, Buckley would dismiss cavalierly not only security risks but also "policy misfits." "The world," opines Mr. Buckley, "has always been crowded with pestiferous blunderers who are incapable of acting in such a way as to promote even their *own* ideal society, much less *the* ideal society."[11] We are offered George Marshall as an example of such a blunderer. Buckley concedes that McCarthy probably was a little harsh in attributing treasonable motives to Marshall, but "To the extent that McCarthy, through his careful analysis of Marshall's record, has contributed to cutting Marshall down to size, he has performed a valuable service." McCarthy cut Marshall down to the size of "America's most disastrous general."

In the prologue to this extraordinary book, an appeal is made to those "who share McCarthy's sense of urgency." This is like appealing to arsonists who love a brightly burning fire. The appeal is broadened at the end of the book. We are reminded that McCarthyism is a weapon in the American arsenal, and then reassured that "as long as McCarthyism fixes its goal with its present precision, it is a movement around which men of good will and stern morality can close ranks."[12] Since men of good will and religious leaders of virtually every major religious group have condemned McCarthyism, we see why Mr. Buckley may be alarmed.

The *Los Angeles Tidings*, a western version of the *Brooklyn Tablet*, was the first to break the news that William Buckley intended to publish a new magazine for conservatives, which would "forthrightly oppose the prevailing trend of public opinion, and its purpose would be to change the nation's intellectual climate." It was spring, 1955. Mr. Buckley answered a few questions. What would be his magazine's policy on liberation? He was "pro-liberationist." Just how? "We favor the abandonment of cocktail talk with Communists. We favor fomenting trouble for them. . . .

10. *Freedom of Speech in the West*, Oceana, 1960, p. 424.
11. *McCarthy and His Enemies*, p. 301.
12. *Ibid.*, p. 335.

I believe that the assumptions of Communism are such as to make coexistence impossible."

Commonweal became concerned about how this prominent young Catholic layman would spell out concrete application of his principles. "We hope he will be able to solve the major problem facing conservatives today: the problem of bringing their principles into working relationship with a world where slogans mean nothing if they remain divorced from the awful responsibilities of power."[13] Given Buckley's opening remarks about our Soviet policy, their concern was not misplaced.

By circulating "The Magazine's Credenda" among prospects, the intrepid Mr. Buckley got 120 investors to underwrite $290,000 for his *National Review*, a weekly, conservative journal of opinion. As publisher and editor, Buckley controls the major stock interests. Family friends must have been a big help, since *Time Magazine* reported that Buckley Sr. has a $100 million fortune in Latin American oil. The conservative "Credenda" gives us a pretty good idea of what was to come. Government should confine itself to protecting the lives, liberty, and property of its citizens. Our most pressing crisis is the conflict between the "Social Engineers" and the "Disciples of Truth." Fabian operators are out to dominate both political parties. As for foreign policy, co-existence with Communism is "neither desirable, possible, nor honorable." The United Nations? "Better to grant independence to each of the forty-eight states than to surrender U.S. sovereignty to a world organization."

In his "Publisher's Statement," Buckley said the *National Review* ". . . stands athwart history yelling Stop, at a time when no one is inclined to do so, or to have much patience with those who so urge it." Liberals might take comfort considering what frequently happens to youngsters playing at railroad tracks. The credo affirms the virtues of "republicanism versus centralism." (Centralized France is not a republic?) Oliver Wendell Holmes is described as "The benign old wrecker of the ordered society." Then we get a good feeling of the tone of the publication: "Drop a little itching powder in Jimmy Wechsler's bath and before he has scratched himself for the third time . . ." This is followed by

13. *Commonweal*, March 4, 1955.

another reassurance that all the errors of the Liberal Establishment will be ruthlessly exposed. ". . . And that, ladies and gentlemen, leaves us just about the hottest thing in town."

Buckley's articles usually have an urbanity and wit not always found in other departments of the *National Review*. The writing is not quite so grim as Dwight MacDonald sees it: "National Review editorials are as eloquent as a poke in the nose, as cultivated as a camp meeting, as witty as a prat fall." But Buckley's editorials are unyielding. He "shadow-debates" every article and can't resist occasional vulgarisms to score points. His subscribers love it. They have discovered that the epée is even more fun than the broadsword. Joe was never like this. The zestful sophistication is terrific—even if you don't understand all the words.

Between articles in his own and other magazines, T.V. interviews, public debates and lectures, and his most recent book, *Up From Liberalism*,[14] William Buckley has succeeded in publicizing the case for New Conservatism as frequently, and probably as eloquently, as anyone has. Consider the conviction with which he intones his conservative apologia: "Conservatism is the tacit acknowledgment that all that is finally important in human experience is behind us; that the crucial explorations have been undertaken, and that it is given[15] to man to know what are the great truths that emerged from them. Whatever is to come cannot outweigh the importance to man of what has gone before. . . . Certain questions are closed: and with reference to that fact the conservative orders his life and, to the extent he is called upon by the circumstances to do so, the life of the community."[16] That was only toward the beginning. On the last page of his book he says: "I will then use my power as I see fit. I mean to live my life an obedient man, but obedient to the wisdom of my ancestors; never to the authority of political truth arrived at yesterday at the voting booth."

Such uncompromising ultraconservatism has cut off Buckley from the mainstream of both political parties. Eisenhower is seen

14. Obolensky, 1959.
15. Buckley believes in arriving at truth through intuition.
16. *Up From Liberalism*, p. 154.

as the quintessence of this abhorrent "age of modulation." His thinking is bland, and he deals in "blurred images" and "diffuse sentimentality," which ends up in "aimless mushheadedness." So much for modern Republicanism. Buckley wouldn't frighten off too many Southern Democrats of the Tidewater school. He feels that for the present time the southern white community is entitled to prevail, since the present leaders of American civilization are white. If Negroes got more votes, they might make more demands on the white man's property (that is, the tax dollar). "I believe it is a man's right to use his political influence to protect his property."[17] Anyway, why is something suddenly unconstitutional after being constitutional for ninety years?

Buckley does admit that the race problem is cultural and educational rather than biological. But how do you break the circle? The Federal government should not interfere. The Negro isn't ready for the vote. (If their separate educations have been as equal as the whites claim, why aren't they ready?) Apparently, even if they were ready, we have to restrict their suffrage because the Negro might plunder the white man's property by asking for more welfare aid. "Militant hectors" of the South are denounced for trying to impose the abstraction of equality and for not facing up to social realities.

The idea of political freedom itself is belittled because it is anchored in the ideal of equality. Buckley condemns liberals for being obsessive, "even fetishistic," about democracy. This, he says, is because of their larger absorption in method, "and Method is the fleshpot of those who live in metaphysical deserts." This is the old argument over whether democracy should have a content. Liberals have generally insisted that democracy was a process in order to prevent the reading in of subjective versions. Radical democrats have held out for pure and simple majority rule because of their stress on the idea of equality: everyone is good enough to vote and hold public office. Moderate liberals stress what they call rational freedom: let's have a literacy test and a merit civil service. Radical democrats stress referenda, long ballots, rotation, short tenure, or direct election of judges. Moderate liberals emphasize the legislator's discretion, short ballots, a longer

17. *Op. cit.*, p. 129.

and more efficient tenure, or the role of the Supreme Court. Both believe in and try to implement universal suffrage.

On the other hand, Mr. Buckley speaks of "the reckless stampede to inflate the election lists. Being able to vote," announces Buckley, "is no more to have realized freedom than being able to read is to have realized wisdom." But all we are trying to get Mr. Buckley to admit is that both are absolutely indispensable first steps. Our chances aren't too good. In an interview with Eve Auchincloss, Buckley confided that universal suffrage is a mockery of true democracy. He isn't too sure just how he would restrict suffrage, but he is certain that he would rather be governed by the first two thousand names in the telephone directory than by two thousand members of the Harvard faculty. His oligarchy is not going to be ruled by the wise.

Mr. Buckley is indulging in dangerous nonsense. Eliminate universal suffrage from democracy, and you are left with an oligarchic shell whose authoritarian contents can be supplied by the strongest interests passing by. This slipshod thinking about democracy is especially irresponsible when you consider the extremist nature of some of *National Review*'s audience.

Great emphasis is put by Mr. Buckley on his fidelity to Catholicism. He is most certainly keeping Catholic circles in motion. Ever since his first book, he has waged private wars with the editors and writers of *Commonweal, Catholic World*, and *America*—the three leading Catholic journals of opinion. *Commonweal* pointed out in 1952 that Buckley's economic theory is repudiated by the popes and his theory of the state solemnly condemned in official Catholic documents. In addition, the General Secretary of the National Catholic Education Association repudiates Buckley's contention that Catholics should not have to pay full taxes for support of public schools.[18] The Reverend Christopher Fullman writes in *Catholic World* that Buckley treats religion as an idea hermetically sealed off from economic life, and does not sufficiently appreciate the co-inheritance of the individual and society. Buckley replied that Father Fullman is too eager to see God on the side of the New Deal, and he quotes

18. June 27, 1952.

papal denunciations of centralization.[19] In a debate with William Clancey in *Commonweal*, Buckley said, "Promulgation of the Negro's civil rights at the recommended speed will not help him to save his soul." Clancey answered that we must not be so smug in our own virtue that we are content to let the earthly city, quite literally, go to hell. He added that conservative Catholics have condemned liberals because the *reasons* for their struggles have been wrong. Why don't they supply the right reasons rather than turn their backs on the battles?[20]

Kevin Corrigan in *Catholic World* wrote that Buckley's refusal to see any difference between a "common good" and a "sum of individual goods" cuts him off from any claim to natural law, and then he mentioned the legitimate control that is needed in all human endeavor because of man's fallen nature.[21] Buckley's reply the following month was furious. He claimed the magazine was trying to anathematize him, and closed his remarks peevishly with "When they get *me*, they'll get the previous editor of *The Catholic World* too, who held—he told me—identical views."

Then, during a Boston debate, Buckley charged the editor with using "rhetorical vulgarities" against him. The editor replied that he had never published an editorial on Mr. Buckley. "In my introduction to Corrigan's article, I asked: 'Is Bill Buckley's position on social and economic questions orthodox?' Neither I nor any *Catholic World* writer has ever questioned his loyalty and devotion to the church." The charity in this controversy seems one-sided: You begin to wonder just how many bishops' pronouncements and papal encyclicals Buckley can ignore short of bettering the record of Paul Blanchard.

Mater et Magistra on Christianity and social progress was released by Pope John XXIII in the spring of 1961, and opened Buckley's most heated controversy with the Catholic press. In a one-paragraph unsigned editorial in the July 29th issue of *National Review*, Buckley gave his comment. He said this encyclical may become important to the Church; but he thinks they will regret it in the future, just like Pius IX's Syllabus of Errors. Then

19. May 8, 1952, and August, 1952.
20. Dec. 16, 1960.
21. January, 1961.

he said, ". . . it must strike many as a venture in triviality coming at this particular time in history." The real menace today is Communism, and the Pope did not say enough about it. In another column the magazine suggested a play on the title: *Mater, Sí; Magistra, No;* that is, that we accept the Church as mother but not teacher.

This time Jesuit *America* was furious. "It takes an appalling amount of self-assurance for a Catholic writer to brush off an encyclical of John XXIII as though it had been written by John Cogley." They ended with as much bite as Buckley could ever achieve: "Of course, playing the role of the great conservative is no cinch, and we shouldn't expect even a man of Buckley's talents to achieve the impossible. But why complicate the job of playing Atlas by doing it in blackface?" They considered the *National Review*'s statements slanderous, and claimed the magazine owed its Catholic readers an apology.

Buckley's unrepentant reply was an article entitled "Whatsa Mater *America?*" in which he claimed his antagonists were exploiting *Mater* merely to succor their own political positions. In an open letter to the editor of *America*, Buckley tells what really hurt him. "After all, the *New Statesman* and *Manchester Guardian* hailed the conversion of the Pope to Socialism: What on earth would you expect an ecumenical Christian journal to do under the circumstances! Curtsy and go away? . . ." He also thinks *America* is being a spoilsport for refusing to accept any more of *National Review*'s advertising.

No wonder Buckley was bothered. Pope Leo XIII in *Rerum Novarum* (1891) held that the state cannot keep aloof from the economy and that the competition of economic liberalism was unchristian. Then Pius XI in *Quadragesimo Anno* (1931) suggests profit sharing, hits unbridled competition, and comes out for world organizations. Now, Pope John not only calls for more social justice in *Mater et Magistra* (1961); he actually says: "When the state fails to act in economic affairs when it should, or acts defectively, incurable civil disorders are seen to follow. Likewise, unscrupulous men of power . . . take advantage of the weak for their own wicked end." And he has to add, "Socialization . . . is also the fruit and expression of a natural tendency to unite for the purpose of obtaining objectives which each ambitions but which are beyond the capacity of individuals." Socialization does not reduce men to automatons. "It is on the contrary . . . a creation of men who are free agents intended by nature to work in a responsible manner."[22]

Remember that "it is part of the conservative intuition that economic freedom is the most precious temporal freedom," is the message of *Up From Liberalism*. Mr. Buckley has criticized President Kennedy for not taking papal encyclicals more seriously. How long can Buckley continue blithely to champion unabashed, classical, economic liberalism and retain that Catholic orthodoxy he so jealously guards? If Mr. Buckley becomes *persona non grata* at the Newman Club, people may begin to wonder just how much difference there is between his brand of rugged individualism and Ayn Rand's. Judged from the conclusions they have reached rather than the principles from which they proceed, Miss Rand and Mr. Buckley already occupy considerable common ground.

Both Miss Rand and Mr. Buckley are recruiting from an audience of serious and sophisticated young people. The atheism of Miss Rand alienates many of the young who feel that religion must never be repudiated, even if you don't especially believe in it. Mr. Buckley's influence among the politically interested young Catholic intellectuals has been somewhat compromised by the *Mater et Magistra* dispute, but it is still strong.

Mr. Buckley's brand of religiosity is fashioned for riding the crest of the postwar campus religious revival that was marked by its sophistication, coolness to liberal theology, and aversion to sackcloth. For the young conservative eager to be worldly as the age demanded, while not jeopardizing his orthodoxy, Buckley suggested an approach. Affirm your religious orthodoxy, castigate heretics and apostates, but conserve your moral indignation for Communism. Expending it on anything less might trap you into some liberal sentimentality such as a Freedom Ride.

The young conservatives desperately needed a young intellectual who had the nerve to face up to Arthur Schlesinger, Jr. Buckley took him on in a debate in Newton, Massachusetts. Al-

22. *Catholic Mind*, Sept.–Oct., 1961.

though he did not win the contest, his very attempt filled his followers with visible pride. Here was someone eager to stand up to James Wechsler, Norman Mailer, or any other liberal champion. Since the young of any persuasion always relish a good fight, it is easy to understand why Buckley became such a popular hero of the New Right. Buckley was drawing blood, and all the young conservatives had hoped for was a few lucky punches.

Above all things, a student fears to be considered gullible, dreads to be "taken in." Those who were too young to remember very much about the vicious techniques of the late Senator McCarthy often find them difficult to comprehend in print. They have to be experienced to be believed. Fortunately no one quite captured his technique. It is much easier to understand the target of his attacks: the alleged softness toward Communists. This is a continuing problem of the cold war.

Buckley has done a masterful job of ignoring McCarthy's results while he keeps alive his charges. Being duped is bad enough. Being "taken" by the Communists would be too much. As always, the student is determined to avoid the likelihood, and many will go to great lengths to prove his incredulity. Those out to prove themselves are naturals for Buckley's student-tailored anti-Communism. It meets student requirements by being relatively urbane and witty, definitely aggressive, usually sarcastic, and always appearing to know the score.

Except for rare moments of restraint, Buckley merely consolidates the ranks of liberal young people, but he is magnificent at rallying young conservatives, and is especially expert at spotting targets of ridicule in liberal positions. It's hard to find a man quicker on the draw. His editorials, quips, and asides become easy snack-bar talk among students.

Student highbrow conservatives give Buckley a mixed reception. Most of them consider him too brash and imprudent. These traditionalists are, of course, a small percentage of the total student conservatives. The bulk of Buckley's support comes from among the middlebrows: young people who admire his activity and get a kick out of Buckley being an intellectual.

Part of William Buckley's glamour comes from the exciting events, places, and people he always seems to be among. Any young man of the Right would be bound to admire and envy a handsome, wealthy young conservative with writing talent who had such a ready "in" with the business community and knew so many politicians and celebrities. And it all began over difficulties with a nonconformist student in an Ivy League school.

If William Buckley, Jr., had written *God and Man at Slippery Rock State Teachers College,* how many young men would be Right today?

CHAPTER 5

Robert H. W. Welch as Activist

BEFORE leaving his brother's candy company
to become one of the major but noncommissioned salesman of
the far Right, Robert Welch had been a successful sales manager
in a highly competitive industry for over thirty years. Welch
wrote *The Road to Salesmanship* in 1941. In his preface, he insists that salesmanship is not a trade but a profession, as important
as law, medicine, or teaching. One of the virtues of the profession
is that it allows "survival of the fittest" to work to the fullest
extent. The salesman can see through phony arguments instinc-
tively, and because he is accustomed to meeting and arguing with
people he is more likely than other members of the community
to speak out on issues. Welch feels the trend toward socialization
might be turned back by salesmen who can convince people that
they need more products that can tickle their fancies and gratify
their acquisitive instincts. "It is these things, materialistic if you
wish, which the vast army of salesmen tries to make the American
people hunger for and strive for, instead of the bread and circuses

handed out to idle mobs by politicians. . . . Those who disagree with us aspire to a philosophy of life which is more oriental than occidental" (page 8).

The salesman should not be apologetic for stimulating materialistic desires. This is his legitimate function. Moreover, "the salesmen and their families constitute one of the most solid and sensible segments of the middle class" (page 13).

As the son of a Southern Baptist minister, Robert Welch is an eager example of what Max Weber meant in writing about the amalgam of Protestantism and the capitalist ethic. When material interests are bounded by thrift, diligence, and sobriety, it becomes easier to speak of dedicating them to God's service. Custodianship becomes stewardship. Worldly success is evidence of God's smiling approval and perhaps an indication of eternal election. The theoretical and historical accuracy of Weber's thesis is disputed. But many people live their lives as if it were beyond question.

The middle class has been the pride and the shame of Protestantism. It has been harnessed to bourgeois virtues and saddled by its vices. R. H. Tawney has suggested that Calvin did for the middle class in the sixteenth century what Marx did for the proletariat of the nineteenth. That is, Calvin supplied through his doctrine of predestination a universal assurance that the middle class was correct in its theory of stewardship, just as Marx later reassured the workers that they were on the side of history. Hence we find modern Protestant critics of liberal persuasion accusing their coreligionists of self-righteousness, smugness, and indifference to problems beyond their comfortable class.

It was inevitable that middle-class Protestants, who accepted, consciously or not, the coincidence of their religion and capitalism, should begin to trim economic and political ideas to fit a highly literal religious mold. An individual's responsibility for his soul before God was used to preclude responsibility for one another's selves before men. There was no need for a social gospel in the face of such unrelenting personal stewardship. Charity—men playing God—yes; but social justice—God playing man—no.

Whereas Reformation theology had repudiated natural-law theory, fundamentalism began to restore it. Personal and social relationships became very precisely defined. Literal readings of the Scriptures produced simple answers to complex social problems. The fundamentalist is essentially a reactionary in that he has a nostalgic picture of religion, the individual, the family, and society as they used to be and should be again. This helps explain the curious distinction he draws between social and economic legislation. Laws against drinking, gambling, divorce, integration, or the teaching of evolution are favored. Laws for economic regulation, health and education, integration, and foreign aid are generally opposed. Why?

Sumptuary legislation, which attempts to coerce morality, is favored because this is essentially getting people back on the straight and narrow road to salvation. God calls for justice, and justice is retribution. The law punishes; it does not reward. Reward comes through grace, and grace is doled out privately. There can be no New Deal on grace. Providence rewards in its own inscrutable way. After all, how is a public housing project going to bring people closer to God?

Immunized to the social gospel, the fundamentalist finds it difficult to fathom the "economic crime," especially since the scene of the crime is shrouded in natural law. Nothing "artificial" can be done. Frugality, diligence, and prayer are the trusty resources. When faced with economic disaster, the fundamentalist turns Christian Scientist.

Civil liberties pose a further difficulty. With centuries of tradition of religious dissent behind him, why isn't the fundamentalist more of a political dissenter today? Why is he so apt to favor censorship, harsh government security measures, and limitations of free speech?

Historically there has not been too close a relationship between religious dissent and political liberalism. It has been very much a matter of fortuitous convenience. From Luther down, the religious dissenter has often eschewed liberal politics. One reason for Fundamentalist illiberality has been an oversolicitous regard for Romans 13, which warns that all power is of God, and whoever resists the power of government is challenging God's power. Perhaps Paul had in mind an irresponsible element that was trying to hasten the millennium through anarchy. In any case, John

Knox didn't let this passage faze him when he went ahead with his rebellion. But most fundamentalists aren't taking any chances. It is pretty clear to them. Unfortunately, it has often devolved into an uncritical support of any *status quo* authority. Hence there is a predisposition to favor the government over the individual.

Biblical literalism tends to spawn purism in other areas. Purity in politics to the fundamentalist means purging alien elements contaminating the country. Xenophobia is a predictable result. Besides alien persons, you must watch strange ideas. Strangeness is the prelude to newness. The extreme fundamentalist is fearful of being violated or poisoned by an infiltrated agent from "out there." Nothing is safe.

If you can associate the political noncomformity with any one, or combination, of alien influences, the fundamentalist has a prima-facie case against dissent. It can be a pretty tight system.

Robert Welch is a cultural product of this fundamentalism. He no longer believes it, but he uses it. "I first broke through the intellectually restrictive bonds of the unusually narrow Southern Baptist fundamentalism, in which I was raised, more than forty years ago," he writes in his *Blue Book* (page 152). "I loved everything about it except the specific details of its dogma." Having emptied fundamentalism of its religious content, Welch goes on to confess his indebtedness to men of the past who labored and sacrificed to give him a moral code, humane tradition, accumulated knowledge and material comforts. "The substance of my conscience . . . was gratitude and a corresponding sense of responsibility."

Ironically, Welch's religious belief borders on Unitarianism. "The keystone to my own religious belief, I think, was best delineated by Tennyson in just one great line: 'For I doubt not through the ages one increasing purpose runs.' "[1]

What is the purpose? Welch turns to the poet Harry Kemp, who sums it up "in just one brilliant line: 'Thou has put an upward reach in the heart of man.' " To make us truly religious, says Welch, "we do not need to know anything more about God, man, and man's relationship to God than is given by a reverent

1. *Blue Book,* p. 146.

understanding of that line." And it doesn't make any difference how each of us feels that this upward reach has been inculcated into the heart of man.

At the top of the list of factors that great religions have in common, Welch happily finds: That man shall not steal, "which further means that man shall recognize and respect property rights." Also in the list: kindness, charity, respect for age and experience, gratitude for favors received, and "an ennobling sense of responsibility." After presenting this array of goodies, Welch asks, "And gentlemen, what firmer foundation can we possibly need for the faith on which to build our new age and with which to inaugurate the dream that is coming to birth?"

The *Christian Century* has called Welch's theology "tawdry syncretism," and they ridiculed his use of second-rate poets who define God as Evolution, Autumn, Longing, and Consecration. The John Birch Society is then dismissed as "merely another of the nonbelieving clusters of our nihilistic generation" (May 31, 1961).

Welch had to secularize his fundamentalism. He needed the universality of its symbols: stewardship, literalness, conscience, frugality, purity, industry, and single-mindedness. He could not risk the particularity of its substance: the New Testament Christ, Biblicism, the Blood of the Lamb, and so on. Welch is essentially a salesman exploiting the symbols of fundamentalism.

When the eleven patriots were first called to Indianapolis on December 8, 1958, to hear the prospectus for the John Birch Society, Welch went out of his way to reassure his friends that he respected their religions. In a grand mixture of religions and metaphors, he affirmed, "The true fundamentalists in our midst, whether Catholics, Protestants or Jews, are the moral salt of the earth—of an increasingly savorless earth where such salt is like a stream of clear water in a desert."[2] He goes on to say, "And nothing I say now, nor any of the plans I outline tomorrow, is intended to question, weaken, or disturb any fundamentalist faith in the slightest; or to discount one iota its tremendous worth as a core of strength for all that we might hope to do."

He laments the diminishing number of fundamentalists, cau-

2. *Blue Book*, p. 58.

tions that "fully one-third" of the Protestant clergy are not true believers, and warns that we are living in a spiritual vacuum. But the faith to which we are asked to return is, in substance, not the faith of Our Father in Heaven but of our forefathers in America. The major threats to this faith are collectivism and Communism. If you think there is a danger of defining collectivism too broadly, wait and see what he does with Communism.

To combat these twin evils, Welch decided to form an American Action group. His society might even have been called American Action or American Rally, except for an accident of research. While reading through the *Congressional Record* for data on the American betrayal of China, Welch came across the case of John Birch. As a Southern Baptist missionary, Birch had spent years in China. His dedication and idealism are unquestioned. Before joining a unit of the United States Air Force in China, Birch was said to have assisted in the escape of General Doolittle. He was given the Legion of Merit for his Intelligence work. While on a mission a few weeks after the war, he was killed by Chinese Communists. Welch claims the killing was cold-blooded. William Miller of *Life* feels it was hot-blooded. According to Miller, Birch was provoked at being held up and disarmed by the Reds. At one point, he got very angry, seized a Red officer by the collar, and cried, "You are worse than bandits!" And they shot him.[3]

Welch felt that the United States Government deliberately hushed up the episode to prevent offending the Chinese Communists. He considers John Birch's death the first American casualty in the cold war. It was a perfect coincidence of symbols. John Birch was a young, redblooded American solider willing to stand up to the Reds. He was also a dedicated fundamentalist. The government trying to cover up his death was corrupted by collectivism and playing the Communists' game in China. American perfidy in Asia is a favorite Right-wing theme. Welch subtitled *The Life of John Birch*: "In the story of one American boy, the ordeal of his age."

Armed with copies of his inspirational biography of John Birch, another Welch polemic on betrayal in China called *May*

3. *Life*, May 12, 1961.

God Forgive Us, selected back issues of his magazine *American Opinion*, and his *Blue Book*, Welch inveigled eleven of his friends to sit through a two-day monologue at Indianapolis in December, 1958. With this converted nucleus of business and civic leaders, Welch hoped to form his American Action society in the name of John Birch. Until Ayn Rand's John Galt appeared, John Birch would have to do.

This meeting is described in the introduction to the *Blue Book*. The main body of this 178-paged polemic is what the *Christian Century* refers to as a "sub book," akin to the *Protocols of the Elders of Zion*. It is basically the expansion of a speech called "Look at the Score," which Welch had been giving to audiences all over the country. Welch admits: "I am an alarmist. I hope to make you alarmists, too." Before he closes the speech with the last stanza of "The Battle Hymn of the Republic," Welch has sounded an impressive chorus of alarms.

Listen! Russia brought on World War II to become an ally of the West and thus to be in a better position to infiltrate us. Nehru and Nasser are Communist agents. Norway is practically Communist; Iceland and Finland are. The Mediterranean basin will be Communist as soon as the Algerian rebels win. Only the South American dictatorships are safely anti-Communist. The Communist-controlled communications union could cripple the Pentagon network overnight. The United States is already 40 percent under Communist control. The Soviet threat of all-out war is 100 percent bluff. A shooting war would set off a simultaneous uprising of the subjugated peoples, and the Soviets wouldn't last three months. We are wasting billions of dollars and facing the socialization of our economy "with this completely phony threat of outside war as an excuse."

Looking deeper into the world's problems, Welch decides we are fools for not taking Spengler more seriously. Oliver Wendell Holmes is labeled "an eternal sophomore" for ridiculing *The Decline of the West*, and Arnold Toynbee is called a hack and "one of the worst charlatans who ever lived" for trying to displace Spengler as a historian. It took Spengler to see that collectivism was the secret cancer of the West. We are urged to get out of the bed of a Europe dying with cancer. (If collectivism is no more contagious than cancer, there is no worry.)

Eliminating Communism is just the short-term task. More important is the long-range goal of saving our "Christian-style" civilization from destruction. This is why Welch feels the John Birch Society will have a role to play for hundreds of years. And as Welch says, we mean business every step of the way.

The organization must be monolithic. You can't defeat the Communists with a collection of debating societies. These members "who cease to feel the necessary degree of loyalty" can either resign or will be put out before they start splintering the movement. Personal leadership of the society is essential. It can hold together a following in the way that organizational leadership never can. This feature of the society has alarmed even Barry Goldwater. In a footnote to the fifth printing of the *Blue Book*, Welch confesses, "This plea for personal loyalty is always embarrassing for me to make before any group." But, he goes on to explain, "this personal loyalty is the cement that holds the John Birch Society together, while other groups crumble around us."

One of the drawbacks of personal leadership is that the cement tends to stick to whatever you touch. Since Welch has placed himself so conspicuously at the top of the organization, whatever he does or writes becomes identified with the society. Nothing has plagued him more than the "Black Book," alias "The Politician." This was written back in 1954. It began as an effusive letter but eventually ran over three hundred pages. Never published, it was put out in offset type and bound with a black spiral cover. Carefully sealed copies were sent by registered first-class mail to select friends for comments. None were sold. Each was considered a loan and to be read in confidence.

There are now only about fifteen surviving copies, and these are kept under wraps at headquarters. Few people beneath the rank of district coordinator could hope to read one. The only entree an outsider has to the fantasies of the "Black Book" is to be found in the *Congressional Record*. Senator Milton Young of North Dakota had been harassed by the John Birch Society because of his support of the Federal Reserve System, C.C.C., and veterans' hospitals. In retaliation, Senator Young published thirteen choice pages of the "Black Book" in the *Congressional Record* for April 12, 1961 (pages 5268f.).

Here is what we find: "In my opinion, the chances are strong that Milton Eisenhower is actually Dwight Eisenhower's superior and boss within the Communist Party. For one thing he is obviously a great deal smarter." Later Welch claims, "Or to put it bluntly, I personally think that he [Ike] has been sympathetic to ultimate Communist aims, realistically willing to use Communist means to help them achieve their goals, knowingly accepting and abiding by Communist orders, and consciously serving the Communist conspiracy for all of his adult life." He insists that Eisenhower is a Communist on the basis of evidence so extensive and so palpable that it seems to put this conviction beyond any reasonable doubt. After all, says Welch, Eisenhower was raised with this mentality of fanaticism, for as recently as 1942 his mother was arrested for participating in a forbidden parade of Jehovah's Witnesses.

Roosevelt, says Welch, was used by the Communists without his knowledge. Truman was used by them with his knowledge as the price for their electoral support. With Eisenhower, the Communists have one of their own actually in the presidency.

Allen Dulles, former C.I.A. Director, is the most protected and untouchable supporter of Communism next to Eisenhower himself, and the C.I.A. is the most Communist-infested of all the agencies of our government. John Foster Dulles is seen as a Communist agent who was assigned the role of always saying the right things and doing the wrong ones.

Arthur F. Burns, former Economic Adviser to Eisenhower, was "born and raised in Russia." (It was Austria.) He is seen as probable liaison man between Eisenhower and his Communist bosses. Typical of Burns's pro-Communist remarks: "Our system of free and competitive enterprise is on trial."

Other prominent Communists mentioned in this brief sample are Max Rabb, who masterminded the steal of the Republican nomination of 1952, and Chester Bowles, once part owner of the pro-Communist publication *P.M.* Charles Bohlen and Philip Jessup get off as Communist sympathizers.

No wonder Mr. Welch chooses not to publish or repeat any of this in public. Now we know what Welch meant when he paused halfway through the *Blue Book* and exclaimed: "Fantastic? Of course it's fantastic. But everything I am talking is fantastic. We are in circumstances where it is realistic to be fantastic" (page 112).

The "Black Book" can not be dismissed as an early indiscretion that we should be charitable enough to forgive. It is too typical of Welch and the society. Listen to the reasons he uses to accuse Max Rabb of Communism: "Proof that he is a Communist would not be easy except as a logical deduction from his overall actions and visible purposes." In the Republican Convention at Chicago in 1952, "he followed so faithfully and cleverly the exact Communist technique of always accusing your enemy, first and loudly, of the very crime which you yourself are committing, that the long arm of coincidence would be strained in reaching so far."

Here we have an equation of the rough-and-tumble politics of a nominating convention with Communist tactics. Politics is essentially the art of compromise, and compromise is used exclusively as a pejorative by Welch and his society. No wonder he speaks of democracy as "a weapon of demagoguery and a perennial fraud." He makes it quite clear that the society must steer clear of the political parties and their "ubiquitous opportunism." In the Blue Book he concedes that the society will have to use, support, and create politicians. "I am thoroughly convinced, however, that we cannot count on politicians, political leadership, or even political action except as a part of something much deeper and broader, to save us" (page 121).

When Bircher Kent Courtney "nominated" Welch for President in 1964 as the head of a third party, it was considered embarrassing publicity because the society prefers to do its fighting primarily on an educational front. At one time Welch toyed with the idea of challenging Saltonstall for his Senate seat, but abandoned such plans when the society was formed.

Welch has commented on the "Black Book" in at least two issues of his monthly Bulletin. In August, 1960, he spoke of his "severe private opinions" in "The Politician." He claims that two-thirds of chapter members had never heard of the book before the Chicago Daily News "exposed" the society. "There are some who feel I made a mistake in being so outspoken, even in a confidential statement of opinions. They may be right. But who knows what is right in this gathering nightmare of our times which none of us have wished?" This is an extraordinary statement to come from someone who has always boasted such clear purpose and firm resolve. Such plaintive disorientation is hardly becoming to a member of the John Birch Society.

The society's *Bulletin* for May, 1961, included a magnificent example of editorial obfuscation. Once again Welch referred to his long private letter that his enemies had resurrected. He had hoped that it would fade away. In a deft assist to oblivion, Welch writes: "But the considerations involved in connection with many such matters are varied, overlapping, involved, and with too many ramifications to be explained in short compass. There are even times when, for reasons of strategy, we take an oblique approach to a specific objective, and fully to explain every step of our course would seriously handicap our effectiveness."

As proof that the spirit of the "Black Book" is far from dead, we have that annual exercise in flamboyancy, the "Scoreboard Issue" of *American Opinion*. In 1960 this issue was called "A World Gone Crazy: A panoramic survey of the degree of Communist influence in each of 107 countries." Welch claims that this will prove to be the most important publication in the whole field of anti-Communist literature since *Seeds of Treason* (Victor Lasky and Ralph de Toledano). We are assured that the report was compiled by "real experts," and if this doesn't awaken and alarm your complacent neighbors, nothing ever will. It is asserted that every fact in the report could be authoritatively footnoted, but there was not space enough.

The naked facts are more embarrassing than alarming. A percentage of Communist control is cited for each country. The stark figures are clothed in pathetic shreds of evidence. Great Britain is now 50 to 70 percent Communist. Why? Macmillan is Khrushchev's toady, running around arranging summit meetings. The population is deluded by the "sluttish joys" of the welfare state. Field Marshal Montgomery is a shameless Communist propagandist. Parliament cynically censured the Union of South Africa and assaulted the public schools. Her intellectuals are cowards, and her trade unions increasingly more Communistic. Maybe they're 75 percent Communist.

With similar evidence, we find Belgium is 50 to 70 percent Communist; so is Norway. Canada is 40 to 60 percent, Saudi Arabia 60 to 80 percent, West Germany 30 to 50 percent, Japan 40 to 60 percent, Finland 60 to 80 percent, and poor Iceland is 80 to 100 percent gone. As of June, 1960, twenty-nine countries were "in danger." Thirteen were "teetering on the edge." Twenty-eight were "sliding into the abyss," and twenty-five were "under Communist slavery." Only three countries in Europe are relatively safe: Ireland, Portugal, and Spain. Portugal is "the most stable government in Europe. . . . It is hoped that Salazar has prepared a successor of comparable wisdom."

We also learn that Trujillo's government was the best and most humane the Dominican Republic has had since 1821. Nasser was a traitor to his king. His Arab League is a Communist-front organization, and Arab nationalism in North Africa is essentially a hoax. The Russian Trade Fair in Addis Ababa was merely an opportunity for black Africa to shop for new ideas on how to exterminate white men. By striking down Massu and Soustelli, De Gaulle has alienated his strongest supporters. The battle being fought in Algeria is for the control of Europe. And a secret report from Peking discusses a master race by cross-breeding Arabs, Mongolians, and Negroes. Did I mention that the United States is 40 to 60 percent Communist? In justifying that 50 to 70 percent figure for Norway, the report says, "But we believe the approximate correctness of this estimate is too well recognized for any analysis. . . ." When Welch can boast of such a "report," it is difficult to understand why he is so reluctant to publish the "Black Book."

Another example of abandon is Welch's "principle of reversal." According to this nightmare formula, things are just the opposite of the way they appear. Eisenhower was an effective Communist agent because he appeared to be so American. Or, the real reason the Russians sent up Sputnik was to increase our defense spending. Incidentally, Welch is skeptical that the Russians ever invent any weapons of their own. They steal the parts in this country and assemble them at home. This prompted A. J. Liebling to remark, "When they walked off with the parts of our heavy-rocket boosters, they might at least have left us the plans."

Welch's principle of reversal, of course, convicts him of being the greatest Communist agent at large.

Most of the people who join the Birch Society, however, are not especially concerned about the "Black Book" or any Marquess of Queensberry rules about logic. They are interested in action. They agree that you cannot fight Communists by throwing pillows. Welch is selling the only program of direct action that the membership feels is sufficiently hardheaded. Welch admits that some of the tactics are mean and dirty, but the Communists are meaner and dirtier. In the *Blue Book* Welch speaks of things he would do if he had a dedicated following of one million members —"if I were 'the man on the white horse' on our side in this war." He hastens to add that the war is still political and educational rather than military.

First establish reading rooms, similar to the Christian Science reading rooms, which could serve as rental libraries for conservative publications. Get books and magazines into public libraries, school libraries, and fraternity houses. Then help circulate conservative periodicals. "Dan Smoot Reports" should be in doctors' and dentists' offices. *American Opinion* might be good for barbershops. Widen the audiences of such programs as Fulton Lewis and Clarence Manion. Write to sponsors and networks praising the programs. Effectively coordinate letter writing to legislators, administrators, editors, T.V. sponsors, educators, foundations, and so on. A letter-writing campaign got United Airlines to remove United Nations insignia from their planes. Organize fronts—little fronts, big fronts, temporary fronts, permanent fronts, all kinds of fronts. For example, "ORFIT," for the repeal of the income tax, A Committee for Withdrawal of Recognition (of U.S.S.R.), or Committee to Investigate Vassar College.

Start shocking the American people. The best way to do this is by exposure. If you aren't sure of your victim, use the question technique to embarrass him. Send hecklers and plant them in the audiences of liberals who have to allow question periods. Sponsor a roster of speakers for the circuit of church, P.T.A., service, and fraternal groups. Begin organizing in foreign countries. (The

Birchers claim lodge brothers in Algeria and the Belgian Congo.) And finally, put your weight into the domestic political scales as fast and as far as you can. Don't expect any help from "modern Republicans."

The White Book (any sales pitch has to come in assorted colors) is an annual of the monthly *Bulletins*. These provide you with homiletic inspiration and an agenda of action for the month. Each chapter leader is supposed to send in "M.M.M.s," members' monthly memos, to headquarters reporting action taken, literature distributed, letters written, and so on. January, 1960, started off with a bang. Paul Fisher of Fisher Pen Company, who had served twelve days in prison rather than hand over his payroll to Internal Revenue agents, was going to furnish "freedom pens" ($1.95 ball points) to members of the society free of charge. Welch added in gratitude, "It is up to us to use this mightiest weapon even more effectively than do the Communists."

Here's what you could do to keep busy for January. Read at least one book on the approved list during the month. Check with your public library to see if they have approved books in stock. This month we are pushing Widener's *Behind the U.N. Front* and Workman's *The Case for the South*. Our new front is "College Grads Against Educating Traitors at Government Expense." Send in lists of patriotic friends to whom we can send the *Blue Book*. Write the airlines, making it known if you are a commuter or stockholder, urging them to put *Human Events* in their reading racks. Then go after the railroads.

Write Senator Stephen Young of Ohio and tell him what you think of his intemperate words to the American Legion. (Young told off the Legion when they protested his speaking before the Emergency Civil Liberties Committee.) Then praise the National Commander of the Legion for speaking out. We must offset pressures to "soften" the Legion. Prevent Christmas from becoming a United Nations "one-world" celebration. We can imagine few things more unpatriotic for a good American citizen today than to own United States Government bonds. This merely contributes to the embezzlement of the American people. Try common stocks or gold in Canada as a hedge against inflation.

February was a good month, too. Kohlberg made Senator

McCarthy's collected speeches available free to all chapters. Members were reminded to send birthday cards to Syngman Rhee, now in Hawaii. Subsequent *Bulletins* offered kits of antifluoridation literature, appropriate for saving any town. It is an article of faith that there is more danger from fluoridation than fallout. Readers were asked to write the Metropolitan Opera and protest the commissioning of an opera by pro-Communist Marc Blitzstein on the Sacco-Vanzetti theme. Farley has rated Truman among the great Presidents. Write him.

Help get *your* church out of the National Council of Churches. Continue to infiltrate the P.T.A. Write to James Roosevelt urging him to start a movement to abolish James Roosevelt and sign it "Not yours, truly." Watch nails. They are being shipped in from Yugoslavia. We found some in Stamford. Let's have an all-out drive to abolish foreign aid. It was started by Stalin.

Demand Secretary of State Herter's resignation. Mail him some blank "stiff note" paper or some powder puffs. Ask the Boy Scouts why the Reverend Edwin Dahlberg, President of the National Council of Churches, was selected to speak before the national jamboree in Colorado Springs. Tell Purex Company what you think of their T.V. Dutch Cleansing of Sacco and Vanzetti. Demand that Nixon, if elected, appoint J. Edgar Hoover Attorney General. When your congressman is home, visit him with a small delegation. Insist that your post office stock issues of the new Taft four-cent stamps. Speak up at meetings of your school committees. Buy and use our stickers "This is a Republic not a Democracy/Let's Keep it that Way." Boycott movies we adversely review. Don't let them raise the Panamanian flag over the Canal Zone. We'll start to call for Herter's impeachment if he doesn't stop.

We're compiling a file on liberals and "Comsymps," a good word because you don't have to specify the degree of Communist belief. Members will please send in 8½" x 11" sheets listing such names ["of people who never will be missed"?], for example: Vera Dean. Regarding the summit meeting, send a wire to Ike: "Dear President Eisenhower—if you go—don't come back!" Christmas is remembrance time. Boycott UNICEF Christmas cards, and write a letter to Westbrook Pegler telling him what a fine job he has been doing all these years.

And so, armed with *Blue Book* and ball point, the months might pass.

Welch himself keeps up a furious pace. He frequently puts in all-night sessions to get out editions of the monthly *Bulletin* and his magazine *American Opinion*, whose stock has been donated by Welch to the John Birch Society. (He admitted the stock had only sentimental value.) The office staff seems to adore him. He frequently eats sandwich lunches with them in an office corner, and he still passes out boxes of candy and five-dollar bills as local charity.

The two-floor office has over fifty full-time employees and twenty-odd volunteers. It is one of the few offices that boasts an American flag over its water cooler. But the staff is not paid off in Necco Wafers. The John Birch Society has over a $12,000 weekly payroll. They have as many as seven full-time district coordinators in California. But one does for all of New England. There is not so much money around as most people believe. The thousand-dollar life members are very rare. Few eastern chapters can sport any.

As might be predicted in a group strikingly similar to the "Poujadists," the Birch Society draws most heavily on small businessmen. "The government is taking care of Big Labor and Big Business." A typical Massachusetts chapter could report no professionals who were members, although the chapter leader did hope soon to win over a priest and a clergyman. More money was needed for projects.

This chapter leader reported that his group was mostly Catholic and composed of members between thirty and forty years old. He admitted that the meetings would be dull to most outsiders. The "Black Book," which he had not read, did not particularly interest him, and he had a spotty knowledge of the *Blue Book*. He felt the country had taken a wrong turn thirty years ago, and Welch was bringing it back to its senses. The Russians must be beaten to the punch. He was not afraid to die or to have his six children die. Fallout shelters were opposed because he felt they created a defensive psychology. Details of the organization did not bother him. The important thing was that they knew where they were going, and they were going to *do* something. Other organizations he had been in had only talked.

While the call to action has attracted members to the society, it has also raised storms of protest. The campaign to impeach Chief Justice Earl Warren is probably the best publicized. Welch has long felt that the Supreme Court was "one of the most important agencies of Communism." But his impeachment-of-Warren crusade has lost the support of even such a staunch friend as Fulton Lewis, Jr., who thinks it is quixotic. Birch Society headquarters does not. Drop in any day, and a dark-suited young man will show you their variety of "Impeach Warren" literature with the aplomb of a clerk moving a size 10-C bedroom slipper.

The telephoning incident in Nashville, Tennessee, was also well publicized. It was charged that Birchers were making anonymous telephone calls warning people that your "own next-door neighbor might be a Communist." But this episode, which was reported in *Time* magazine, was denied by Welch. Never denied was the allegation that student members of the society in Wichita were being instructed to report to their chapter leader any "Communist influence" noted in the classroom. A businessman was intimidated from giving money to the University of Wichita because he feared a Birch Society telephone campaign against his business.

State Attorney General Stanley Mosk of California tells of seventy or eighty Birchers showing up at a meeting sponsored by four local clubs. They cheered on cue and shouted the word "republic" when the speaker said "democracy." A peaceful meeting at Encino Community Center was infiltrated by so many restive Birchers that police had to be called in to restore order. Five thousand Birchers marched four abrest through the streets of Los Angeles protesting a major speech being made by President Kennedy.

These are the developments that alarm people who wonder what the Birch Society might do next if emboldened by the million dedicated members it is seeking.

How is the John Birch Society being received? An April, 1961, Gallup Poll showed that 39,000,000 people had heard of the society: 47 percent did not approve of it, 8 percent did, and 45 percent were undecided. This means Welch has only to reach one out of five of the 5,500,000 people who were favorably impressed. No membership figures are given out, but the annual income from dues was divulged as being about $1,333,000. Discounting life members, and figuring on the basis of a $24.00 annual membership, this means there are not many more than 60,000 present members. About another third of a million comes in from literature sales and "goodwill" contributions.

The rate of recruiting might depend upon what the opinion-formers are saying. Reading from Right to Left, it goes something like this. William Buckley admits that the organization is vulnerable on some points but that its objectives are laudable. "The press is trying to discredit the entire American Right through Welch. . . . I hope the Society thrives" (*National Review*, April 22, 1961). Goldwater said many people in his home town have been attracted to the society and that he was impressed by the type of people in it. "They are the kind we need in politics" (*Time*, April 7, 1961). Cardinal Cushing of Boston declared, "I unhesitatingly recommend him to you and endorse his John Birch Society. I do not know of any more dedicated anti-Communist in the country than Robert Welch" (letter to C. M. Crawford of Los Angeles, April 28, 1960).

Conservative Senator Thomas Dodd of Connecticut called the society "an affront to decency and intelligence" (speech of March 31, 1961). Nixon has written off the society as "subversion on the Right," as has Otis Chandler, conservative publisher of the *Los Angeles Times* (*New York Times*, March 19, 1961). The anti-Communist Freedom House held that the John Birch Society was not really fighting Communism. "Those who join are serving the cause of destruction and chaos, requisites for a Communist advance" (statement in *America* June 3, 1961). Editorially, *America* claimed, "We can hardly conceive of a more singularly ineffective way of fighting communism" (April 15, 1961). The *Christian Century* sees the society appealing to those unable to bear any longer the attrition of the cold war, and those "compelled by hatred too long contained to crucify somebody" (April 12, 1961).

Nation says this society is not merely of the radical Right; it is of the idiot wing of the radical Right, "than which there is nothing sillier in the vast reaches of political absurdity" (April 8, 1961). But they do not want them investigated. The Moscow *Literary Gazette* hailed "the predictions of Lenin being materialized in the United States:" first McCarthy and now Welch. They feel Welch might do the American Communist Party almost as much good as Senator McCarthy (April 4, 1961).

Welch has struck a responsive lowbrow chord. His John Birch Society is the current expression of what Alan Westin has called America's "warmhearted, Main Street vigilantism." For those who feel prompted to act because of their very respectability, here is a program. The society's motto of "Less government and more responsibility" appeals to those longing for the days before the government began alphabetizing agencies. Who cares if Mr. Welch used to be an O.P.A. consultant for the candy industry? Today he is Defender of the Faith of Americanism to those who refuse to draw a line between faith and mania.

The John Birch Society has published a recommended reading list called "One Dozen Candles." No candle burns before Lord Morley's classic *On Compromise* (1874). Pharisee and salesman have conspired to bring forward Robert Welch as the champion of political fundamentalism.

Robert Welch's intellectual appeal to young people is just about nil. Even middlebrows ridicule him. The society itself is sometimes spoken of in kinder terms, but then only by young people who feel that some kind of action against Communism is necessary regardless of what form it takes. It takes a very unusual young person to join up, given the almost universal repudiation the society has evoked.

One young man in the home office in Belmont, Massachusetts, was a real enthusiast. He had just graduated from a Catholic college, and this was his first real job. After he took his position, he admitted that none of his former teacher-priests were very pleased. They told him he was actually harming anti-Communism by helping the J.B.S., but he stuck it out anyway. He would joke about the conspiratorial reputation of the society and insist that all it wanted to do was to put its case before people. Proud of his recruiting and fieldwork, this young man showed the dedication of a young Fuller Brush salesman eager to exceed his quota.

Part of Welch's difficulty in recruiting young people is that he is still trying to round up a sales staff. He wants young salesmen who will work dreary long hours, believe in the product, put up with exasperating guff from buyers, and work completely on the basis of commission. His followers are expected to put in more time than most activist groups require. They must be committed to a demanding creed of Americanism, be ready to handle the hostile arguments of those they are trying to convince, and be willing to wait indefinitely for any gratifying results.

This type of rugged individualist is rare even among young conservatives. Welch's continued attempt to find them shows how far out of touch he is with contemporary society.

The alleged martyrdom of John Birch himself has elicited no response among the young. Perhaps his death symbolizes a phase of our Far Eastern foreign policy that is too remote to appeal to today's young. It takes an older, more sentimental generation to respond to this kind of appeal.

Young conservative disillusionment with Welch is universal but mixed. Some are genuinely alarmed at his violations of the rules of the game, and his outlandish accusations. Others are just disappointed because he muffed a good thing. William Buckley and Company have dropped Welch from the team, but you get the feeling that it is only because he kept fumbling lateral passes, not because he was prone to run the ball toward the enemy's goal line.

Accepting the Birch Society minus Welch (which the founder will not abide) is usually on the grounds of its active record. These young conservatives believe that, at the time, no other Right group was so effectively anti-Communist. These people were *doing* something. Here the society might have had an effective appeal, but they were soon superseded by the more activist Young Americans for Freedom, a movement exclusively for the young and without the J.B.S.'s nearly lethal publicity.

Only the ultra-Right young man who also likes Billy James

Hargis or Kent Courtney could go along with Robert Welch, whose appeal seems to be confined to youthful lowbrows.

Industrial baronets and respectable businessmen have responded quite well to Welch's sales pitch. Why doesn't it work for the young? Except for anti-Communism, which is now carried by your neighborhood dealer, Welch's movement is throughly antiquarian. Its businesslike techniques thinly veil a movement organized on the forlorn virtues of the traveling salesman. The antimajoritarian implications of J.B.S. have a limited market today; the same is true of the irresponsible, unsubstantiated charge.

A movement so devoid of sophistication and balance might have an appeal to older, more frightened businessmen; it could hardly catch on among young conservatives who treasure their sophistication if they have it and generally respect it if they don't. Young conservatives may continue to use J.B.S. materials and occasionally support similar issues, but they are very unlikely to join its ranks.

CHAPTER 6

Senator Barry Goldwater as
Catalyst

WILLIAM BUCKLEY is a galvanizer. Robert Welch is a gadfly. Neither could assume Goldwater's role. Nor could Richard Nixon. Nixon is a politician with a sensitive ear, perfect pitch, and a beautiful sense of timing. But he leads a following; he doesn't create one. Henry Wallace, Adlai Stevenson, and Robert Taft had this political mystique that creates followings. So does Barry Goldwater.

No one else has so successfully accelerated a right-Wing synthesis. What Eisenhower failed to do in restructuring the G.O.P. for the center, Goldwater has tried to do from the Right. Three months after his break with Eisenhower in the spring of 1957, Goldwater said on the Senate floor, "I am happy to note today that the word 'modern' has disappeared from the language of the Republican Party."

The breaking point came when the faithful were asked to

support the administration's $72 billion budget in May, 1957. Goldwater called it a budget to wake the dead. "Our party's aims should be to cut spending, balance the budget, reduce national debt, cut taxes—in short, to live within our means and allow our citizens the maximum personal benefits from their economic endeavors."

I have never believed, Goldwater continued, that our people were fundamentally receptive to government by bribe. We are saturated with the New Deal doctrine of squanderbust government. How attractive do we make the ideal of freedom to the rest of the world with our $71.8 billion budget?

To cap his point, Goldwater asked unanimous consent of his colleagues to insert in the record an anonymous "study" called "How Freedom Vanished in the Ancient World by Popular Vote." The article decried Pericles's P.W.A. and giveaway programs. Cleon is compared to Huey Long. It was the rise of Big Government with its one and only policy—government spending—that ruined Athens. Diocletian is compared to the La Follettes. Listed among the steps toward ruin are centralization of credit, bringing into cultivation of wastelands and improvement of soil by means of a common plan, or the equal liability of all to labor. The latter would lead to industrial armies, W.P.A., or C.C.C.

Aside from this extraordinary addendum, Goldwater's speech was a pungent delivery of the classic Republican anathema on government spending. The modern Republicans had gone too far. Someone had to cry halt. Goldwater saw it as his duty. When pressed for a reply to this attack, President Eisenhower said we can't turn back to 1890, but differences of opinion are part of the American political system.

After panting into office on the strength of Eisenhower's plurality in 1952, Goldwater was a conscientious supporter of most of the administration's policies. He balked at Bohlen's confirmation, favored Senator McCarthy, and held some rugged positions during the Taft-Hartley debates. For example, he felt it would be quite fair to require a union to have 95 per cent support of a plant's employees before it could be recognized as a bargaining agent. Also, states should be allowed to outlaw collective bargaining. But generally he went along. He favored the

St. Lawrence Seaway and upping congressional salaries from $15,000 to $22,500.

Now Goldwater felt free to prove that Taft was really right. America wants and needs conservatism. This was assumed as self-evident in a series of speeches Goldwater gave following his 1957 declaration of independence. With the editorial co-operation of his Arizona campaign manager, Stephen Shadegg, Goldwater put the speeches together in a little book called *The Conscience of a Conservative*. Shadegg evidently has a flair for elegant but folksy titles. His later biography of the senator is called *Barry Goldwater: Freedom Is His Flight Plan.*

In the foreword to *The Conscience of a Conservative* we are reassured not only that America is basically conservative but also that the young are especially yearning for a return to these principles. He regrets the need so many conservatives feel for apologizing. For example, Nixon saying we must be "conservatives with a heart"; or Ike: "I'm conservative when it comes to economic problems but liberal when it comes to human problems." Other Republicans refer to themselves as "progressive" conservatives, implying that "ordinary" conservatism is opposed to progress.

The apologies are unnecessary if you accept Goldwater's spiritualization of conservatism. Conservatism, he says, is not an economic theory, though it has economic implications. It is socialism that subordinates all other considerations to man's material well-being. Conservatives take account of the whole man. Liberals look only at the material side. The enhancement of man's spiritual nature should be the prime concern of our political philosophy.

Both sides can be confusing on this question of materialism versus idealism. There is a moral and an economic aspect to both individualism and socialism. The moral socialist indicts the moral individualist for being too egocentric and having an insufficient social conscience. Here is a tension between two versions of idealism. The economic mechanism of process may end up stifling the ideal motives of either the individualist or the socialist. Thus a materialist could result on either side of the fence. Neither position is immune.

Anyone owing a desert showplace, a Laguna Beach pleasure

dome, a Washington apartment, and three department stores (only recently sold) has to tread carefully on the issue of materialism. Gore Vidal asked the senator if he really thought the desire to do good was entirely economic in origin. Goldwater said of course it was. "I then asked him to explain how it was that two people as different as ourselves worked hard, though in neither case was the spur money. He was startled. Then he murmured vaguely and slipped from the subject" (*Life*, June 9, 1961).

If the moral socialist really wanted to have his ire raised, he should have heard Goldwater addressing the National Association of Plumbing Contractors. After denouncing the last thirty years of "economic fakery," Goldwater urged his audience not to seek more business through supporting Federal aid to school construction or more public-health programs. Invent some new gadgets, he advised, that everybody has to have in the bathroom. "We don't make our money selling things people have to have. When I think of all the gadgets I put into my new house four years ago! That is the kind of thing I talk about when I talk about research."

The conservative's reluctance to entertain new speculative ideas finds strange compensation in a fond penchant for new things in practical affairs. Irate at the allegation that he was not modern, Goldwater protested from the Senate floor: "My brother and I have just built a new store. I fly an airplane. I like new things and new gadgets."

A new mercury light switch or an electric pencil sharpener gives you a lift and a feeling that you are riding at least a small wave of the future. These pleasant undulations at the surface of progress do not disturb any deep currents of social thinking. Whether you go stereo or stick with monaural, nobody really gets out of line. Change in the realm of practical things can be harmless, and it's great for business.

Pride in personal ownership is important to the conservative because it connotes so many of the reassuring virtues of fundamentalism: industry, thrift, stewardship, and so on. Goldwater is trusted and respected because he sincerely believes and reflects these attributes. His friend Stephen Shadegg wrote an article back in Phoenix which Goldwater had reprinted in the *Congres-*

sional Record. It is a testimony of stewardship called "God's Time." In it Shadegg tells of lending a friend a power tool. "He used it with great care. . . . Each night he put it back in its case with the chips and sawdust brushed away. When he returned it to me he said, 'I was mindful each time I used this thing that it belonged to you.' "

Whether you are being solicitous about a power tool, a front lawn, or a payroll, you are playing the part of the good steward. Property comes from hard work. Hegel spoke of private property as being an extension of one's personality into the realm of matter. Even Marx defined labor as "man's metabolism with nature." But Marx refused to go on and say that property relationships are therefore protected by natural law. The conservative does. If you alter the rules on property, you run the risk of violating the natural order.

Goldwater deeply believes this. Apparently conservatives feel that no other public official is more sincere than Goldwater in this belief. It is a key factor in understanding his catalytic effect on the Right.

Even before the lonely crowd was disclosed, people loved sincerity in their heroes. Every quarter seems to agree that Goldwater is amply endowed. Often the qualities you speak of in others are the ones you value most yourself. When Senator Richard L. Neuberger of Oregon died, Goldwater delivered a euology of him in the Senate. He singled out three qualities of his friend and political opponent. First to be prized was his sincerity; next was his honesty—that is, devotion to the honesty of his convictions. "I have never known Dick to deviate one inch from a principle in which he believed." His third characteristic was the sincere application of his thinking and the dedication of his life to the principles in which he believed.

These, of course, are the very qualities the public sees in Goldwater. He is seen as not only sincere but consistent. He sticks to his guns and is more interested in principles than in pluralities. This senator uses less cant and more candor than most politicians, and firmly believes that fences are for indicating sides and are not to be straddled.

This is evident in his remarks before the Platform Committee of the 1960 Republican Convention. "The American people," he argued, "will be far more eager to place their destiny in the hands of a man who announces his beliefs and principles than in the hands of a man who promises and promises and promises." He denied that there was any great public demand for Federal aid to depressed areas, public education, or support of the economy.

As one magazine might put it, forthright was his position on Russia. "To our undying national shame, there are those among us who would prefer to crawl on their bellies to Moscow rather than to face the possibility of an atomic war."

Nixon's decision to confer with Rockefeller was described by Goldwater as a Munich meeting. This convinced him that Eisenhower Republicans had no ideological backbone. Goldwater boasted that if Nixon had waged a truly conservative campaign, he would have won every state except New York, Michigan, and Massachusetts. The conservatives lost this Republican convention but they were out to capture the next.

Addressing the Cattlemen's Association in Dallas, Goldwater claimed that we are maintaining a herd of boarder cows at public expense. The speech had opened with his leitmotiv: "It's encouraging to see people who have not been taken in by that beguiling promise of something for nothing, which is the universal bait employed to secure citizen consent for federal intervention." After a remarkable number of clichés for 1960, including "Waste not, want not," the finale goes: "We can return to those principles of thrift, industry and person-to-person charity which conquered this hostile continent and made America the goal and the beacon light for all men everywhere."

The United Press International Conference of Editors and Publishers was told that we don't need new goals. "We have one: 'life, liberty, and the pursuit of happiness.' The blueprint for Fabianism is speeding through Congress at this very moment in the form of a depressed-area bill and the minimum-wage law. Gentlemen, there is a breaking point, and I believe the American people are reaching it more rapidly than is generally supposed."

Two weeks later Goldwater tore into the tractor deal with

Castro at Rockford, Illinois. "How sick do we have to get? . . . How rotten can we be? How low can we sink as Americans before Americans rise up and say, 'Look, our heritage demands more than this.' "

These speeches revive conservative hopes trampled by a generation of liberals. Work hard, persevere, and provide for yourself. After hearing Goldwater's words, those conservatives who were able to refuse W.P.A. groceries in the threadbare thirties can feel a new pride. Those who have finally tidied up major surgery bills with a second mortgage can preen themselves on their frugality. People who have long believed in the chaste reputation of our foreign affairs welcome the assurance that this is no time to begin compromising. And the reassurance comes, not from a cranky mossback, but from the only member of the United States Senate licensed to fly a jet airplane.

Conservatives tend to reduce the problem of human freedom to a simple formula. Whatever is freely intiated by the self is essentially good, as long as it does not intrude on the rights of others. Whatever attempts to regulate the individual is bad, unless it is preventing him from harming others. For example, charity is superior to a welfare measure because it is freely given.

In his *The Conscience of a Conservative*, Goldwater decries the harm done to individuals even when they do not realize it. The idea spreads that the government owes the benefits it confers. "How different it is with private charity where both the giver and the receiver understand that charity is the product of the humanitarian impulses of the giver, not the due of the receiver. Let us, then, not blunt the noble impulses of mankind by reducing charity to mechanical operation of the federal government" (page 73).

Private charity means the benefactor is to determine the object, nature, extent, and occasion of charity. To say that an individual, or even a private agency, is always going to determine justly to whom, in what form, how much, and when assistance is to be given is putting quite a strain on the human nature that conservatives believe to be so corrupt. The moral ambiguity of private charity as opposed to the relatively more objective demands of social justice has been discussed in an earlier chapter.

The point is that, whether through commission or omission, much that originates from the free self is essentially not good.

How about the charge that unless you are restraining an individual from harming others, you have no right to regulate him?

Senator Strom Thurmond yielded the floor for Goldwater to say, on August 17, 1961, that the common denominator between governments other than governments of free men is control. "We are witnessing in our government today more and more the realization that control must be had if the programs are to be consummated. . . . Each piece of proposed legislation on which we work in this body and in the other House has in it elements of control over people. . . . Communism, Socialism, egalitarianism, monarchism, dictatorship or—and forgive me— the New Deal, Fair Deal, or New Frontier. They all have one thing in common—they must have control."

This is an extraordinary remark to come from a member of a mid-twentieth century legislative chamber. The blanket condemnation of "controls" brings to mind the comment of a nineteenth century English conservative, James F. Steven: "To exalt liberty, in the sense of 'absence of restraint,' at the expense of restraint, is like praising the centrifugal force in the solar system and blaming the centripetal." Political coercion, and even social custom, is not hostile to the individual merely because the control comes from "others." The question should be of the nature and tendency of the force, not of its origin. A most destructive force might be emanating from the self. A liberating force may be supplied by "others."

If Senator Goldwater held to this view consistently, he would be the absolute darling of both Ayn Rand and the John Birch Society. Fortunately for his political future, he doesn't. In practice, that is, by his vote, he seems to realize that political coercion is a matter of degree and convenience. In the Senate he has favored Federal funds for construction of 140,000 housing units, introduced a resolution for stockpiling of extra-long staple cotton, sponsored a bill to enlarge government holdings in Grand Canyon, pushed for subsidies on wool and wheat and support prices on copper and tungsten. He wanted more Federal money for flood-control improvements on the Gila and Salt rivers in

Arizona. He could use a little for construction at Buttes Dam and Reservoir, and let's not forget the Colorado River development fund.

Then there was his bill to provide Federal loans for the construction of sea- and brackish-water-conversion plants. One of his pet projects is to provide Federal funds for acquiring riparian rights from Arizona to the Gulf of California for the piping and pumping of water to his home state for irrigation purposes. Besides favoring the $2 billion highway construction bill, he has gone along with Federal subsides for oil, magazines, and the merchant marine. He has even introduced a bill for the Veterans Administration to permit retired officers and enlisted men to use available hospital facilities. What can you do when you are a member of both the V.F.W. and the Thunderbird Post 41 of the American Legion?

Certainly Goldwater does not oppose the use of force in foreign relations. He included Teddy Roosevelt in his list of the six outstanding American conservatives because "he showed that the proper use of power could preserve the peace" (*New York Times Magazine* July 31, 1960).

After the above voting record, Senator Goldwater faced then Representative Stewart Udall in debating whether Arizona should participate in the National Defense Education Act. Goldwater was opposed to Federal subsidies for education on principle. "I'm not out to rob New York for the benefit of Arizona." Then he clinched his point with the admission, "Yes, I fear Washington more than I do Moscow" (*New Republic*, January 4, 1960).

At the top of his form Senator Goldwater can be an effective custodian of public funds. Prepared with an impressive display of facts, he tore into the request for a $7 million supplemental appropriation for rebuilding a navigation lock at Wheeler Dam, part of the T.V.A. in Alabama. This lock, Goldwater claimed, failed because of inexcusable ignorance in engineering. Excavation for the new lock was alongside and not far removed from the old one. When the new excavation cut below the strata upon which the old lock was built, there was slippage on the clay seam, and a part of the old lock slid into the new excavation. This could have been prevented by proper exploration work and by keying together the various stratas of limestone.

Why should we pay for this inexcusable negligence in engineering? A good question.

On the same day (September 23, 1961), he asked why T.V.A. was opposing the attempt of the Southern Railroad to obtain lower rates on grain shipments? (Use of new high-capacity aluminum freight cars made lower prices possible.) If the new rates were approved, barge lines carrying T.V.A. fuel and construction materials could not compete with the railroads. "It seems to me T.V.A. is getting a little out of character when it objects to the lowering of the rates on anything." So it is.

Debate like this could win the senator a considerable following of moderates.

But Goldwater seems more inclined to court forces to his Right. In part he is doing this by an outrageous exploition of the old radical theory of direct democracy. According to this romantic notion, the only safe power is that in the immediate hands of the people. The more decentralization, the better. This is fine for Goldwater. It gets power out of Washington. As he says in *The Conscience of a Conservative* (page 22), "Our tendency to concentrate power in the hands of a few men deeply concerns me."

On the previous page his conservative conscience was bothered by the observation that "we have gone the way of many a democratic society that has lost its freedom by persuading itself that if 'the people' rule, all is well." He uses a theory of direct democracy to challenge the existing system of representative government. Then he warns us of the dangers of radical democracy. It is all the more confusing when we recall that Goldwater believes our country is a republic and not a democracy.

One minute Goldwater is talking himself out of a job as senator because we can't trust representatives of the people. The next moment he is talking us out of a democracy because you can't trust the people.

Part of Goldwater's difficulty is his belief that anytime power is decentralized it is a victory for individual freedom.

This might surprise Negroes in the South. It certainly would have been news to the serfs under feudalism. The centralizing nation state has often been a positive force in liberating Western man. As Burke put it, "Nothing turns out to be so oppressive and unjust as feeble government." Decentralized power may or may not bring more freedom. There is no necessary correlation.

Gilbert Harrison has noted how frequently Goldwater will indulge in the old device of proof by definition. He will set forth a premise, such as "the less centralization, the more freedom," and treat it as a fact. It is a grand way to infuriate the opposition. Just as your opponent is ready to argue your premise, you have waltzed off to another "fact."

Conservatives frequently strike a romantic note of the heroic. Sometimes the occasion for a heroic stance is so convenient that you wonder how much of it is quaint credulity and how much is sheer hypocrisy. A year before Goldwater admitted to Gore Vidal that the desire to do good was economic in origin, he was debating Senator Gore on the question of Federal aid to teachers' salaries.

Goldwater felt that low salaries were not a primary problem. "I know of many officers in the Air Force who could resign tomorrow and receive better salaries with private companies, but because of patriotism and love of their work they do not do so." He said he was convinced that salary was not the driving force for people. "Some persons go into business because they feel I can make myself rich, and others go into business with a feeling that they can do something for their country" (Senate, February 3, 1960).

Anyway, Goldwater insists, what the schools need even more than money is the continued personal concern of parents and citizens. Mere money won't produce closer cooperation. Federal aid would actually make local citizens less interested in school affairs, since it would deprive them of control. What controls? Senator Gore claimed that in forty years of operation the Smith-Hughes Act had no undesirable controls.

The National Defense Education Act of 1958 has been singled out by Goldwater as an example of legislation that would control the schools. Yet Title I of this act prohibits control over "the curriculum, program of instruction, administration, or personnel of any educational institution or school system." This would hardly dishearten the P.T.A. The act calls for establishing a priority program approved by a state agency. Hearings for applicants are to be held before state agencies. Laboratory and other special equipment must meet state standards. If anything, the states would appear to be getting the best of the bargain.

Goldwater has his own remedy. He has introduced a Senate bill that would give tax credits on the income-tax form for local school taxes paid. If the local authorities felt more money was needed for education, they could then tax these rebates. The first result of this scheme, according to Senator Clark, would be a Federal deficit of about $4 billion. The first three years of Kennedy's education bill would run only $3 billion. New tax loopholes would be created for the wealthy, and there would be nothing to ensure that adequate funds would be available for education.

According to Goldwater, the important thing is not to blackmail, bribe, intimidate, or in any way coerce a local school system into spending more money than it thinks is necessary. He calls the Federal grants-in-aid program "a mixture of blackmail and bribery." Somehow certain subsidies, depletion allowances, and tariffs escape this condemnation.

To say that education is strictly the private affair of one community is like saying that health is nobody else's business. Ignorance is as contagious as disease. The educational limitations of Alabama are as much a threat as hoof-and-mouth disease in Texas. Border guards in California check on diseased oranges but not on ignoramuses. Yesterday's submarginally educated child in Picayune, Mississippi, may end up as tomorrow's problem citizen in Phoenix, Arizona.

Federal aid to education does not disturb Goldwater as much as the power of labor unions. The senator has made greater yardage on no other subject in the *Congressional Record*. Few of labor's peccadilloes escape his scrutiny and none of their crimes his scorn. Again his basic difficulty is with an incredible view of power. He warned the Chamber of Commerce in Washington, D.C. (May 1, 1957), that "power itself is the enemy of freedom." This is an extravagant case of converting a debate topic into a datum of experience. "Power," he continues, "is invariably created as a collective effort and then exercised by one or two individuals using the power of the collective to enforce their personal wills. . . ." Power is denied any neutrality, and apparently any collective effort is doomed to tyranny.

Freedom is being menaced by labor leaders who have established political power as the total objective of their organizations. "Today certain labor leaders bring to the bargaining table, not only the strength of their arguments but the power of politics." The union leader most out of line is Walter Reuther, whom Goldwater accuses of exploiting the labor-union movement to create a machine for personal political power. Reuther is considered more of a threat to trade unionism than Dave Beck or Jimmy Hoffa.

In testifying before a Senate Committee hearing, Hoffa confided to Goldwater: "When you separate the political from the economic you and I could have a different discussion." The Teamsters' boss said labor leaders had no business trying to influence politics. Goldwater responded: "Well, Mr. Hoffa, just to wind this up, I think we both recognize that in the writing in the clouds today there is an individual [Reuther] who would like that to happen in this country. I do not like to ever suggest to let you and him fight, but for the good of the labor movement, I am very hopeful that your view prevails" (Hearings of Labor Subcommittee, August 20, 1957).

When Goldwater submitted a minority report for the Senate Labor Rackets Committee, he claimed that corruption, misappropriation of funds, bribery, extortion, and collusion with the underworld exist within the U.A.W. as they do in those other unions whose derelictions have been so widely publicized.

This brought a generous response from the conservative *Detroit News* (February 13, 1960): "We don't approve of Walter Reuther's insatiable desire for power. We don't like his social philosophy. We think his free pouring of union funds to control elections both violates the law and threatens our democratic system. . . . But the U.A.W. is no Teamsters Union and Reuther is no Hoffa. We doubt if any major union has been more free of corruption and collusion with the underworld. We do not believe Senator Goldwater . . . has the facts to prove the contrary."

Goldwater's vendetta with Reuther is just a colorful reflection of his general opposition to modern unionism. Unions are fine, says he, but they should be denied industry-wide bargaining, the union shop, and political activity. He sees trade unionists as America's new second-class citizens, a new serfdom because they are forced to join a union and to make political contributions. Addressing the Traffic Club in Pittsburgh, Goldwater spoke of this denial of rights to the laborer as the deadly civil-rights problem in the North, which is just as bad as the South's.

Yet in N.L.R.B. elections from 1947 to 1951, union-shop authorizations won in 97.1 percent of the plant elections. There appears to be a marked preference for the union shop among workers. It's heroic of Senator Goldwater to champion the position of 2.9 percent of the labor force, but it is questionable whether national policy should be determined by such support.

In *The Conscience of a Conservative*, Goldwater attempts to answer the question Why should nonunion workers benefit from union achievements? by arguing that since the Red Cross benefits us all, why aren't we forced to make donations? One retort is that a donation to the Red Cross is assumed to be an altruistic gesture, disinterested in the sense that unless you happen to live on a flood plain in a cyclone belt, you usually do not expect an immediate return on your investment. We expect benefits from the Red Cross to be incidental and accidental. A trade union exists to further one's economic self-interest. Its benefits had better be essential and deliberate. There's a difference.

Reuther has defended the A.F.L.-C.I.O.'s Committee on Political Education (COPE) by saying that what you win at the bargaining table you can lose in the legislative halls. He told his U.A.W. that the people you elect to write your tax legislation affect your income just as much as the bargaining committee you elect to work on your wage contract. Senator Goldwater's attempts to muffle COPE are no more desirable or likely of success than would be Walter Reuther's attempts to silence the National Association of Manufacturers.

If Goldwater's labor policy brings on hearty cheers from

conservatives, his foreign policy evokes deafening applause. His basic premise is that no American foreign policy is feasible unless it presupposes a program for the defeat of world Communism. How? The affairs of nations, Goldwater wrote in the *National Review* (March 25, 1961), are not determined by goodwill tours, almsgiving, gestures of self-denial, rehabilitation projects, and discussion programs—but by power.

"The United States has proceeded on the assumption that virtue is its own rewards. . . . Having the world think well of us is sluggish sentimentality." The theme occurs again in *The Conscience of a Conservative*. "The American government does not have the right, much less the obligation, to try to promote the economic and social welfare of foreign peoples. . . . Foreign aid has not made the world stronger; it has made America weaker" (pages 95, 99). Nothing of value has been produced in the fifteen years that we have been engaged in it.

He went on to tell the Congress of American Industry (December 8, 1960) what they already knew. "We have nothing to apologize for in this country. We are a good people and a sound people. We have been a people who have always helped the world. We have allowed other countries to determine our foreign policy, where we should have been determining theirs as much as possible. Respect is what we should be seeking. In fact, we should be demanding it. Since we have the greatest military and economic power in the world, there is no reason why we can not earn the respect of other nations."

This was from a speech against the $500 million authorization for Latin American economic aid. Contrast these rodomontades with the criticism of the same bill offered on the Senate floor by Senator Long (August 19, 1960). He stressed the bill's loose construction and the fact that it had no limiting date like the Marshall Plan. How are we going to prevent a privileged few from hogging the benefits? Are we going to force land reform? How? There must be guarantees of tangible benefits.

Of course, such reasoned criticism presupposes that foreign economic aid per se is feasible. Goldwater does not. He generally prefers a more dramatic alternative.

On the Jack Paar show, Goldwater said the government

should be trying to get United States citizens free who are jailed in Red China.

Paar: "What could we have done outside of atomic war? It would have been war, wouldn't it?"

Goldwater: "Well, what if it would? Can American people live in the kind of peace we would have if Communism were dominant in this world?"

In the event of another Hungary, issue an ultimatum forbidding the Soviets to intervene. Be ready to move in nuclear weapons. We could bluff the Soviets out of fighting. Throw an economic and naval blockade around Cuba. The Kennedy Administration finally obliged with a selective naval blockade of offensive weapons in October, 1962, after discovering Soviet missile sites on the island. Assist the rebel forces in any way. Ignore South American riots protesting our policy, and Castro would fall in six months. As for Africa, we can't afford to jump on the bandwagon of anticolonialism. "We are the bearers of Western civilization, the most noble product of the heart and mind of man." He continued informing the faithful of the *National Review* by reminding them nuclear tests are harmless because the danger of fallout from stratospheric testing is nonexistent (repeated in *The Conscience of a Conservative*, page 110).

The cultural-exchange program is a Communist confidence game. Anyway, we should be withdrawing recognition from the Soviet Union rather than fraternizing with her. The United Nations? "We begin by not taking it seriously." The United Nations provides a unique forum for Communist propaganda, places an unwarranted financial burden on American taxpayers, and may be leading to an unconstitutional surrender of American sovereignty. Our national interests usually suffer when we subordinate our policy to the United Nation's. But withdrawal is "probably" not the answer.

The Right wing believes that Washington is not earnestly engaging the Communists in cold-war battle. Goldwater attentively voices this distrust. He announced on the Senate floor (March 15, 1960) that "a craven fear of death is entering the American consciousness. Our enemies have understood the nature of the conflict, and we have not. . . . Our leaders have not made victory the goal of American policy because they have never believed deeply that the Communists are in earnest. . . . unless you contemplate treason, your objective, like his, will be victory. Not peace but victory."

This was followed up three months later by the explosive "Suggested Letter to Khrushchev," which demanded apology from Mr. Khrushchev for insulting President Eisenhower at Paris. Goldwater felt the State Department should have sent one like it. In it he chastized the Soviet leader for his temper, warned him that we can still outproduce him two to one. We have better armaments and could survive more than one harvest year without facing the threat of starvation. We have been outwitted at peace, but we have never lost a war. The peace is up to you. "How do you stand, sir?" (This question became the title of Goldwater's syndicated column.)

The reckless, almost apocalyptic, approach to the cold war becomes even more irresponsible when you consider a remark Goldwater made in his speech against Latin American aid. In denying the efficacy of foreign aid, he made the astounding statement: "No assemblage of men, no bureaucratic form of regulatory government established in any one central place, can solve a crisis. All they do is compound the crisis." Goldwater's bent for decentralization often shows alarming signs of devolving into a proclivity for anarchy. Are the fifty states to conduct their own foreign policies? His phobia of centralized power would apparently deprive us of even the saving grace of the Articles of Confederation.

For those on the Right more interested in beguiling dogmatic consistency than candid logical coherence, Goldwater is a convincing spokesman. A robust personality and handsome profile are enhanced by the stature of senatorial office. As a catalyst of the Right, it is to his advantage not to be an intellectual. Goldwater has come a long way since his first book written in 1941: *An Odyssey of the Green and Colorado Rivers: The Intimate Journal of Three Boats and Nine People on a Trip Down Two Rivers.* Still he regrets his lack of academic background, and defers to Russell Kirk as the philosophical mentor of conservatism.

Goldwater is more comfortable in his role as Legionnaire,

Shriner, and Elk, and so are his followers. He is very much a gentleman of the Southwest, with undeniable charm that often enchants his opponents.

Senator Hubert Humphrey: "Whenever the Senator from Arizona addresses this body I always like to be present, because I know I am hearing good sound Republican doctrine, sincere and honest, and to the point. It is the kind of doctrine which I respect, even though I may not agree."

Senator Goldwater: "I thank the Senator and I assure him that I will not speak in the Senate on the day of the primary in Wisconsin [Laughter]."

Senator Humphrey: "I am deeply grateful even for small favors."

As Gore Vidal put it, his engagingly cranky rejection of liberalism has made him catch on as a personality even if his policies have not.

Few politicians have hit it off as well with young conservatives as Barry Goldwater. No one comes near him in their eyes. He manages to embody all the homely virtues of middle-class conservatism with such finesse that it is almost sophistication. Somehow he never gives the impression of being too pious or priggish. He carries it all off in a regular-guy style that would make Robert Taft weep in envy. If Taft was conservatism's Tom Sawyer, Goldwater is its Huckleberry Finn.

Whether he was in fact or not, Taft often gave the impression of being self-righteous. His acknowledged virtue was worn with awkward grace. Every time you looked at Robert, you imagined a medal on his wide lapel proclaiming twenty-five years of perfect Sunday-school attendance. Barry gives you the impression of having played a pretty good game of hookey.

The Huck Finn dimension might not be apparent to young liberals who consider Goldwater hopelessly moralistic. But to young conservatives he does have a touch of the ingratiating warmth, openness, native deviltry, and occasional humor of a Huck Finn. The analogy can be strained no further because Huck Finn is essentially a liberal character. But to young conservatives who have produced more than their share of Tom Sawyers, even a hint of Huck Finn strikes sparks.

Goldwater has convinced his young followers that you can

be both a successful capitalist and a conservative politician without being a stuffed shirt.

Most of the drive for Goldwater's candidacy at the 1960 Republican Convention at Chicago was supplied by young supporters. (The same had been true of Stevenson's last roundup at Los Angeles.) Youth for Goldwater was so enthusiastic about its hero that it refused to acknowledge defeat and go home. Instead the nucleus of this group rallied and formed Young Americans for Freedom, under the tutelage of William Buckley, Jr.

Goldwater the politician is conservative youth's idol because he fits the bill so perfectly. He carries conservatism just about as far Right as you can go and still win elections. As head of the Campaigns and Elections Committee for Senate Republicans, Goldwater has acquired a reputation for political acumen [not shared by G.O.P. liberals]. The young conservatives must believe that they are championing someone who can win. Goldwater gives them a tactical security they have not enjoyed before. Without showing some sign of winning more political battles soon, conservatism was in danger of losing youthful support. Goldwater changed this.

Never the intellectual, Goldwater appeals to the young middlebrows in business and on campus who find a diet of Ayn Rand too rich and disturbing and who prefer their capitalism and patriotism defined and defended by someone closer home to middle-class virtues. They admire the courage and verve of a politician willing to champion these virtues with such apparent consistency and composure. Young conservatives want to believe the capitalist folk myths about success and virtue. Goldwater makes it easier.

Genuinely impressed by the response he has evoked among young followers, Senator Goldwater speaks at fifty or sixty college campuses a year, and draws large crowds. As godfather to Young Americans for Freedom, the senator favors them with a liberal allowance of his time, which is in such great demand. Although he speaks only the familiar words, they love him. At last young conservatives have a leader who acts and looks like a white knight. And most important of all, he is mounted and charging, whether he is tilting at dragons or windmills.

Certainly Senator Goldwater has demonstrated that he has

the requisite qualities to accelerate a synthesis of the political Right. Like a catalyst, he has been a small force reaching a large audience and is perfect for his element—anathema to others. How unchanged he will himself remain will be in part determined by his susceptibility to the moderating winds of presidential ambition. The question of major importance is how he fulfills the last property of a catalyst. Although he has increased the rate of reaction, can he really alter the final political equilibrium? It can't be done in chemistry.

CHAPTER 7

The Soft Sell: Peter Viereck and Clinton Rossiter

FOR masters of the conservative soft sell, we might turn to two historians: Clinton Rossiter at Cornell and Peter Viereck at Mount Holyoke. One wins you by his politic realism. The other captivates you by his poetic humanism.

PETER VIERECK

As historian, Peter Viereck has an enviable catalog of data at his command. As poet, he makes such surprising juxtapositions of ideas that you are sometimes startled into accepting his thought-images for their esthetic rather than for their logical value. Viereck can't browse through old ideas without putting them back on the shelf in new positions. After reading Viereck, you might not agree with his conclusions, but it is pretty hard to say why.

Goldwater's arguments have just the edge to make liberals

111

more self-righteous than ever. Viereck's idea-associations have the discomfiting effect of making liberals realize how conservative they are.

Both socialism and conservatism, Viereck believes, work in America as a diffusion, not a movement. They do not have a social base, a party, or a class. When they do become a movement, they become small, comical splinter groups. This diffusion will be jeopardized if the conservatives try to localize it into the apologetics for any one class. Viereck speaks of a "diffusion" because he thinks conservatism is essentially an ethical and cultural force. It may seem strange to ignore the obvious economic factors and think of both conservatism and socialism as ethical and cultural forces, but this is the way Viereck plays it.

In his plea for *The Unadjusted Man: A New Hero for Americans,* Viereck warns of the short step involved from the well-adjusted to the overadjusted, the "public-relations personality of public smile and private blank." The overadjusted has an abnormal desire for normalcy as an end. The unadjusted is not to be confused with the maladjusted man, nor with the never adjusted, the merely crotchety. Ideally, man is a wayfarer in the present but not part of it. "Unadjusted Man is adjusted to the ages, unadjusted to the age, has lasting roots and ephemeral surfaces." The true conservative must always be unadjusted in this sense.

Admitting that the current return to orthodoxy, values, and tradition is 90 percent toadyism and opportunism, Viereck urges the New Conservatives to stop becoming what they accuse liberals of being: rootless doctrinaires. Conservatives still adhering to the economies of Adam Smith are guilty of arbitrary, rootless abstractions. Take conservatism away from those who think primarily of economic man.

"The Taft worshipper is that kind of American failure known as 'a success in life.'" He has been successful only at grabbing gold rings. Earlier in his *Conservatism Revisited,* Viereck said that the conservative function is to insist on distinguishing value from price, wisdom from cleverness, happiness from hedonism, and reverence from success worship. Too many of today's conservatives have difficulty distinguishing between the extrinsic and the intrinsic.

A true conservative sympathizes with aristocracy, says Viereck, but never with plutocracy. The "McKinley-style pseudo elite of Taft Republicanism" can hardly be called aristocratic or conservative. It links individuals by the cash nexus: "inadequate, disenchanting, a nexus psychologically unsatisfying." Viereck entitled an *Antioch Review* article "Will America Prove Marx Right?" (September, 1952), and admonished us not to have a triumph of cash-nexus thinking. A new shallowness regarding values would play into Marxist hands. "What is merely useful, rather than innately good, must never be regarded as sacred, beyond criticism, beyond future change."

Conservatism, Viereck points out, ought to mean "the zest of rediscovery." One of the things to be rediscovered is that there is no antithesis between conservatism and socialism. Democratic capitalism requires occasional doses of Disraeli's "Tory socialism." Richard Oastler is quoted to the effect that a Tory is tenacious of the rights of all, but most of the poor and needy, because they require the shelter of the constitution and laws more than other classes. Therefore, a compassionate and humane approach to economic suffering is the logical outgrowth of the oldest Christian, Jewish, and Hellenic ethic. We are urged not to allow an insensitive capitalism to prove that Marx was right.

Who are the new conservatives? Viereck points out to the exurban throngs who voted for Eisenhower. Why did they turn Republican? "Perhaps the reason these unthankful sons are so eager to associate the New Deal with Alger Hiss is because they don't want to admit the association it really suggests to their mind: Horatio Alger" (page 114). Their rise in income was faster than their increase in social standing. Consequently these radicals of prosperity overassimilated and became 200 per cent American nationalists.

The new Right, claims Viereck, is the most anticonservative uprising in native Americana since the Whiskey Rebellion of 1794. This bombshell comes through the courtesy of one of Viereck's very favorite specters—direct democracy. The new Right is the form taken today by direct democracy. It is a form of coercive American overadjustment.

According to Viereck, Rousseau's "Noble Savage" (common

man), his admonition to keep power directly in the hands of the people, and his distrust of sophisticated bureaucracy are best found preserved in the Populist and Progressive movements, which believed that original sin stopped west of the Alleghenies. This people's movement, according to Viereck, has engendered anti-intellectualism and isolationism. It is a triumph of value-defying egalitarianism that has produced such demagogues as Governor Huey Long, Father Coughlin, and Senator Joe McCarthy.

Viereck's analysis flusters liberals who had looked upon radical Populists-Progressives as natural allies, and confounds conservatives who had no inkling of such radical support. But it gives him a formidable base from which to attack McCarthyism. The *Pacific Spectator* (Summer, 1955) contains Viereck's "The Conservative Case Against McCarthyism."

Too little of an ideologue to be a fascist, Viereck sees McCarthy as a new type Left-wing Populist or Jacobin agitator who, by an infallible instinct, subverted those institutions that are most organic and conservative. He attacked the Constitution, most decorated military leaders, most ancient universities, most strongly established religion, and best families—the most patrician aspects of society.

Whereas most Right-wingers welcomed McCarthy in the fight against Communism, Viereck alludes to such extreme Right-wing anti-Communists as "White Bolsheviks." Even McCarthy's penchant for lie detectors is used as evidence of the connection between the senator and the demon Direct Democracy. The lie detector is seen as an egalitarian leveler, not overawed by traditional honor or rank, not duped by big words, nor taken in by any well-earned reputation for public trust and service.

McCarthyism is seen as symptomatic of what both Tocqueville and Pareto spoke of as "status resentment." The resentment of the would-be antiradical of the new Right is not economic; it is resentment against social, educational, and sectional aristocracy. It is Overadjusted Man preferring new stereotypes over traditional archetypes, conforming rather than conserving. This is the cardinal sin to be committed against Viereck's version of conservatism. As he puts it, the old Populist cry of "you internationalist Anglophile snob" was replaced by the deadlier "you egghead security risk."

While you might dispute Viereck's derivation of the new conservatism, its character and direction are described with devastating acumen.

Why does the new Right usually accuse only non-Communists of Communism? Because, suggests Viereck, its quarry is not Communists but old constitutional traditionalists. They want to be the new determiners of culture patterns, taste patterns, and values. The new would-be rulers included unmellowed plebeian western wealth and their big, gullible mass base of western sticks and eastern slums. Nationalism is their means to power.

These philistines are part of a third-generation Babbittry (the second generation was the stereotype liberal). If you want to make Babbitt III purr with pleasure, prompts Viereck, introduce him as "Squire" Cabot Babbitt. He maintains a Hunting Lodge Salon for Cultivating Choice Old Values, makes retrogression a deliberate principle, and reflects no concern with the human predicament but an in-the-swim glibness. This sounds like Gerald Johnson's critique, but it's Viereck's.

In case you wonder whom he has in mind, Viereck gives us a prime example in his *The Shame and Glory of the Intellectuals*— William Buckley, Jr. Buckley's movement is seen as combining a militant plutocratic ingroup with an intellectual outgroup. Underdog is linked with top dog. Buckley does see a need for principles, but he misapplies them. What is his alternative to collectivist materialism? The sterile tradesman-materialism of the McKinley era. "He enshrines as equally sacrosanct Adam Smith and Jesus." Even mild social reform is treated as crypto-communism. His movement has brought forth a "motheaten mouse of petty economic privilege." Buckley is seen as intelligent, sincere, and wrongheaded. He has yet to demonstrate sensitivity, compassion, and an inkling of the tragic paradoxes of life. Again this sounds like an editor of the *New Republic*.

Listen to Viereck appraising the New Deal as an "Overdue Deal." According to Viereck, the New Deal was conservative in its substantive aspect (antirevolutionary and antiplutocracy), but radical in its procedural aspect (direct democracy, Supreme

Court packing, bypassing the Constitution). True, the New Deal was infiltrated by Communists. But because its Communist sympathizers were often so conspicuous, the New Deal hindered Communism, helped Wall Street, made the masses more conservative than before, and preserved our traditional institutions.

The year 1933 killed radicalism and Communism in America. Someday conservatives will rank 1933 with 1688, a revolution averted. And Franklin Delano Roosevelt was really a crypto-conservative trying to combine aristocracy and yeoman traditions.

There's more. Viereck seconds August Heckscher (former editor of the *New York Herald Tribune;* Kennedy Cultural Coordinator) who spoke of Adlai Stevenson as "the most consistent and philosophically mature conservative in this century." He is the restorer of the intellectuals, with a unique feeling for the way separate groups could be brought into the service of the whole, and he articulates the highest standards of statesmanship currently available.

Then Viereck goes all the way. Adlai Stevenson is the first presidential candidate in American history to recognize fully the danger of the American Overadjusted Man.

In case there were any survivors after that volley, Viereck moves in with a *coup de grâce.* The radical Right hates the liberal ingroup more than Communism, which indeed benefits from their attacks on foreign aid, United Nations, and the middle road. They resent liberals because they are an ingroup, aristocratic and accepted, while they of the nationalist far Right are a moneyed but status-resenting outgroup. Their continued attack on the ingroup aristocracy is a blessing, for it will continue to keep its conserving function incognito.

At this point outraged Right-wingers might picture Viereck as a demented Medea eloping with Jason the Liberal and viciously tossing back pieces of her conservative brothers Welch, Buckley, and Goldwater to slow down the pursuing Old Guard.

But a coupling of Viereck and the liberals might be as stormy as the liaison of Medea and Jason. *The Shame and Glory of the Intellectuals* was written largely because Viereck feels the liberals are not fighting the Communists' tyranny in the glorious way they did the Nazi terror. Time is a taxidermist, says Viereck, and has made rebels stuffy. Later, in *The Unadjusted Man*, he feels that the *avant-guard* has become rearguard, and speaks of "the arthritic somersaults of aging *enfants terribles*."

Reminding the liberal that he isn't so frisky as he used to be is not especially bothersome. Real trouble starts when Viereck's basic conservatism shows up. The conservative, affirms Viereck, realizes that values can never be captured by general formulations. "Imprecise necessities," like the words "freedom" or "religion," ought to be used imprecisely. Reality itself is unsymmetrical, ungeometrical, imprecise. Conservatism embodies; it does not argue. Therefore, admits Viereck, a good conservative always loses theoretical debates with liberals and radicals. The conservative draws his insight from epigrams, isolated nuggets, and "helter-skelter jottings." We are given Yeats: "Man can embody truth, but he cannot know it."

Poetry is the forte of the disorganized conservative mind, prose the weapon of the liberal. Life is not to be defined and blueprinted; it is to be lived and savored. This is what alarms the rationalistic liberal. How far can you go on preferring life to logic, to "abstract speculation," without abandoning yourself to irrationality?

The message of Viereck's *Metapolitics—From the Romantics to Hitler* (1941) was that romanticism can easily lead to authoritarianism through the inviting but deceptive "Cult of Life." The villain Richard Wagner is condemned by Viereck for exalting "Life against law, content against form, instinct against reason, synthesis against analysis, the organic against the atomistic. . . ." (page 107). Just how immune is Viereck to this very romanticism? When he speaks of the liberal's "mania for categories," the "inarticulate roots" of true values, and the "wise stupidity of conservative temperament," you wonder if Viereck is really serious about Athene or is secretly lusting after Isolde.

We are asked to accept "the priority of beauty-seeking" rather than "the manipulative aspects of intellect," and are told that "only art can deal with flesh." Any hope of overcoming man's doom by founding a more exact social science is sheer self-deception. Viereck's vice as a political theorist is his virtue as a social critic. He is gloriously consumed by a love of beauty. He teaches the necessity of ethics as a restraining factor but preaches the desirability of lyricism as a liberating force. "One lyrical gesture of the joy and bitterness of the human heart can still give us implicitly more moral insight than 'all the sages can.'" Love and lyricism, he insists, are the only flame that fuses form and content, aesthetics and ethics, without sacrificing either. And lyricism requires unadjustedness.

Viereck's campaign against protean Babbittry, pettiness, and ugliness would be welcomed by all intellectuals. Everything must be done to encourage grace and sensitivity in a society that tends to ignore their importance. His cultural criticisms is valid and a joy to our ears. We all want to sing along with Viereck.

But how do you use aesthetics to judge ethics? This in theory is what Viereck is asking us to do. Is a gracefully opened well-wrought crematorium door any excuse for the roasting? One camp did play Beethoven symphonies. How and when are our aesthetic sensibilities going to tell us we are doing wrong? Not being very strong on abstract speculation, categories, or general schemata, Viereck leaves us at loose ends. He is not one for a score. Everything must be played by ear.

Fortunately, he himself has an excellent ear, but this is not much comfort to the less gifted. Perhaps this is why he continually pleads for an aristocracy of spirit, which possesses decorum and "an inner check of *noblesse oblige*."

A commendable example of Viereck playing it by ear was his fight against awarding the Bollingen Prize for American poetry to Ezra Pound in 1949. The New Critics were defending the award on aesthetic grounds. It was just good poetry. Viereck countered that Pound's *Pisan Cantos* were anti-Semitic. "Our entire civilization," said Viereck in *Dream and Responsibility* (1953), "including poetry, depends almost completely on our constantly maintaining a moral heritage which Nazi anti-Semitism would destroy." Didn't the Soviets use a similar argument for denying the Nobel Prize to Pasternak?

But we won't quibble. Here aesthetics was restrained by ethics. How a "moral heritage" is preserved without an appeal to abstract ideals is a problem for Viereck to wrestle with. You keep feeling that he is peeking at the score.

One of the most endearing examples of Viereck's elegant ethic is to be found in a graduation address he made to a class of college seniors. Suppose you vow, suggests Viereck, never to associate either in personal friendship or in any close political alliance with any individual or group that advocates Nazi-style or Communist-style mass murder or that apologizes for it or that appeases it? Let individuals take this vow quietly without exhibitionism. It is time to return to that inelegant virtue: righteous indignation. It is never time for that elegant vice: self-righteousness.

Viereck then called for improving things by friendly persuasion and a sense of humor. Organization would misdirect the aim of such a vow by sacrificing long-run inner change to short-run success.

I wonder how many in that senior class have since joined the program of the John Birch Society?

The conservatism of Peter Viereck is very tempting when he reduces it through his classical humanism to read: "Our cause . . . is gray not white; it is the cause of the second best against the worst . . . when the best is historically impossible."

It is irresistible in poetical orbit:

The earth is a freer place to breathe in, every time you love without asking or calculating any return. It is freer every time you feel spontaneous sympathy for strangers. It it freer every time you make your drudgeries and routines still more inefficient by taking plenty of time out to experience the shock of beauty, whether in nature, poetry, music, or the fine arts. . . . In the long run whatever enriches your inner sensibility with the unguessed suprises of beauty and love is a moral act and even a political act. . . .[1]

The trouble comes after you have grounded the poetry. When you turn from personal to social regeneration, you need more prosaic standards to guide your actions. If you feel that society requires not only change but reform, then an occasional blueprint might be necessary; and Viereck would not be your man. But those shopping for a modern conservatism chastened by wit and wisdom would seldom find it more elegantly expressed.

1. *Dream and Responsibility,* University Press of Washington, D.C., 1953, p. 42.

CLINTON ROSSITER

The *Seedtime of the Republic* (1953) established Clinton Rossiter's distinction in the field of American history. His reputation as a political scientist followed books on the presidency, the supreme court, political parties, and the problem of constitutional dictatorship. Rossiter brings urbane sophistication to the roles of meaty historian and detached political scientist. His mastery of subject matter preserves him from becoming smug or contentious, as the less well grounded, and hence more nervous, polemicist might be. Rossiter's business is footnoted objectivity. He speaks from the strength of academic heights. For him intellectual tolerance is not a tactical concession; it is a strategic conclusion. This is what irritates the far Right and endears him to the Center.

Try this on for conservatism: "Awareness, reflection, traditionalism, and at least some degree of disinterestedness—these are the qualities that distinguish the genuine conservative from all others who bear this label."[2] This could almost be a definition of scholarship. He requires a degree of detachment rarely achieved by conservatives or liberals. It is a plea for an ideological wayfarer seldom seen in this vale of political original sin.

This paragon is further described as one who blends reverence, distaste for materialism, high morality, moderation, peacefulness, and the aristocratic spirit. "The shady deal, the shoddy job, the easy way out, the cheap trick, the fast bargain—the conservative is shocked by these evidences of moral softness." Again, with some reservations about aristocracy, this could be a description of a well-intentioned liberal. It is almost going too far when Rossiter insists that a conservative must be like Milton's *Penseroso* "sober, steadfast, and demure." I dare the first demure Rightwinger to step forward.

Actually, this was an unfortunate selection of words. "Demure" means not merely decorous but affectedly modest. I am sure Rossiter would not want to encourage this note of hypocrisy.

The difference in mood becomes clearer when Rossiter goes

2. *Conservatism in America*, Knopf, 1955, p. 8.

on to say that the conservative must have a feeling of deep respect tinged with awe for authority, history, law, institutions, and traditions. He is finally off the runway. The liberal is more apt to feel respect for authority tinged with gall. (A lot should depend upon what authority and tradition are up to.)

We see the conservative mood really crystallizing when the role of reason is discussed. Rossiter is as reluctant as Viereck to assign it much significance in the conservative apologia. "The principles of American conservatism are not thoughts or reflections or hypotheses; they are assumptions, prejudices, myths, vague longings and slogans—above all slogans. I have heard its critics argue cogently that it has no philosophy. I say this as a truth I have come to reluctantly, not as a libel that I was anxious to prove from the start." Later he concedes that "in the realm of ideas, American conservatism has proved an impotent failure."[3] Thus the conservative mood is almost ineffable. You can sense it, but it is difficult to articulate it.

Then what is all the noise on the Right? Rossiter quite frankly admits that much of it is precisely what Lionel Trilling meant when he referred to "irritable mental gestures which seek to resemble ideas." For example, such slogans as "Liberty versus Socialism," "States' Rights versus Centralized Tyranny," or "We are a Republic not a Democracy." Other irritating gestures would be the antics of the D.A.R. or fellow travelers of fascism. Pure individualists such as John Chamberlain or Ayn Rand who fight the "iniquity" of income tax and the "fraud" of social security are dismissed as reactionaries or "opportunists at a time when anti-radicalism offers the most mileage."

George Sokolsky and Fulton Lewis, Jr., are identified as the radio voice of the ultraconservatives who have a penchant for radical methods. Unfortunately, laments Rossiter, Russell Kirk has now begun to sound like a man born 150 years too late and in the wrong country. Both the extreme "choleric Right" of the John Birch Society and the more respectable "ultraconservatism" of Senator Goldwater are labeled as too "aggressive, restive, and materialistic."

For Rossiter these are the conservatives who use such distort-

3. *Op. cit.*, pp. 187 and 235.

ing devices as the false equation that equates Keynes and socialism, the false dichotomy that demands black and white choices,
or the easy generalization that hopelessly oversimplifies. However,
their chief sin is championing economic individualism. "Sixty
million bathtubs are a colossal achievement; they are hardly the
firm foundation of a conservative tradition." This calamitous preoccupation has obscured the fact for too many conservatives that
social progress is itself a key element of stability.

Both Viereck and Rossiter feel strongly that plutocratic
thinking with its one-sided emphasis on economic man is playing
into the hands of Marxists. Furthermore, it distorts what both men
would like as an elite. They believe that a small ruling group is
inevitable and desirable, as long as it is open-ended and supplied
by a democratic base. But they are as repulsed as Khrushchev was
by the vulgarism "You look like a million dollars!" Public policy
should be determined not by men of business who have met
payrolls but by men of experience who have mined traditional
and cultural pay dirt. Rossiter speaks of "the beneficence of an
aristocracy of talent and virtue, one that is trained for special
service and thus entitled to special considerations."[4] He adds that
it takes more than one generation to make a genuine aristocrat.

William Newman in *The Futilitarian Society* (1961) is concerned about how the transition is to be made from plutocracy to
aristocracy. Newman presumes that Rossiter is suggesting an elite
civil service corps similar to that of Great Britain, and he warns
that its most noteworthy characteristic is fixedness. Of course,
this is not necessarily true of either Rossiter or the British civil
service; but because of his failure to spell out how a new aristocracy is to be implemented, Rossiter leaves himself open to such
interpretations. Most liberals would be alarmed at the idea of any
kind of aristocracy, and most conservatives would be peeved because they would not qualify.

Picture the consternation of conservatives you know when
Rossiter says that he is revolted by plutocracy and moved to tears
by *noblesse oblige*. This does not make him a sentimentalist. Conservatism, he says, should pride itself on its common sense, realism,
adaptability, and respect for unpleasant facts. The *oblige* must

4. *Ibid.*, p. 24.

be sparingly applied. Rossiter says that the humanitarian function of government will always remain secondary to its great duties to keep the peace, establish justice, secure rights and property, and raise the level of morality. Yet Rossiter is really too much of an Aristotelian at heart to question the necessity of political power. He says he could never fall prey to the simple doctrine that the best government is the least.

The shibboleths of economic individualism bother him more than its diatribes against the state. Laissez faire, enlightened self-interest, and the profit motive make him uncomfortable. The profit motive, he maintains, should be recognized for the selfish thing it is and be kept within reasonable, socially imposed limits. To achieve both justice and stability, says Rossiter, we must seek a mixed economy. The true conservative knows that "government for all its imperfections is the instrument most fitted to reduce the coercions visited upon one another by imperfect men."[5]

In a *Harper's* article, in April, 1957, on the new American conservatives, Rossiter insists that conservatism must free itself from cant about the nature and role of government. It is time, he says, to admit that government gives a more equitable distribution of the wealth that private enterprise has produced. We are reminded of John Adams: democracy depends upon widely diffusing among the people knowledge, virtue, and property.

Earlier, in a *Yale Review* article in March, 1955, Rossiter asked, "Is equality of opportunity really the best answer the conservative can make to the contradictory demands of the American dream and American Reality?" It is all that remains to those who have mesmerized themselves into believing that the state really is a horrible behemoth. The old cliché of conservative forums, "Liberty versus Security," is denounced by Rossiter as a false polarity. Security in property or job or pension is necessary to liberty. Liberty, he insists, can be defined only with the aid of words such as "opportunity," "creativity," "productivity," and "security."

These words of advice might be confusing to the conservative because Rossiter says later that the conservative thinks of liberty as something to be preserved and defended; the liberal

5. *Ibid.*, p. 42.

thinks of it as something to be improved and enlarged. It might be difficult for anyone to define liberty aided by words such as "creativity," "productivity," and "opportunity," and think that he is merely defending, and not enlarging, liberty.

The boundary between the preservation and expansion of liberty is an elusive one for moderate liberals and conservatives to draw. How much of the refurbishing of liberty is radical departure from the old form? When conservatives claim that nothing worthwhile is really very new, things get difficult. If the conservatives can maintain that the freedom won in the American Revolution was really just a revival of the rights of Englishmen and that the New Deal is in fact conservatism risen Phoenixlike from the ashes, the liberals are going to be hard pressed to win this game.

Rossiter admits that there is a limit beyond which a man cannot push for social and economic reforms. After this point he must surrender his claim to be considered a conservative. For example, says Rossiter, Senator Clifford Case of New Jersey is too willing to take bold steps into the future to be called a political conservative. The same is true of Adlai Stevenson. These men, we are told, are really conservative liberals.

Then what can we expect from change? How does Rossiter combine Burke's "disposition to preserve" with his "ability to improve"? We'll do it by slow steps, says Rossiter. First, change must have preservation, and if possible even restoration, as its object. It must be limited in scope, fulfill an indispensable need, and be worked out in careful stages. Conservative auspices would see that it was carried out in deference to the customs and laws of the people.

We are supposed to try to discover the order that inheres in things, says Rossiter, rather than to impose an order upon them. This almost suggests that society consists of a fixed inventory of ideas that may be lovingly dusted, expectantly held to the ear for new sounds, and occasionally rearranged to simulate the latest fashion. It's quite safe.

One of the reasons why Rossiter is so kind to liberals is that he realizes his indebtedness. "When the one glorious thing to be conservative about was the Liberal tradition of the world's most liberal society, how could a conservative be expected to be conservative?"[6] As usual, the conservative is expected to take his consolation in practice rather than in theory. Although the liberals win nine times out of ten in political thought, admits Rossiter, in political practice the conservatives win out almost as monotonously. How? Simple: the Constitution and our party system, the most conservative in the Western world. The victorious party can hardly ever put through thoroughgoing reform. Ask Presidents Truman or Kennedy. Our Constitution and laws make almost as much of conservative duties as our tradition does of liberal rights.

With *The American Presidency* (1956) and *Parties and Politics in America* (1960) Rossiter could not help recruiting a following from the vital center. In this latest book he speaks of the Democratic party as the oldest full-bodied party in the world, a party that, among other things, has experienced glory under Jackson and F.D.R., greatness under Polk and Truman, and has scraped the stars with Wilson and Stevenson. Of course, he cites Democratic shortcomings, but who can hear them?

The Democratic party is praised for persuading the country to face up to new government responsibilities, for social welfare and economic health, and for simultaneously facing up to the new diplomatic responsibilities of this century. Could you find a more charming definition of the Democratic party than "It has shocked the fastidious, discomfited the established, comforted the disinherited, and amused the detached"?[7] One of the failures of the Democrats, says Rossiter, was their absence of moral capacity to check the upsurge of the spirit of plunder under the Republicans in the 1870's and 1880's.

Republicans are praised for their fertilization of American enterprise in the late nineteenth century and for their accepting, "none too soon but also not too late," the burdens of the New Economy and the New Internationalism of the middle of the twentieth century. The G.O.P. is criticized for allowing a maldistribution of the fruits of our industry and for dealing ineffectively with the breakdown of old domestic and international orders.

Rossiter sees the Republicans leaning to the ideological side

6. *Ibid.*, p. 224.
7. *Ibid.*, p. 74.

of politics, the Democrats to the practical. This, of course, is an inversion of the conservative and liberal roles. Largely because of their attachment to economic individualism, it is the Republicans who are more prone to abstract slogans. It is the Democrats who are now playing it by ear. It is to be hoped, muses Rossiter, that Walter Lippmann might become to the Republican party what John Dewey has long been to the Democrats.

This choice of apologists is symptomatic of Rossiter's dilemma. Dewey was an innovating backfield man, good at end runs, and a whiz at forward passes. Lippmann is more the aging coach who thinks the forward pass is cheating and never expects the team to do anything right but who fascinates everyone by his brilliant Monday-morning quarterbacking. The Republicans could use more Saturday-afternoon victories. Shouldn't Rossiter be urging a stronger backfield man or a more optimistic coach not so addicted to drives through the line. The metaphor is not doing justice to Walter Lippmann's critical acumen. It is merely suggesting that he is not the man for this particular job. Rossiter's problem is to produce for the G.O.P. an issue-oriented conservative idea man willing to compete on the field. His critique of conservatism suggests this may be impossible. It is especially poignant since he believes that we need more ideology and less group diplomacy in party politics.

If most conservatives were astonished by Rossiter's susceptibility to Democratic virtues, you can imagine their consternation at the publication of *The American Presidency*. This was Rossiter at the zenith of his political realism. The unusual growth of the executive power under the New Deal was inevitable, necessary, and desirable. Most Americans, he claims, counted the presidency "a mighty weapon in the struggle for liberty at home and security abroad" (page 109). This growth of authority is hardly the outcome of a shameful conspiracy on the part of the three Democratic Presidents of this century. It was in response to the mounting burdens of peace and war.

Rossiter lists five fresh ingredients of the presidency: his strong posture of legislative leadership, his new channels of opinion, his increased concern for domestic peace and prosperity, his emergence as a leader in the struggle for personal liberty and racial equality, and above all his conversion into an institution. Few conservatives would be pleased at those addenda. He just won't stop. "All the great political and social forces that brought the Presidency to its present state of power and glory will continue to work in the future" (page 237). The presidency in our future must be that of Roosevelt and Truman rather than of Harding and Coolidge. The people have made the presidency their peculiar instrument. "They can take comfort and pride in the thought that it is also their peculiar treasure."

Modern conservatives have always downgraded and even demeaned the presidency. Its increase in power, they believe, *was* the conspiracy of Democratic Presidents. This growth, they insist, was unnecessary, undesirable, and potently unconstitutional.

To Conservatives jealously guarding every vestige of congressional power, Rossiter must appear a ranting radical. Lippmann agrees with Rossiter on the presidency, but they would be hard pressed to muster a House of Lords' quorum (four) of support among other conservative theorists. This is considered liberal talk on both sides of the fence. As for most conservatives, you couldn't talk this way even with a smile.

How does Rossiter maintain his club card in conservatism? If pressed for the password in the dead of night, Rossiter could always invoke his "Twenty-one Points of Conservatism" as General Orders. Point Five speaks of the need for a ruling and serving aristocracy. Point Six stresses the fallibility and potential tyranny of majority rule. Or Nine reminds us of the duties of man: service, effort, obedience, cultivation of virtue, self-restraint—as the price of rights. Then Seventeen comes through with the primacy of the community—"a wondrous, divinely ordained union of lands, laws, and customs" . . . Add his strictures on inflation, plus his championing of private property, and at least his Affiliated Membership should be valid indefinitely.

Because both Rossiter and Viereck adhere with commendable fidelity to what Rossiter calls "tireless fact-finding and dauntless fact-facing," these men will continue to have considerable influence among young intellectuals who are in any way disenchanted with liberalism. After all, Viereck is gunning for the same game: Babbittry. At the close of his *The Shame and Glory of the Intellectuals,* Viereck hopes that someday Babbitt Junior (the Liberal) may stand in front of his mirror saying of Pound in bedlam and Hiss in prison, "There but for the grace of God go I." For the sake of their misapplied courage and their misapplied idealism, may God have mercy on two miserable sinners (page 309).

There is no telling how many liberals can be persuaded to recant, or, as Rossiter puts it, to realize how conservative they really are. But few conservatives theorists could be more effective. The college student might well find Lippmann and Kirk stuffy and/or anachronistic. The sophisticate is apt to say "quaint." This lethal epithet is difficult to apply to either Viereck or Rossiter.

Conservatism must not overlook the sensitive young intellectuals, some of whom are temperamentally inclined to the Right. The quickest way to lose them is to push cant instead of logic. Such young people demand intelligently fashioned arguments. Although their elders might be shocked, these young men admire the lechery of a scholar denuding an idea. They want to be relentless in their pursuit of facts, and expect others to be similarly devoted.

Viereck and Rossiter are incalculable assets to conservatives in intellectual warfare. They are not dogmatic, and they write with style, precision, and a respect for inductive inquiry not always found among conservatives. These are traits young conservative intellectuals must value if they are going to take on their liberal peers in debate.

In a skeptical age, arguments demand considerable sophistication. The young know the embarrassment of naïve conviction. It is the vocation of intellectuals to expose this naïveté wherever possible, especially whenever it masquerades as unquestioned doctrine. Moderate conservative writers like Viereck and Rossiter are deft at exposing fraudulent dogmatics, Left or Right. They speak eloquently in the respected idiom of their time. Their knowledge of the opposition's weaknesses may convince some conservatives that they are really mercenaries not to be trusted.

Unfortunately, many young conservatives have rejected Rossiter and Viereck as too liberal, and have abandoned as unclean ground the center area so meticulously farmed by these two theorists.

When D. Van Nostrand Company decided on twin paperback editions of *Conservatism* and *Liberalism*, Peter Viereck was paired against J. Salwyn Schapiro. When the Columbia Broadcasting System did a feature program on the far Right, Clinton Rossiter was brought on to add a note of conservative moderation. Both were discreet steps taken for the sake of discriminating audiences. As intellectuals who have avoided sloganeering and clichés, Rossiter and Viereck are especially immune to ridicule. Highbrow, and as "U" as conservatives are allowed to be, they may well become the new mentors of any young intellectual as he casts his first furtive glance to the Right.

CHAPTER 8

Appeal of the Conservative Press

Suppose a Chief of Police were a fanatic liberal who had the temporary indulgence of the community in carrying out a purge of Right-wing publications. Where would he start?

According to *The First National Directory of "Rightist" Groups, Publications and Some Individuals in the United States* . . . (Fourth Edition, Noontide Press, San Francisco, 1962), there are nearly one thousand organizations in this country that may be called Rightist and that regularly publish or distribute quantities of Right-wing literature. The State University Library of Iowa has an extensive collection of their publications.

Some would be easy. Gerald L. K. Smith's *Cross and the Flag* is blatantly anti-Semitic. Newsletters like "Counterattack" or "American Legion Firing Line" are about as irresponsibly nationalistic as Billy James Hargis's *Christian Crusade*. Magazines such as John L. Rice's *Sword of the Lord* or William Herrstrom's *Bible News Flashes* picture all the liberal clergy as "devil's doormats."

At least 550 locals of the Citizens Councils in the South distribute literature, or perhaps what libraries would call "ephemeral material." Kentucky features the *American Eagle*, Florida the *Crusader*, West Virginia the *Alarm*. The *Alabamian* and the *Virginian* are cousins-in-arms, as are Horace Miller's *Aryan Views* and E. E. Williams's *Sons and Daughters of Free Men*.

Qualifying for political pornography might be pamphlets such as Pat and Deane Mernagh's "Mammy Liza's Appeal to Her People on the Question of Integration in Southern Schools," W. E. Michael's "New Jazz Plot to Seduce Youth" and "Corrupt Races Exposed," or Mathew Ravenshaw's "Sickle-Cell Anemia." But these seldom circulate outside the South.

What would the censor do about better known and more respectable magazines such as Leonard Read's *The Freeman*, Russell Kirk's former quarterly *Modern Age*, or Russell Maguire's *American Mercury?* Then there are the *Clarence Manion Forum* and the "Dan Smoot Reports," and so on. These may be highly "suggestive," but are they really beyond the pale?

Fortunately, no such police chief exists, and the lines do not have to be drawn. Except for rare lapses, political literature has escaped the censor in our country.

Given the plethora of Right-wing publications, what is the young conservative reading for periodicals? Except for regional zealots, very little of the above. According to the word of campus leaders and such authorities as William Buckley, Jr., and M. Stanton Evans (*Revolt on the Campus*), most of the current-events reading of young conservatives centers around four well-written and cleverly edited serials: a fortnightly "little magazine" —Buckley's *National Review;* a mass weekly—David Lawrence's *U.S. News & World Report;* a Washington newsletter—Frank Hanighen's "Human Events"; and America's only national daily newspaper—the Dow-Jones *Wall Street Journal*. They are generally preferred in the order given.

William Buckley, Jr., founded the *National Review* to prove that he really meant business when he wrote *God and Man at Yale*. Brother-in-law L. Brent Bozell (co-author of *McCarthy and His Enemies*) became an editor with James Burnham (*Managerial Revolution*), Willmoore Kendall of Yale, and Frank S.

Meyer and William F. Rickenbacker who later helped found New York State's new Conservative party. Sister Priscilla L. Buckley came on as managing editor. Will Herberg, Henry Hazlitt, Russell Kirk, John Chamberlain, and Richard Weaver became contributers.

James Wechsler charged that the *National Review* became something of a house organ for all the know-nothing groups that had never before had an urbane statement of their resentments. The Down-Right Irreverent Dwight MacDonald suggested that the magazine was recruiting from the intellectual underground and underprivileged. He pointed out that the only "names" of intellectuals sending in greetings were the conservative economists Von Mises and Ray Moley. Others were Adolphe Menjou, Gene Tunney, and Cecil B. de Mille.

Buckley answered MacDonald, who has occupied more than one ideological position, by referring to him as "The Tommy Manville of American politics," and warned that as a liberal he was a security risk.

The polemical, peevish, and jejune quality of many of the articles invited a lethal MacDonald harpoon: "If italics were horses, intellectual beggars might ride."

This is a bit harsh. A respectable intellectual front is presented by middleweights Russell Kirk, philosopher; Willmoore Kendall, political scientist; John Chamberlain, historian; and Will Herberg, lay theologian. In one article, Herberg grasped his chalk boldly and tried to enlarge the family circle by including Reinhold Niebuhr (co-founder of Americans for Democratic Action) as a conservative. Some of the family's readers were not too pleased. Herberg has been fairly successful in moderating the bitter conflict between Buckley and the editors of *America* over *Mater et Magistra*. He felt Buckley's *Mater Sí; Magistra, No* was a piece of theatrical cleverness that created misunderstanding.

Russell Kirk's Burkean conservatism sometimes baffles rank-and-file readers. While in England, Kirk wrote an article called "Multiple Shops" (September 23, 1961) in which he complained that English chain stores were displacing the picturesque old shops. He lashed out at hydraheaded impersonal corporations whose primary concern is profit. "Collectivism is not the less disagreeable because it retains the label 'capitalism.'" Then he complained about ". . . nasty, pretentious, big stores selling dreary wares."

A New York reader associated with the G-E-X Stores objected to Kirk's adjectives. "Far from being 'dreary,' our stores are truly exciting, bright, clean, and cheerful." Anyway, he wanted to know what right Kirk as a philosopher had to criticize stores. What does he know about merchandising?

When a Michigan town raised a storm by deciding to use McGuffey Readers in its school system, Kirk defended it. He thought the century-old readers with their religious and puritan homilies were "quite sensible and usable," although he admitted they were not perfect. What he really wants is a revision of the "inane" textbooks used in grade schools—all part of his war against progressive education. Most intellectuals would probably agree that substance should not be constantly sacrificed to "readability," but few would take comfort in a McGuffey Reader. In problems of higher education, Kirk has a disarming objection to Federal aid to colleges. He claims half those now in college should not be there. More Federal money would just kill the colleges with kindness.

While Kirk regularly surveys education "From the Academy," James Burnham writes "The Third World War." This column reminds us that we are in it, and since the Kennedy administration it has acquired a leitmotiv: the Stevenson-Cleveland-Rostow clique is playing the neutralists' game. To break out of this, we must assume the tactical offensive. A move in Asia would divert pressure on Berlin. Why not support partisans in Tibet or drop more arms into Communist China? Better still, why not intercept all those Soviet ships carrying arms and propaganda to Guinea, Cuba, Indonesia, Ghana, or North Africa? With inspections, boycotts, and embargoes, we could have as much fun harassing the Soviets on the high seas as they do molesting us in Berlin. The selective blockade of Cuba supported by nineteen American states in October, 1962, came as a result of an upset in the nuclear balance of power. It was defensive military strategy, not a harassing political tactic.

"Who knows," says Burnham (November 4, 1961), "a sampling, even on a limited tactical scale, might revive in our commanders their traditional taste for the strategic offensive as well." Then we would really be in business.

Apparently believing that collegiate conservatives have a high kindling point, *National Review* ran a short story by Victor Gold called "Football is a Lonely Battle" (November 4, 1961). You guessed it; it's about the cold war. Coach says: "I have also ordered an absolute embargo on any alumnus popping off in public. Do you know what one of those birds said last week? He said we were out to beat State. Repeating—to *beat* State! How the hell can I justify that one to the American Association of University Professors?" Coach is also afraid of getting the other team sore. "A good defense is the best offense." This is Containment football. "If you don't have the ball, you can't fumble. Right?" The point is that no matter what the scoreboard shows, there are no winners in modern football.

If that doesn't do it, *let* them join the A.D.A.

No opportunity is lost to demonstrate the inevitable decadence of liberalism. On December 7, 1955, even the Third World War was interrupted to feature on the front cover "The Strange Case of Dr. Dooley." This was the only article mentioned on the cover. It concerned a Connecticut doctor who used homosexual practices on several young boys for therapeutic purposes. The boys had been incorrigible delinquents, and the doctor alleged remarkable cures. Because some liberals in the locality defended the doctor, *National Review* used the occasion to lay this unique therapy on the doorstep of liberalism. The entire relativist tradition down to Dewey and progressive education was blamed for this transgression. In a seven-page tirade, the editors insisted that this eccentricity was the logical result of the "anything goes" spirit of liberalism.

A book review of Miller's *Tropic of Cancer* (August 12, 1961) is used as an occasion for attacking abstractionism in general. The review closed with this remark: London once displayed a prize-winning model of a memorial to the Unknown Political Prisoner. Abstract strings and wires criss-crossed—no form, no substance. A genuine unknown political prisoner came along, a Polish D.P., looked at the model, reached over and smashed it with his fist. "While there are men like that Pole about, there is still hope!"

Editorially, *National Review* has urged that the United Nations cease to be a political body. They have backed Moïse Tshombe in the Congo and asked "Will Formosa Liberate the U.S.?" Shirer's *The Rise and Fall of the Third Reich* was condemned for jeopardizing our German alliance. On the other hand, General Walker is reprimanded for calling Dag Hammarskjöld a Red and Welch censored for leading conservatives into "irrelevancy and ineffectuality."

Back in one of his early "Ivory Tower" columns (December 29, 1955), Buckley suggested that students send in evidence of their professors' bias. For example, does your teacher of politics insist upon or press a particular idea as to the desirable relationship between the executive and the legislative branches? ". . . The magazine will award the two students who submit the most revealing material $100 each."

National Review is frequently criticized for its questionable taste in sarcasm. The *Mater et Magistra* incident has been mentioned. Stevenson had a dose. "Adlai Stevenson says he is not sure what critics mean by the phrase 'no-win policy.' It's the policy advocated by Presidential candidate Stevenson in 1952 and 1956, and with the same results. Okay, Adlai?" (March 13, 1962). Secretary Udall came in for some because of his landing on a private Kansas farm when reconnoitering by heliocopter. ". . . Since taking office, Udall has been thrown out of a few places for being dressed like a bum [with Supreme Court Justice Douglas while on a hike]. He has now been thrown out of another place for acting like one. Maybe he'll eventually be thrown out, period" (December 16, 1961).

So has the liberally dominated National Students Association. "The National Students Association—which by the way why doesn't somebody burn it down?—is always strutting about claiming to speak for 1.3 million students" (June 3, 1961).

You really have to be on Mr. Buckley's side to put up with this sort of thing.

But lighter moments are ahead. You will never realize how

much fun it is to be a conservative until you turn to *National Review*'s classified ads. Special real estate is on sale for conservatives only. You can get an "I AM A RIGHT-WING 'EXTREMIST'" button for fifty cents. How about having your very own PATRIOTIC SLOGAN, one or two lines, hotstamped on a Lindy ball-point pen? Did you know that Madame Chiang Kai-shek is now available on tape? Or do you want to get some "I AM A CARD-CARRYING AMERICAN" cards with the flag on one side and Pledge of Allegiance on the other?

There are special job opportunities for conservative draftsmen and sales representatives. A conservative art studio needs an apprentice. You can help form a Conservative Repertoire Theatre. Join Public Action, Inc., which for $2.00 keeps its eye on bills before the Congress and alerts conservatives when it's time to act. "Are your workers pilfering away your products? Read: How to Stop Pilferage in Business." The Evanston Panel is "Alerting Parents: American youth are exposed to pressures in a ruthless attempt to destroy love of country and engender a preference for world government."

If you really want to be prepared, try "Someday a gun could save your life. We have them. Write your needs. How to buy them legally." Finally, for some good sober reading, you might send for Hartnett Reports put out in Tuckahoe, New York. These expose infiltration of "T.V., Stage and Movies by Communists, and anti-anti-Communists."

Obviously *National Review* is many things to many people. It is especially important to the young conservative intellectuals who generally look upon it as their most presentable face. The editorial offices in Manhattan's east sixties are a Mecca for young conservatives in their off hours. Students from Fordham and Hunter come down and help out with the dedication shown at a campaign headquarters of Volunteers. A surprising number of young writers are broken in on *National Review*'s staff. The first issue of this "little magazine" was written entirely by people under thirty years of age.

But the magazine has been losing about $125,000 per year. Even though its 1962 printing of 90,000 copies per edition made it the largest of any of the "little magazines" of opinion, it had a

$100,000 deficit for the previous year. In February, 1962, Editor Buckley sent out a six-page letter to subscribers opening with the sentence "We have $5,532 in the bank, and unpaid bills amounting to just over four times that sum." Once again readers were asked to make up the deficit. Despite paying out one million dollars more than it has taken in since 1955, *National Review* shows every sign of mastering its crises. Its survival seems assured by readers who write: "Congratulations on your sixth birthday. Glad you were born with a full set of teeth and an appetite for raw meat, hence the increase in circulation."

U.S. NEWS & WORLD REPORT

Early in 1962 Editor Buckley announced to his readers that four-color ads for the back covers of *National Review* had been secured for the entire year. *U.S. News* would never have to make such a boast. Issues come secured between ads for Shell Oil and Salem cigarettes as a matter of course. Sandwiched between are ads for Beechcraft and Piper airplanes and hints at shortcuts to executive skills. With its million and a half circulation putting it second only to *Time* as a national news magazine, *U.S. News* exudes the confidence of eminently successful enterprise.

It styles itself a magazine "For business and professional people and their families." While *Time* sought its bowdlerized version of *New Yorker* sophistication and *Newsweek* tried to sound like *Time*, *U.S. News* banked on the homeliness of the old *Literary Digest* and *Pathfinder*. It's life with financially successful Father sounding off at the breakfast table about the latest obstacles some nincompoops have thrown in the paths of business.

Articles are presented in graphic, terse, meager sentences—the clipped, authoritative, declamatory sentences of a telegram from the home office. There are seldom notes of doubt or indecision. It is generally a forthright matter of following the directions on the package. There is a busy, bold use of graphs and charts. Colored borders and color-blocked introductory paragraphs arrest the eye. Its format includes five two-paged newsletters: "Tomorrow," "Worldgram," "Business Around the

World," "Trend of U.S. Business," and "News You Can Use." Each is printed on a different colored paper. In the pink "Worldgram," tilted chevrons emphasize each brief, double-spaced paragraph, and crucial sentences are underlined.

Family articles are done on compact cars and how to finance a college education. Home hints are given on recognizing termites, collecting for storm damage, or how to trade in your house like a used car. You are kept posted on the latest in tax deductions, interest rates, home accidents, and even a weather-outlook map for the month. An especially welcomed feature for subscribers is "News Lines: What You as a Businessman Can and Cannot Do" as a result of recent Court and administrative decisions. This column takes the sting out of bureaucracy by informing you of your opportunities as well as reminding you of your limitations.

In news coverage, *U.S. News* gives twice as much space as *Time* or *Newsweek*, which summarize more and carry more cultural features. The Syracuse University School of Journalism showed that in 1956 *Time* printed 34,000 words of campaign news, *Newsweek* 14,000 and *U.S. News* 150,000. This study showed that *Time* was biased toward the Republicans 75 percent of the time, *Newsweek* 28 percent, and *U.S. News* only 1 percent. In questioning these figures, Ben Bagdikian wrote in the *New Republic* (February 2, 1959) that this Syracuse study looked only for editorially inserted words of bias. How about the selection of speeches and their arrangement, he asks? On the autoworkers' demands, there were textual reprints from heads of car manufacturers but none from labor. Eleven out of the twelve speech texts were those of conservatives.

It is understandable that *U.S. News*, a journal for businessmen and their families, should be less than enthusiastic about labor's demands. More difficult to understand is the magazine's position on the race problem. After the Supreme Court's segregation decision, Mr. Bagdikian found that 75 percent of the integration coverage in *U.S. News* was critical, either showing it as a failure or as causing trouble.

The step-by-step chronology of events leading to the Little Rock crisis has 66 percent of its three pages devoted to direct and indirect quotations of Governor Orval Faubus. A five-page layout, "Political Leaders and Editors Size up Little Rock Crises" is 80 percent against integration moves. Readers could find no mention of Billy Graham's condemnation of Little Rock and endorsement of integration, even though he had been featured on a cover story the week before. Meanwhile, Editor David Lawrence was writing eighteen consecutive articles on the evils of enforced integration in his nationally syndicated column.

There seems to be more than the usual conservative objection to the Federal government's role in integration. On August 14, 1961, considerable space was given to an article by a psychologist at the University of Virginia who claimed psychological testing showed the Negro inferior. Racial differences in mental ability and perhaps also in character are innate and genetic, he claimed. Another feature-cover story, "Why Are People Brown or Black or Yellow or White?" (March 26, 1962) spoke of the blood differences between whites and Negroes. "It is likely that other significant differences in blood make-up will appear to help define races." Mixed marriage, the article said, particularly between whites and Negroes, is not generally acceptable to either race. Even the United Nation's "Statement on the Nature of Race and Race Differences" was criticized.

Ironically these theories uphold the Soviet geneticist Lysenko and defy the accepted position of Western scientists. It would be one thing for the magazine to cite these "new" ideas as news items. When these peripheral ideas are exploited as feature articles, you begin to wonder why U.S. News is so anxious to increase sales in Jackson, Mississippi. They are trying to prove more than a states' righter has to prove.

Frequently a guest expert or panel of experts will discuss a controversial question. James Conant was used very effectively when he did a piece on the difficulties of the integrated classroom and stressed the socioeconomic handicaps of the Negro child. Conant himself fully endorses integration, but his article could be used by the segregationists. It got feature billing. A great coup was carried off back in 1953 when four articles Rebecca West originally wrote for the London *Times* were reprinted in U.S. News: "As a Briton Looks at McCarthyism"

(May 22nd). Miss West admitted the absurdity of the name "Un-American" Activities Committee—". . . the name suggests unreasonable prejudice against yodeling or pagoda building"— but urged American liberals not to be silly or dishonest in facing up to the facts of Communist infiltration.

The article was written, said Miss West, to counteract anti-Americanism in Britain. "Witch hunts" have taken over where "lynchings" used to be talked about. Consequently, she demonstrated that not all of HUAC's charges were groundless. Despite the title *U.S. News* gave to her article, Miss West was not discussing McCarthyism. "I dealt solely with pre-McCarthy investigations. I neither attacked nor defended McCarthy. I don't know him and have never read a complete speech of his," said Miss West in a subsequent memo to the magazine. However, by associating Rebecca West's eloquent defense of some of the pre-McCarthy investigations with the title "As a Briton Looks at McCarthyism," many readers were left with the impression that Miss West was defending McCarthy.

Liberal readers were again unsettled by the treatment accorded "Operation Abolition," the film on the San Francisco student riots. Under the question "Was Film on Communist Hearings Distorted?" you find HUAC's reply to charges but no mention of the more trenchant charges made in the pamphlet put out by the National Council of Churches' Department of Religious Liberty. The article was published in January, 1962, yet no mention was made of the fact that the student, Robert Meisenbach, who had been accused of triggering the riots by beating a policeman, had been cleared of all charges nine months before. Asking HUAC if the film had been distorted is like asking Bluebeard if he had really molested all those women.

The 1960 campaign was covered with commendable restraint. "Liberal" Democrats were treated to inverted quotes. But Charles Herman Pritchett and James M. Burns were called upon to do articles on political conventions. In August readers were asked "Which Party Means Higher Prices?" The October 31st issue warned that almost every change in the White House in the last half-century involving defeat of the party in power has been followed by serious consequences. And there were twenty-four articles on the religious "problem." but the past election "Loss, Strayed or Stolen: Millions of Votes" dealt with election mechanics with no attempt at recriminations.

Much of *U.S. News*' effectiveness consists in changing the declaratory statements of the *National Review* into questions. "The U.N. Should Get Out of Katanga" becomes "Should the U.N. Get Out of Katanga?" The message comes through both ways, but it sounds more objective the second way. A prize for cramming the verdict into the case citation might go to an article in the December 25, 1961, issue: "In the Congo, a Strange War—Started by the U.N. . . . and around the world, sharp debate rages—with Moscow and U.S. on the same side." It was not quite accurate, but it does get over a point.

Much of the conservative's enthusiasm for *U.S. News* comes from reading the editorials of owner David Lawrence on the back page. No pretense at objectivity is required here, and straight Lawrence can be a heady concoction. Since 1919 David Lawrence has been syndicating his own column. It now runs in 270 papers, and is considered to be the most widely read of all serious columns.

U.S. News & World Report grew out of a paper Lawrence founded in 1919 called *U.S. Daily*, which was concerned exclusively with government. In 1940 it was converted into a weekly news magazine with its present title. It is claimed that Otto Kahn, Simon Guggenheim, and Ruth Hanna McCormick nursed it along with about $2 million dollars. By 1960 the magazine was taking in $11 million worth of annual advertising. This was only $3 million behind *Newsweek* and on a par with *Good Housekeeping*. It was a profitable investment in conservatism.

David Lawrence would never ask "Should We Get Out of the U.N.?" With Zarathustrian authority, he declared, "The U.N. is dead—it was killed by the Korean War" (July 3, 1953). Typical of Lawrence sentiment is "U.N.—Mediator or Meddler?" the point being that the United Nations has no power to tell sovereign states what to do. As it is, United States foreign policy is too preoccupied with phony promises of "peaceful co-existence" and "disarmament." (How he loves snarling quotation marks!)

Lawrence summed up the foreign policy of a good number of conservatives in an editorial on "Prestige" (February, 1960).

"If we can only remain dedicated for all time to human freedom and maintain our record of unselfishness, we shall not need to be concerned about the short-range readings on the barometer of prestige." Confidence in the United States record of unselfishness is one of the mainstays of Right-wing foreign policy. The only severe strain in this confidence that Lawrence has publicly shown was in a conscience piece called "What Hath Man Wrought" written after we had dropped the first A-Bomb. "Man has at last brought forth a weapon that reduces war to an absurdity. . . . our guilt is also the guilt of all mankind which failed to find a way to prevent war" (August 6, 1945).

This former pang of conscience seems to have been dissolved in the enormity of technological advance. The nuclear age has revitalized Mr. Lawrence's confidence. "We have allowed ourselves to be propagandized into an obsession about the alleged dangers of nuclear tests," says Editor Lawrence in 1962 (March 26th).

President Kennedy's administration was treated to a reprint of a 1949 Lawrence column called "Conservative Liberalism v. Radical Liberalism." Not all Right-wingers would adhere to Lawrence's conservative-liberalism, since it does recognize the need for farm price supports, minimum wage, and government loans to business in time of crisis. The Right would have no difficulty applauding Lawrence's stereotype of radical-liberalism. The radical-liberal loses interest in the worker at the factory gate. He has no business sense, opposes automation, and believes that anything big in business is necessarily criminal. When in public office, he dispenses favors to lobbyists. Finally, the radical-liberal would impose state socialism by means of taxation and destroy private rights and liberties (January 15, 1962).

Lawrence insists that today's liberal is a radical. On another occasion he said the real difference between a conservative and a radical is that the radical wants to experiment with new ideas; the conservative knows from bitter experience they won't work. To conservatives this is the song their mothers taught them. They can't hear it enough.

As Lawrence shows, many conservatives can be extraordinarily obtuse when it comes to party and group politics. Lobbying is regarded as unsavory. A good President, he says in another column, would avoid party ambition and the self-interest of groups and blocs. Administration pressure on Democrats to vote its way was described as "gutter politics." The irony is that Lawrence accuses the administration of revealing "an impatience with the democratic system" (February 13, 1961).

Possessing an abundance of the good business sense he despairs of ever seeing in "liberals," David Lawrence will undoubtedly continue to maintain *U.S. News & World Report* as a dependable, conservative beacon among the mass weeklies.

"HUMAN EVENTS"

When General Robert E. Wood, chairman of Sears, Roebuck and Company, Colonel Charles Lindbergh, and W. H. Regnery, Sr., conservative publisher, co-sponsor a luncheon, it is a pretty safe day for Americanism. The luncheon was held in Chicago in 1944 to launch "Human Events" as a new Washington newsletter. Frank C. Hanighen, formerly of *Reader's Digest*, was to be its editor and publisher. Much later M. Stanton Evans, author of *Revolt on the Campus*, became managing editor. The acorn was a subscription list of 120. By 1962 there was a paid circulation of over 90,000.

"Human Events" is one of the few publications that comes in convenient throwaway form. Each of up to six sections is a self-contained news sheet or feature article. It's like receiving a weekly packet of mail-order flyers full of colorful suggestions. The format is to encourage readers to mail choice pieces to deserving friends. One drawback to the idea is that libraries receiving such a packet would generally classify it as ephemeral material, and this is located next to the "circular file."

Such featured articles as Ayn Rand's "JFK: High Class Beatnik?" James Kilpatrick's "Lyndon Johnson: Counterfeit Confederate," or Frank Chodorov, "Senator Kennedy's 'Right to Loaf' Bill"—this happened all in one week—can be had in bulk—ten for $1.00, up to 5,000 or more for $25, and they can be ordered by airmail. "Human Events" tries to think big. Readers were invited to send subscriptions to twenty-five friends—only

$7.50 per week. In another issue subscription blank spaces were provided for fourteen prospects. Payment can be in one of three ways: "Payment Enclosed," "Bill Me," or "Bill My Company."

For gift subscriptions you are urged to consider your "employees, suppliers and customers, persons in your industry, officers of your chamber of commerce, civic and service clubs, patriotic organizations." Apparently you can forget about the fellow at the next lathe. The class bias of "Human Events" is more blatant than that of *U.S. News*. But wonders of circulation have been achieved by these methods. At the top of a page you sometimes find the slogan "MULTIPLY YOURSELF by mailing to someone each section of 'Human Events,' after you have read it." No lavish giveaway schemes were used to increase circulation. However, as a bonus for ordering $65.00 or more in gift subscriptions, you can get the annual bound volume of "Human Events" free.

Conservatives who were delighted at seeing *National Review* slug out issues with six-ounce gloves are thrilled at "Human Events'" barefisted encounters. Liberals fumed when Negro Carl T. Rowan was kept out of Washington's Cosmos Club. "Human Events" gave a blunt defense of the blackballing. Rowan was kept out, an article claimed, because "he is bumptious, self-enamored, and a tasteless fellow. . . . People like people of like interests, like religion, and like racial origins. . . . No race is more clannish than the American Negro" (November 24, 1961).

An impressive cast of journalistic prizefighters is employed to keep the punches flying. Westbrook Pegler, Holmes Alexander, Fulton Lewis, Jr., and Frederic Nelson, who used to write the editorials on the back page of the *Saturday Evening Post*, are among the more prominent. Some of the footwork is pretty fancy. In a recent issue, Frederic Nelson attacked Senator Kenneth Keating of New York for advocating the repeal of literacy tests for voting. "This sounds like one of the most virulent attacks on the Negro race that has come from a Senator since the days of Ben Tillman. . . . The suggestion that New York Negroes could not pass a literacy test comes strangely from the lips of a Northerner. . . ." (April 28, 1962).

If you think that one was tricky, try H. Alexander on Alexander H. On June 9, 1961, Holmes Alexander became especially resentful of President Kennedy's accumulation of powers, and wondered aloud if Kennedy had ever read any Alexander Hamilton, who warned against too strong a President. Since Alexander Hamilton led the fight for the broadest possible interpretation of the Constitution and wanted George Washington to be a constitutional monarch, one wonders if Mr. Alexander is aware of whose corner he is headed for?

The jabs at President Kennedy are often erratic. We are told that when *Sunrise at Campobello*, the film of F.D.R.'s painful convalescence from polio, was shown to Kennedy at Palm Beach, he was bored and had the projector turned off. Then we are reminded that one of the favorite musical selections of Jack and Jackie Kennedy played over a Washington radio station was the "Coronation Scene" from the opera *Boris Godunov*.

Kennedy's "Alliance for Progress" was subjected to a neat example of bobbing. "By what right does the U.S. government propose to Congress that it appropriate an immense sum to an international agency to engage in internal intervention in the affairs of nations which have been our loyal allies?" Then we are asked, Has the United States achieved complete success in taxation, housing, education, welfare, and so on? Anyway, "land reform" is in essence a Communist proposal (March 31, 1961).

The same issue treats us to Congressman John H. Rousselot of California and of the Birch Society who is eager to set things straight on "The Truth About 'Operation Abolition.'" There is no end of authorities.

A special report reassured subscribers that the publication had "listening posts" everywhere. "News flows to 'Human Events' from every bureau and agency in Washington. In many government offices regarded as 'hotbeds of liberalism' there are officials or employees who are avid devotees of 'Human Events.' They phone—sometimes from outside pay stations—to tell us about the 'goings on.'" Imagine what Mort Sahl could do with this? To prove they were not kidding (still in the March 31st issue), we are informed (probably via an outside pay station) that Secretary of Agriculture Freeman has been reading Machiavelli's *The Prince*.

The sense of urgency is everywhere: "If the left-wing super-party is not stopped, everything which the American people do not want will be imposed upon them." This logic is not too baffling when we consider a definition of democracy suggested in a later issue. "Democracy is counting all the heads empty or not."

To remind us of the things we don't want, "Human Events" (February 17, 1961) ran a piece called "Cut Your Income Tax . . . You Decide How Much." A series of suggested expendable items follows. You pick your own: Return our ground troops from Europe. Cut foreign aid two-thirds, as well as the U.S. Information Service. "Sweden and Switzerland are more popular than the U.S., and they spend almost nothing." If the Soviet Union wants to give away its resources to backward countries, why should we object? Or, as it was put in another issue, "Whom are we trying to sell—the riff-raff who join Communist street mobs, or honest-to-God people?" (November 3, 1961).

Billions can be cut from farm supports. Public housing can be abolished, civil defense cut by one-half, and the Federal payroll reduced 15 percent. As a final thought, abolish the Small Business Administration and farm extension service. Ayn Rand may be jumping for joy, but why are all those voters who were being imposed upon so silent?

The vigilance of "Human Events" is unrelenting. Take the abuse of cultural exchange. The Bolshoi Ballet contained one known spy. And then there was that Soviet tourist who wrote under a picture of the Golden Gate Bridge, "Often those who are disappointed with the American way of life jump from it." To top this, two almost unmentionable articles were written by Soviet tourists: "Too Many Automobiles" and "Horrors of Insurance."

And what is the F.B.I. doing about all this? "It is now learned that large sections of the F.B.I. formerly working on the Reds have been reassigned, on orders from above, to the investigation of gangsters and other criminal breakers of the law" (June 2, 1961).

The F.B.I. may be relenting. "Human Events" is not. Annually it holds an informal School of Journalism in Washington to help meet the dearth of conservative writers. Scholarships are available. Their first summer session in 1957 produced David Franke, now an assistant editor of *National Review;* Douglas

Caddy, executive director of the Young Americans for Freedom; and William Schultz, who is assistant to Fulton Lewis, Jr.

Another annual function is the Political Action Conference held for two days each summer. In 1962 Senators Barry Goldwater and John S. Tower and Congressman Donald Bruce of Ohio held forth on what could be done to elect conservatives in 1962. The conference fee is $75.00, but students, teachers, and clergymen get in for $45.00. Complete tapes of the conference are available for $80.00, or you can buy individual speeches. The tape recorder has been a boon to Right-wing groups. Perhaps it was born of early association with office dictaphones. "Human Events" tapes Congressional Interviews (about 12½ minutes each) with such stalwarts as Rousselot, Bruce, Bruce Alger, Edgar Hiestand, John J. Rhodes, etc. There are now over thirty such interviews available, and the tapes are offered for $8.00 apiece.

Starting with "The Case Against Socialized Medicine," special double-sized editions of "Human Events" have appeared in four-color layouts. A second special issue is "Tax Freedom Day," representing a private war against the income tax. To counteract the ADA Index of Congressional voting, "Human Events" has published the "A.C.A. Index," Americans for Constitutional Action. It gives critical roll-call votes between 1953 and 1959, and rates congressmen by conservative criteria.

Editor Hanighen is proud to have signed the articles of incorporation for the Intercollegiate Society of Individualists, an organization to propagate conservatism among students. They were given desk space in the "Human Events" office.

In the February 3, 1961, issue, the newsletter asked, "Is 'Human Events' Biased?" Its answer: "In reporting the news, 'Human Events' is Objective; it aims for accurate presentation of the facts. But it is not impartial. It looks at events through the eyes that are Biased in favor of limited constitutional government, states' rights, private enterprise and individual freedom. These principles represent the bias of the Founding Fathers. We think the same bias will preserve freedom in America."

Professed ideological bias is never objectionable, but two weeks later "Human Events" ran an article on Ed Murrow that said in part, "Needless to say, *The Worker* has frequently praised Murrow. This, of course, does not make him a Communist. But the Communist rag does not usually praise anti-Communists." This type of reporting might titillate the Right wing, but it can hardly be considered honest journalism.

In many respects the newsletter "Human Events" is similar to Robert Welch's magazine *American Opinion.* They recommend the same books, urge the writing of similar letters, share a common urgency, and appeal to a like readership. At one time, the two publications were even offered together as a subscription package. Welch is still fighting a campaign to get "Human Events" on all major airlines. But apparently *American Opinion*'s affiliation with the Birch Society has limited its appeal.

The circulation of "Human Events" has increased ten times in five years. Yet on April 21, 1962, "Human Events" admitted it was in serious financial difficulty. As it is going into debt for expansion, it is faced with a $40,000 annual postage increase if the administration's rate increase goes through. Its current deficit is $50,000, and pay raises are necessary because of the competition in the Washington labor market. Instead of increasing second- and third-class mail, the editors suggest a six-cent stamp for first-class mail. So far no congressman has volunteered to campaign on the issue.

As a remedy, "Human Events" is trying to raise $300,000 by selling five-year and lifetime subscriptions. Those faithfully subscribing to both *National Review* and "Human Events" are in a financial squeeze, but the prospects of both look promising. The Right wing cannot suffer either of these voices to be silenced without seriously muting the Cause.

WALL STREET JOURNAL

Conservatives are seldom exasperated by the editorial pages of their daily newspapers. Liberal frustration runs pretty high. A game that any number can play is trying to guess the names of liberal newspapers. Playing time will not take much over thirty seconds. True, as you go farther Right, you find more conservative readers discontented with editorial policy. Poised between the zenith of liberal exasperation and the first signs of Right-wing disaffection is the *Wall Street Journal*. The staunch ADAer considers the paper demonic. The extreme ACAer might agree, but sees different demons. But for the average Right-winger, the *Journal* is the best available conservative answer to the *New York Times*.

It is the only real national daily newspaper in the United States and is printed five days a week in seven cities: New York, San Francisco, Washington, Cleveland, Chicago, Dallas, and Chicopee Falls (Massachusetts). There are more readers of it in California than in New York. New York City accounts for only 10 per cent of its readers. No local news is carried. Its circulation has increased almost twenty times in the past twenty years (now at 710,573 and virtually equal to the daily *New York Times*), making it the eighth or ninth ranking daily in circulation.

Starting in 1882 as a financial bulletin launched by Charles Dow and Edward Jones, the *Journal* picked up feature after research service until it became the most comprehensive businessman's newspaper in the world. It now reports on fourteen stock markets, and its hourly Dow-Jones ticker-tape service reporting industrial averages has become as integral a part of American capitalism as the Harvard Business School.

Promotional surveys boast that one-quarter of the *Journal*'s readers are either owners or presidents of a business, and the readers average an income of $22,648 a year. Half-page ads for Richardson Yachts have been carried. The paper's format is determined by the interests of its affluent readers. Seventy-five percent of the paper's columns are devoted to business and financial news and analysis. Political news is found only on the front page and the editorial page. At most the news items under the front page "What's News" get only three- or four-sentence paragraphs. Readers used to the *New York Times'* saturation coverage would feel cheated. While skimping on general news, the paper goes all out on special leader articles that occupy prime Page One space. These often approach the *New York Times Magazine* articles in length and reflect considerable style and research and may be on anything from used cars and rising foreclosures to urban land shortage.

No American daily has more successfully resisted the temptation to jazz up its front page. There are no pictures on Page One. You get one graph that might tell you that rubber is up, machine tools are down, or freight cars off. The *Journal* seems to have inherited the old *Boston Transcript*'s reputation for gentility and journalistic honesty.

In an editorial called "The Function of a Newspaper" (September 10, 1952), the *Journal* said a paper's primary function is to tell the people what is happening. "Print it, don't censor it." You should offer judgments on passing events, but "we do not think an editor has any duty to mold public opinion." However, he should express an opinion of his own. Any editor who suppresses his true opinion out of "duty to his government" is not fulfilling his function. This anticipated Secretary of State Dulles's subsequent remarks about the press as a legitimate instrument of United States foreign policy.

But it is difficult to confine opinion to the editorial page. Consider the treatment accorded President Kennedy's Transportation bill on April 6, 1962, in the *Journal* and in the *New York Times*. The most important feature of the bill according to the *Journal*'s front-page account was that railroads would now be free of rate regulations in certain areas. The *Times*, besides the rate regulations, headlined the announcement that Federal aid to city systems for developing mass transportation systems in and around cities would be available. There was no mention of this feature of the bill in the *Journal*. The *Times*' reportage and text ran to two full pages. The *Journal* ran six sentences on the front page and approximately half a page inside, and 50 per cent of this was critical, stressing the shortcomings of the bill.

The six lead columns on the front page of the April 6th *Journal* ran as follows: "Conquering Colds," "Rail Operations Should be Freed" (transport bill), "Former Maj. Gen. Walker Assailed Rusk," "Private School Plan Urged in New Orleans to Thwart Integration," "Kennedy Feeds Federal Contracts into Political Hotspots," and "Robot Tax Sleuth" (an I.B.M. invention). Only the Transport bill and the Walker incident were reported in the *Times*. "Three Asian Nations to Unify Efforts for Common Aims" (Malaya, Thailand, and Philippines) was featured on Page One of the *Times*. It was mentioned nowhere in the *Journal*. Maybe it was displaced by that chart on aluminum output.

Editor Vermont Connecticut Royster writes of the *Journal's* fond regard for "19th Century Liberalism." An April 10, 1961, editorial was reacting to the liberals' cry that this is the twentieth century. "We hear frequently these days that old methods cannot cope with new problems, and again comes the assertion that only government can devise and employ the needed new methods. This point of view is certainly reflective of the times, if only because it was so highly regarded by Hitler, Mussolini, Stalin, Khrushchev, and Mao. Surely none of these men ever was in doubt about what century it was, or what the problems of that century demanded."

Here we have the familiar conservative device of equating all government intervention with tyranny. Four days later an editorial said the great threat to man's freedom has always been the state. I wonder how many Negroes think this about the Federal Civil Rights Commission?

The editors went off the deep end in a January, 1961, editorial: "Neither Jefferson nor Hamilton hobbled our country with a national plan." Arthur Schlesinger, Jr., replied, "That was a very funny editorial in the Dec. 5th *Journal* about how Hamilton and Jefferson did not believe in national goals. Hamilton not only believed in setting national goals, he believed in using the federal government's power to achieve them." He went on to mention Hamilton's broad construction of the welfare clause and his interventionist "Report on Manufactures." Jefferson's Northwest Ordinance was specific about how the territory was to be used, and so on. And what about Jefferson's national goal in the Declaration of Independence: Life, liberty, and the pursuit of happiness?

The editorial reply ignored the Jefferson comments, admitted that Hamilton would use federal power, but insisted that he warned us of the evils of long-term debt. Then the editors went on to say, "Yet the principles upon which he believed that action [promoting the general welfare] should rest were hidden from many men of his own time. And it would seem, from not a few since." If this cryptic comment means that Hamilton justified public spending only if the government did not go into debt, Professor Schlesinger is going to have to send the editors to the back of the class once again.

The *Journal* exults in laissez-faire moralizing. It editorialized against a Federal plan to reduce the down payment on a house to as little as 3 percent of purchase price with as much as forty years to pay. "Such an absurd set-up is an open invitation to imprudence . . . what comes that easy can go that easy." They objected to the assumption that life can be made easy for all on Federal terms. "That is a sentimental approach which can only weaken our society, for it seeks to foreclose what good sense and strength of character we may have" (April 6, 1962). This Puritan outrage is similar to the protest that first labeled the installment plan immoral. First thing you know, "Everybody will be somebody, and then nobody will be anybody."

To the editors, economic bias is more important than political slant. The paper does not endorse political candidates. During the 1960 campaign both Nixon and Kennedy were chastised. "If the public has any idea of the differences between Kennedy and Nixon in so far as future policy is concerned, it was acquired mainly by osmosis" (November 8, 1960). Neither candidate treated the public (on T.V.) as intelligent people. "Mr. Nixon was probably more affected by this method of dealing with great issues in ten-words-of-one-syllable. . . . Rarely have two candidates talked so much and said so little."

The day after elections was handled with magnificent nonchalance. On the front page in type only half the size of the headline "Sportswear Makers Sound a New Style Note" was the announcement: "Kennedy Led Nixon in Popular and Electoral Votes Early This Morning."

In critique-ing the election, the editors thought that Nixon should have challenged the liberal philosophy head on. One irreverent reader did suggest that Nixon should have said his "Me too" louder. Obviously the paper was not feeling comfortable with either party. Later, in a January 17, 1962, editorial, the paper said: "When two almost identical products are offered, the public will go for the original. The Republican Party has not learned this yet. . . . It is sad when millions of voters have no party to call their own." Considerable *Journal* space is given to the idea of a "new" Goldwater of softened views who would be able to rally the "silent Americans," that is, the true individualists who are not part of existing pressure groups.

Certainly the *Journal* has not been harsh on the far Right. "There is a danger in being extreme about extremists. . . . These extremists have not sprung up without due cause. There is often a grain of harsh truth. Perhaps that is why they are so irritating" (December 13, 1961). Ten letters were printed in praise of this editorial, none in criticism. The theme of the letters was incorporated in an editorial a month later. "The Left hopes the Far Right furor will cover up their own hotblooded activities for a neo-Socialist State." The same thing was being said in Robert Welch's *American Opinion*. But the paper did go on to say that liberals were trying to link all conservatives with an intemperate few. It was made clear that conservatives must be more discriminating than members of the Birch Society. The *Journal* has given the ultras understanding but not encouragement.

The *Journal* is not too long on humor. There isn't much funny business. Their attempts at humor have generally been about as successful as those forlorn cartoons in the *Christian Science Monitor*. "Wigwarm: what George Washington said to Martha on a hot day when he took it off." Or, "Beat Nick: Department Store Santa Claus at the end of a hard day."

One day the editors got to wondering why the liberals have more of a reputation for being funny: "Maybe liberals have more humor because they have things their own way more often. By the same token, how can the more conservative politicians be expected to laugh when the joke is so clearly on them? And on the nation" (May 12, 1961).

If the *Journal* does not laugh too easily, it often demonstrates a good disposition. There were gracious remarks after Adlai Stevenson's 1952 defeat. "Democrats can be especially proud of Stevenson's words upon defeat. Nothing better revealed in Mr. Stevenson a quality for leadership than the manner of his yielding it" (November 6, 1952). Editor Royster even has kind words for Harry Truman. In discussing Truman's *Memoirs*, Royster says: "A reader may not excuse the blunders but he can understand them. . . . Reading Harry Truman's memoirs in the tranquillity of different times, you cannot help but feel a sympathy for this man who did as well as he was able" (November 7, 1955).

An ultra-Right-winger going over the files might cancel his subscription upon unearthing "The New Deal: Did Roosevelt or Popular Demand Create it?" (April 14, 1938). "This thing called the New Deal seems to have grown out of deep-seated popular dissatisfaction with affairs as they were and were becoming between the peak of the boom in 1929 and the bottom of the depression in 1932. . . . There is evidence to show this dissatisfaction outran Mr. Roosevelt on more than one occasion." This would be commendable coming from the *Journal* in 1958. It is remarkable coming in 1938.

The Tennessee redistricting case caught the editors trying to make their way across a badly charred bridge. They backed the Supreme Court's decision. Of course, it would be best for the states to reapportion themselves. "That would indeed be the right remedy if the states would do it. The trouble is that many states have refused to do it" (March 28, 1962). Two years earlier, in commenting on Senator Eugene McCarthy's new book, *Frontiers of American Democracy*, the senator was condemned for urging the Federal government to do things the states should do but failed to do (November 9, 1960).

Probably one of the things that irritates liberals most about the *Journal*, and endears it to conservatives, is the capacity for saying about the Left wing what is usually said about the Right. The example is dated but the sentiment is classic. Back in 1943, control over the Board of Economic Warfare was withdrawn from Henry Wallace. Warming up to this slap at the Vice-President, a July 17th editorial remarked that Wallace is the archtype of idealist who contributes two things to public office: futility and disruption. "As idealists they [Wallace *et al.*] have their place and function in American life. But what has happened to Mr. Wallace is a lesson that that place and function is not responsible administrative office." This is precisely the condescension now reserved for the Right wing. Perhaps they are necessary as irritants, but keep them out of public office.

If the Harvard Business School is the Citadel of American

Capitalism, the *Wall Street Journal* is its General Orders. It is flourishing in resources, circulation, and prestige. The *Saturday Review* (May 13, 1961) reported a poll of university journalism teachers that cited the *Wall Street Journal* as showing the "greatest improvement" over the last decade in broadening its scope. In their list of the top fifteen papers, the *Journal* ranked third after the *New York Times* and the *Christian Science Monitor*. The *Journal* makes a policy of recruiting young men from college and offering summer scholarships to students working on campus papers. It is a modern major newspaper.

Critics may feel it reads too much like an affluent Sunday-school teacher. Edward Ziegler, writing in the *Nation* (January 2, 1960), suggests that the *Journal* is for the Individual—particularly if he pays his bills. He also objected to the glittering essays on first-rate trivia. But the more carping liberals revile, the more contented conservatives revere the *Wall Street Journal* as the prestige journal of the Right.

CHAPTER 9

Organizations for the Young Conservative

THE last thing a young conservative has to worry about is an organization to join. As soon as he begins to feel lonely, all he has to do is to write to the Alert Americans Association in Los Angeles. They have compiled *The First National Directory of "Rightist" Groups, Publications and Some Individuals in the United States (and Some Foreign Countries)*. Their fourth edition (1962) is twice the size of their third (1957), and boasts "some two thousand listings." By eliminating foreign offerings, individuals, churches, and the multiple entries of Citizens Councils (25), States'-Rights parties (35), Constitutional parties (40), KKK chapters (17), and Young Americans for Freedom (22), the directory is down to 824 groups. This is not correcting for cross-references.

You still have quite a choice. For a start you might turn to the Committee for the Protection of Patriotic Broadcasters, which is fortified by the Network of Patriotic Letter Writers. Backstopping these is the Committee for the American Treatment of the News. It may be comforting to learn that there is a Committee to Restore America to the Citizens. The more militant might prefer the Ultra American Service Association, or you might sign up for Jab a Liberal Series. You would be playing it safe with the Stay American Committee or the American Flag Association. But what do you suppose the Cup of Cold Water Ministry thinks of the Association for the Protection of our Water Supply?

These, of course, are the more extreme causist organizations, and are not particularly geared to the young. Besides scores of local campus groups, there are about a dozen national organizations appealing directly to young people. Some of these groups are *ad hoc* and ephemeral. You are very likely to get letters of inquiry returned with "Moved—Left No Address."

Most of these national student organizations are primarily anti-Communist. Some focus on special causes within the Crusade. The Student Committee for Congressional Autonomy was formed at Northwestern University by two members of Young Americans for Freedom to vindicate the traditional right of Congress to engage in investigations. They specialize in distributing reports from the House Un-American Activities Committee and the Senate Internal Security Committee. "It is no longer an attack on one or two committees," said the student founder. "They have declared war on both the congressional prerogative to inform itself and on the peoples' right to know."

The Student Anti-Communist League (SAL) is based in Phoenix, Arizona, and has a national advisory board which includes Herbert Philbrick, Rabbi M. J. Merritt, and Adolphe Menjou. It is organized on national, state, and local levels to combat Communist influence on high school and college campuses. Their goal is to spotlight Communist propaganda circulating on campus and to point out the fallacies of pro-Communist ideas. A handbook, *Guideline to Action*, claims to be "a complete and concise analysis of Communist campus activities." S.A.L., however, is not so eager as most student organizations to divulge information about itself.

A more forthright but less well-organized group is Students for Freedom which formed in reaction to alleged excessive liberalism on the San Diego State College campus. In October, 1960, they published *Evolve* to vent conservative protest. "Why should academic freedom mean that the professor has the Right to present exclusively the Liberal interpretation on all important issues?"

They have carried on a campaign against the popular American government readings book, *The Politics of American Democracy*, by Marian Irish and James Prothro. In the book's discussion of the House Un-American Activities Committee, it is charged that no favorable evidence is advanced for the Committee. This particular issue led to an exchange with the American Civil Liberties Union of Southern California. The students held their own creditably.

Evolve does well enough from its ads (including Knott's Berry Farm) and contributors to offer the publication free to students on campus. They have 800 paid subscribers in twenty states and two foreign countries.

Playing conspiracy is a tempting game for minority groups. It is one thing for the editors to joke about cautioning their readers to exercise restraint in brandishing copies of *Evolve*. You are playing for keeps when you suggest that a student editor was murdered for political reasons. On March 30, 1961, Newton Armstrong, Jr., newly elected editor of *Evolve*, was found hanged in his parents' home. The San Diego police called it a suicide. *Evolve* writers could not agree. They put out an eight-page special edition with thirteen photographs of clothesline and rafters, trying to prove that the death could not have been a suicide. It was a homicide, they alleged, and probably due to political animosity. Through a private investigation by a former FBI agent, they hope to reopen the case.

Unless Students for Freedom can substantiate its charges, it may find itself limited in future recruiting.

According to the West Coast's Communist newspaper *People's World*, California's Number One anti-Communist is Charles Fox, a young graduate assistant at Berkeley. Mr. Fox organized Students Associated Against Totalitarianism (SAAT) in March,

1961, in reaction to the appearance on the Berkeley campus of Frank Wilkinson, alleged Communist and archfoe of the House Committee on Un-American Activities. The group remained active for about nine months but never received university recognition. The *San Francisco Examiner* (October 25, 1961) reported that Students Associated Against Totalitarianism was being subsidized by the Associated Farmers. This was later denied by Mr. Fox.

After the demise of SAAT, Mr. Fox concentrated on publishing *Tocsin*, which had been started in June, 1960. Subscribers now number over 2,000, and the press run goes over 5,000. Reprints are sold in bulk. In an interview gallantly granted to *People's World*, Mr. Fox listed four varieties of evil: Communist, pro-Communist, pro-Soviet, and liberal (confused). "Of course," he explained, "I see so-called peace activities as being pro-Soviet . . . Also, I see the so-called civil liberties movement as pro-Soviet. There is a group of people who want freedom simply to destroy our freedoms" (March 17, 1962).

Critics have accused the slick *Tocsin* of operating à la "Hollywood Confidential," giving suggestive leads about who was affiliated with what organization and identified with which cause. Unlike their earlier editions of warmed-over articles and speeches, *Tocsin* now does its own researching and prods every left-of-Center organization for pro-Soviet soft spots.

Two feature columns have undoubtedly helped: "Ask Aunt Tanya" and "Letters from Cornelia." For example:

"Dear Aunt Tanya: The girls in our progressive club are frankly fed up with Peace and would like to switch to something else for a while. We did Civil Liberties two years ago.—Funlovers, N.Y.

"Dear Funlovers: Surely you are not so stupid as to be unaware that the Party has ordered Peace until we win this war. Stick with Peace and stop acting like spoiled enemies of the working class."

Or, "Dear Mama: Don't be disappointed if I don't send you my usual Mother's Day card. I am sending you a May Day card instead. . . ."

Tanya is invariably funnier than Cornelia, but any attempt

at humor is rare in the anti-Communist publications under consideration. Collection of "Letters from Cornelia," a well-Red impressionable coed, are reprinted in bulk lots. The exaggeration of these letters to Mama play up the stereotype that the far Right is convinced dominates American campuses. Publisher Fox handles these distortions with considerable finesse. Compared to its cohort publications, *Tocsin* is relatively sophisticated. Unlike most anti-Communist publications, it appears to be secular, and does not stress the religious issue.

For keeping up with what young conservatives are doing, nothing equals the *Student Statesman*, which is a publication of the Reverend Thomas Wyatt's Crusade for God and Freedom. It is over twice the size of *Tocsin* but only half as well edited. *Student Statesman* eagerly solicits articles by young conservatives, and they get them. Thanksgiving, 1961, caught them with a front-page specimen of prose that would shame a conscientious eleventh grader. "I am the U.S. . . . I am the Brooklyn Bridge. . . . I am Babe Ruth and the World Series. . . . I am Eli Whitney and Stephen Foster. . . . Yes, I am the nation and these are the things that I am. . . ." Apparently this doesn't happen too often, but when it does, they print it.

Reprints appear from "Human Events," *Christian Herald, Freeman, This Week Magazine,* and Kiplinger. Speeches from notables like the Hoovers, J. Edgar and Herbert, are used. But most of the writing is done by the staff and student contributors, mostly from western schools. The intellectual count is low because the paper is trying to appeal to both high schools and colleges.

Publisher Thomas Wyatt, a radio minister, loves flamboyant gestures. He sponsored the 1960 Pony Express to Washington carrying a letter engraved in leather alerting President Eisenhower to the dangers of Communism on the eve of Khrushchev's visit. On a tour of Western Europe, Wyatt launched "Operation Airlift" to carry *Student Statesman,* Bibles, and other anti-Communist literature via balloon behind the iron curtain. One of his major editorials was in favor of superpatriotism.

The Policy Statement of *Student Statesman* declares against the tyranny of Right or Left. It also opposes "communism, fascism, radical nationalism, internationalism, racism, Castroism, socialism, and personal and national godlessness." So far the editors have not been able to unearth any tyranny on the Right, nor have they found nationalism too radical anywhere. But they certainly have taken off after internationalism, socialism, and godlessness.

One article (November, 1961) warned against UNESCO, the seed of one-worldism: "Its policies are aimed at destroying American freedom by brain washing our children to disdain their rich historical heritage." Parents are urged to block this master plan of subversion in the schools. "Today modern textbooks have reduced patriotic quotations to a trickle, and even these are almost 100 percent world centered." All this is largely due to the influence of UNESCO. After all, as the article put it, "We believe that education is basically a problem of the home and community, and not of the nation or world."

The May, 1962, issue carried an article on free enterprise from the *Freeman* which claimed that competitive private enterprise was the only political concept consistent with the belief that individuals are endowed by their creator with certain unalienable rights. Presumably Christian Socialists as well as Communists are to take notice.

Everything is fair game for a sermon. When a public cry went up for outlawing boxing after the tragic death of Bennie Peret, the *Student Statesman* editorialized: "It is time for us to pull our heads out of the sand and put first things first. Boxing doesn't threaten our way of life but Communism does. Let's take up the battle cry 'Communism must go.'"

Prominent coverage was given to the remarks of a school superintendent who spoke to a "Wake Up America" rally in Arcada, California (September, 1961). He said Americanism can be taught in the schools by an emotional approach, and it should be. The child can understand later.

A similar approach to the Communist menace is found in one of the brochures of the "Student Statesman Seminar." This is a correspondence course and organizational kit giving you the Policy Statement and telling how to organize a campus chapter. You also get ten attractive brochures, each in a different color, giving you an abbreviated and simplistic course in "world affairs."

Number Five (green) is called "Why Do People Become Communists?" Dr. W. S. McBirnie, the author, suggests two main causes: First, sickness of the emotions. "No one ever becomes a Communist by objective reasoning." Second is the individual's lack of a cause for which to live. Dr. McBirnie urges us to read this again, and modestly adds, "It is the most important single insight you will ever have into the real nature of Communism!" Green ink tells us the contributing causes: Idealism, Envy of the Successful, Blackmail, Ambition for Personal Power, Members of Socially Handicapped Minorities: "social oddballs" and Sex Deviates "getting back" at society. Dr. W. S. McBirnie wrote six of the ten brochures.

Besides disseminating this study material, chapters are urged to fortify themselves with Welch's *American Opinion,* the Reverend McIntire's *Christian Beacon,* and its "own security system of screening applicants and preventing subversive students from infiltrating the Chapter." Members are also encouraged to attend patriotic meetings on and off campus, to invite speakers to student meetings, to write congressmen, and to organize peaceful demonstrations against Communist-front groups both on and off campus.

Copies of *Student Statesman* are sent to the library of every college and university in the United States and Canada. In addition, mass distribution in quantities ranging from 25 to 3,000 takes place on more than 150 campuses. By the fall of 1962, the paper expects to be printing 100,000 copies per month. In 1962 *Student Statesman* was published in England and Mexico and distributed by means of newsstands and by hand on campuses. The editors did confess that "the major difference in the English edition is that it will carry an European viewpoint regarding national and international affairs" (December–January, 1962). Wonder what happens to UNESCO?

The activities of *Student Statesman* pale when compared to those of the National Education Program. This is a foundation set up at Harding College in Searcy, Arkansas, not too far from Little Rock. Harding's Americanism program was inaugurated by Dr. George S. Benson when he assumed the presidency in 1936 after eleven years as a missionary in China. The program really got moving in 1949 with a gift of $300,000 from Alfred P. Sloan, former president of General Motors. Substantial contributions have raised a miniscule endowment to $6,000,000. For accreditation purposes, the NEP has been separated from the college, but Dr. Benson is president of both.

There are two vice-presidents and a staff of eight. Of the annual budget of $200,000, $60,000 goes for postage. Dr. Benson's weekly column "Looking Ahead" is sent free to more than 3,000 weekly newspapers. His monthly "National Program Letter" is sent to 50,000 subscribers. The monthly letter has such articles as "Is Infiltration Possible?" Have we another crop of agents operating around the intellectual elite of the White House? Another, on muffling the military, said that this may be done by Communists, socialists, or misguided liberals. The results are the same: pleasure and satisfaction in Moscow. Americanism Days are urged, such as the one held in Searcy which began with a Boy Scout flag-raising ceremony and was climaxed by the local theater's showing of "Operation Abolition."

A radio program called "Land of the Free" is broadcast on 368 stations. A lecture bureau keeps five speakers in constant circulation from coast to coast. Dr. Benson himself averages 125 audiences a year. Thirty motion-picture films are for sale or hire. A technical triumph is the animated technicolor cartoon "Adventures in Economics." Wages, prices, and taxes are handled with the engaging charm of a Walt Disney production. Seldom has the rigid free-enterprise line been more attractively packaged. Metro-Goldwyn-Mayer distributed the series of ten cartoons to over 15,000 theaters, where they were viewed by more than 35 million people.

Another series of thirteen black-and-white films called "American Adventure" range from Plymouth Colony to corporation profit. Number Five in the series, "A Look at Socialism," promises an objective analysis, and then depicts "the miserable plight of a people living under Socialism." This miserable existence is dramatized by picturing eight pathetic piles of sugar, lard, flour, and so on, which constituted a week's ration under Britain's "Austerity Socialism." The charge is made that socialism and not World War II produced the austerity. All socialism, the film claims, leads to poverty and loss of individual freedom.

"American Adventure" has been incorporated into a great

many state educational systems. It is required for all juniors and seniors in public high schools in the State of Louisiana.

"Communist Encirclement—1961" features the San Francisco student riots and the Cuban take-over. This thirty-minute color film supersedes "Communism on the Map," which is probably NEP's most controversial project. "Communism on the Map," a professional forty-five-minute film that has been seen by over ten million people, shows the United States helplessly exposed to Communist conspiracy. General Marshall is blamed for losing China, Batista is praised as an anti-Communist, and the San Francisco students are pictured as manipulated by Communists. A world map shows all the important nations except Switzerland, Spain, and the United States (a big question mark) going Communist.

Norman Thomas was outraged. "All the material in this film is either false or misleading. Its theme is that socialism and Communism are identical, which could not be farther from the truth" (*New York Times*, May 18, 1961). Ninety-two professors at the University of Washington were equally indignant. "Having seen this film strip, we are shocked by its irresponsible mingling of fact and falsehood and by its gross distortion of historical events. As scholars concerned with the truth, we protest against this harmful and misleading propaganda."

When the superintendent of public schools in Wichita Falls asked for materials, the NEP sent him twenty-four items ranging from films to flannel boards. Full scholarship courses for teachers of American history and social science are available during a five-week summer course. The session awards six hours of graduate credit. One of the courses, History 501, covers the "development of the background of the American way of life from literature and from economic and political philosophy from the Greeks to the American Revolution." They don't just fool around.

The college's American Studies Group conducts a "Week at Harding" each summer for high school students from all over the United States. In 1961 there were 339 high school students in attendance. A series of one-day forums are held during the year.

Forums on Americanism have caught on. Dr. Benson claims that more than one hundred private colleges now have programs patterned after the National Education Program. The two most prominent progeny are in New York and California. Under NEP tutelage, King's College of Briarcliff Manor, New York, has set up a National Freedom Education Center and held a New York City forum in the spring of 1962. It featured over two dozen speakers.

In Los Angeles, Pepperdine College, which concentrates on business majors, has held California Freedom Forums and produced a film, "Communist Accent on Youth," narrated by Harry von Zell, which is in use by groups in forty-eight states. They are now working on a series of thirteen half-hour films on the theme "Crisis for Americans," and are planning a weekly radio broadcast to four hundred stations of an Americanism show featuring Pat Boone and top business and political leaders. Both the King's College and Pepperdine programs have been aided by the parent group at Harding.

Brief mention might be made of the use of anti-Communism forums by the military, since these are obviously intended to influence young men. Such forums are frequently sponsored jointly by the military and local Chamber of Commerce. Reserve officers are given credit points for attending. The nonpartisan pretense of the forum is often strained. At Glenview, Illinois, Naval Air Station, Fred Schwarz was given office space where he tape-recorded a statement criticizing the Democratic candidate for Congress. One Glenview pamphlet, "Background Material That Every Patriot Should Know," attacked the National Council of Churches, NAACP, National Education Association, COPE, and ADA.

A leaflet given out at the Minneapolis Naval Air Station, "What I Can Do to Stop Communism," recommended joining the Birch Society or Fred Schwarz organization, and listening to Fulton Lewis, Clarence Manion, and Billy James Hargis. The Fourth Army and San Diego Junior Chamber of Commerce sponsored a seminar in September, 1961, at which General Wedemeyer accused the Kennedy administration of appeasement. Welch's *Blue Book* was on sale in the lobby. More details of the military's anti-Communism role can be found in the January, 1961, issue of the *Progressive*.

These military anti-Communist forums share Dr. Fred

Schwarz's difficulty. Neither can remain "primarily anti-Communist" without lapsing into attacks on liberalism. Yet both feel uneasy about a Right-wing label. A group that is primarily conservative and therefore anti-Communist has the advantage of appearing less testy and probably will enjoy more long-range success.

The Intercollegiate Society of Individualists might be such a group. It is small and almost unknown outside conservative circles, but it is conservatism's most dedicated intellectual organization. Impressed by the success of the old Intercollegiate Socialist Society, Frank Chodorov of "Human Events" hoped he could accomplish as much for the Right with a similar campus organization. The Foundation for Economic Education (publishers of *Freeman*) promised to supply literature. Since its 1953 founding, the ISI has built up a mailing list of over 13,000 and mailed over one million pieces of literature.

A new campus group is given five or six books as a club library. No charters are issued. Some chapters are sponsored by liberal faculty members. No particular commitment is demanded of student members, although a director at Philadelphia headquarters said they probably would purge a Lincoln Rockwell. Three-quarters of their funds come from individual contributions, the rest from educational foundations. It is said that the Andrew Tuller Foundation of New Jersey is a contributor, but this could not be officially confirmed.

A student newspaper is distributed free to members. Conservative publications are made available at a discount, and a torrent of pamphlets can be had for the licking of a stamp. ISI encourages a discussion of theoretical issues, and sponsors regional "Leadership Conferences." Five of these were held during the first semester of 1961–1962. In April of 1962 a Southern Seminar was held at the University of Virginia on the theme of a conservative approach to foreign policy. Frank S. Meyer of *National Review* gave a speech on the "Illusion of Coexistence," and Dr. Hans F. Sennholz, economist of Grove City College, Pennsylvania, spoke on "Youth for Socialism: The Peace Corps."

Four summer schools were held during 1962. These cost

students only traveling expenses. One at Grove City College will be for academic credit.

The intellectual reputation of ISI is not particularly enhanced by its newspaper, the *Individualist*, which a director said was 99 percent the work of students. Young H. R. Regnery is editor. It tends to be like the G.I. gripe columns of *Stars and Stripes*. One student critic said of liberal professors, "What right have they, entrusted with the sacred education of this nation's youth, to teach what they please and exclude what they like?" These professors are hopelessly unrealistic. ". . . Money is a part of reality, but since they have never had any large sum, ten thousand is the same to them as ten million. They cannot visualize how hard these people would balk at giving it up" (October, 1961). Especially that ten million.

Sometimes the adult contributors are just as wild. In a brief essay, "The Moral Necessity of Economic Freedom," economist Wilhelm Roepke says, "In fact, the collectivist state that supports itself with the patent dishonesties of price ceilings, exchange control and confiscatory taxes [all of which the U.S. has had] acts with greater immorality than the individual who violates these regulations to preserve the fruits of his own labor."

Then there was the day that Chodorov tried an essay on social contract theory called "Source of Rights." We are told that "the basic axiom of socialism, in all its forms, is that might is right." This, says Chodorov, is because socialism believes in a theory of social contract that holds that all rights are derived from the government. This would be a surprise to Marx, who rejected all theories of social contract. It wouldn't help much in explaining why Hobbes, the most authoritarian social contractor, preferred a laissez-faire economy. And poor Rousseau, the source of so much collectivism, never even recognized a contract with government.

Richard Weaver, English professor at the University of Chicago, is on hand to warn of the dangers of "Mass Plutocracy." This is the error of thinking that everything can be solved by money. We cannot spend our way to security or happiness. This is the root fallacy of our foreign-aid program. "I think of the expression of *wantlessness* which I once saw in Mexico on the face of a peasant in from the hills. There is dignity in that too." Weaver quotes Jacob Burckhardt on the curse of industrialization: "Nobody knows how to be poor any more." This sermonizing on materialism is not always too popular with the more rugged economic individualists.

Besides the reprints of speeches and essays, ISI has fathered student publications on campus. The first was *Insight and Outlook* at Wisconsin, then the *New Individualist* at Chicago, and *Analysis* at University of Pennsylvania. Easily the best is the publication at the University of Chicago. A great deal of the ISI's reputation for intellectuality comes from its association with the *New Individualist Review*. The first edition carried a lead article by Chicago economics professor Milton Friedman on "Capitalism and Freedom." It is an excellent presentation of market economy morality.

Friedman points out that the post-World War II Englishman who could not spend his vacation in the United States because of exchange controls was just as deprived as a United States citizen denied entry to U.S.S.R. because of his political views. He also goes on to admit that although economic freedom is a necessary condition for political freedom, clearly it is not a sufficient condition. Russia before World War I and Japan, Italy, and Germany before World War II are offered as examples of private-enterprise economies with little political freedom. This admission of the complex relation of political and economic freedom is rare in conservative literature.

Rarer still is a conservative feud with William Buckley, Jr. Associate Editor Ronald Hamowy rebuked Buckley and his *National Review* in the November, 1961, issue of *New Individualist*. Hamowy charged that Buckley and his review were leading true believers in freedom and individual liberty down a disastrous path and betraying conservatism's principles.

Instead of championing civil rights, Buckley is endorsing "a polite form of white supremacy" and labeling civil libertarians Soviet agents. Instead of advocating peace, Buckley would foment war. "The libertarian principle of peace and non-intervention has been replaced by the heroics of a barroom drunk who proudly boasts that he can lick any man in the room." The Right under the aegis of *National Review* has itself become a leading minion of the state. "They do not so much desire to limit the State as to control it." Hamowy thinks this will produce a conservatism of Pharaonic Egypt, medieval Europe, and the Inquisition.

In reply Buckley defended his antistatism purely along economic lines. Defending colonialism, Editor Buckley said that freedom is not a matter of "Ready, Set, Be Free." It must be earned and sometimes takes centuries. Hamowy asked how it was to be earned and who is the paymaster? "No one *gives* anyone else his freedom," said Editor Hamowy, "nor is anyone indebted to others for it. . . . Freedom is not earned but is the *right* of each human being." According to our Declaration of Independence, this is supposed to be self-evident.

This is the voice of nineteenth century *political* liberalism so infrequently heard on today's Right. Intellectual candor of this caliber will make the *New Individualist Review* a formidable contender in public debate. It makes the writing on the home office's newspaper, the *Individualist*, look pretty sad in comparison.

In keeping with its policy of promoting reading and discussion on campus, ISI has avoided taking stands on issues and tries to remain as nonpolitical as possible. Remaining noncontroversial may prove to be a strain. In the spring semester of 1962 the chairman of the History Department of Grove City College was dismissed under unusual circumstances. J. Howard Pew of Sun Oil, chairman of the board of trustees of the college, is well known for his extreme Right-wing views. The history professor, a Quaker, was well known for his liberal views. It was learned that members of the campus Conservative Club had sent textbooks used in various history courses to the ISI in Philadelphia for evaluation. The eastern field director of ISI is a recent graduate of Grove City College, and John G. Pew, son of J. Howard, is vice-president of ISI.

This raises the question of how long ISI can preserve its amateur standing.

While the Intercollegiate Society of Individualists prefers academic discussion, Young Americans for Freedom is eager to work the precincts. YAF is the brainchild of William Buckley, and reflects his verve and dashing enterprise. The organizational meeting was held in September, 1960, at Buckley's home in Sharon, Connecticut. YAF's manifesto bears the town's name and was drawn up by M. Stanton Evans, author of *Revolt on the Campus*. The nucleus of the group represented disappointed Young Republicans who had crusaded for Barry Goldwater at the Chicago convention that summer. Actually, Buckley was implementing a suggestion of Goldwater himself that this fine group of young supporters be kept alive.

Two twenty-three-year-olds, Douglas Caddy and David Frank (already involved in six other conservative groups), set out to show what a well-inked mimeograph machine and rugged enterprise could do to the "Liberal Establishment." During their first year the ink supply was supplemented by nearly $70,000 in contributions. Respectable contributions came from Charles Edison (lights), Herbert Kohler (plumbing), Roger Millikin (drip-drys), and Lewis Strauss (now with Kuhn-Loeb banking). Each of these gentlemen was later to receive a Freedom Award from a grateful YAF. In addition Captain Eddie Rickenbacker has solicited funds for the organization.

National advisers poured in as readily as dollars. Eleven were supplied from the Birch Society ranks, including Adolphe Menjou. He already counsels the Student Anti-Communist League and ISI. However, YAF has no connection with the Birch Society other than these advisers who, it is assumed, serve in an honorary capacity.

Using the Young Republicans' cut-off year of thirty-nine, YAF does not confine itself to students, and seeks to recruit among young people in the community at large. Of their 190 chapters, eighty-five are off campus. The Greater New York Council alone has about 2,200 members-at-large not yet integrated into chapters. About the same number in New York City are organized into campus and community groups. At this point YAF has a membership of about 20,000, and hopes to have chapters in every college and high school in the country. Work is going slowly at the high schools. So far there are five YAF chapters and 24,226 high schools. YAF objects to being called extremist. "Americans for Democratic Action are more extreme than we are," said Executive Director Richard Viguerie. As proof he quoted the Arthur Schlesinger, Jr., statement that the answer to Communism is the welfare state. Mr. Viguerie, incidentally, believes that Communists should not be issued permits to speak in the community.

Certainly YAF is not extremist on the segregation issue. The Southern Student Freedom Fund is sponsored by the National Student Association to raise money for students expelled from school for segregation protests. Twice the Fund appealed to YAF for support. Months after their original appeal, members of the Fund were told that their request would be submitted to YAF's board of directors for consideration. No further action was taken. Perhaps this is not surprising, since there is not a word in the Sharon statement about civil rights being a problem.

Not all leaders of YAF share this reticence on civil rights. New England Regional Chairman Jack Molesworth supported the sit-in movement and is a member of the American Civil Liberties Union.

In January, 1961, liberal youth groups planned a demonstration against the House Un-American Activities Committee. Pickets were to parade before the White House. YAF learned of the picket plans and managed to get twice as many students to Washington to demonstrate for the Committee. This brought them their first national press coverage. This was to be just the first in a series of harassing attacks on the Left. Challenging a citadel of liberalism, the Greater New York Council of YAF set up its first chapter in Greenwich Village, where they proceeded to show the film "Operation Abolition" to a crowded theater.

There was another clash in Washington at a meeting concerning the organization of the Peace Corps in March, 1961. YAF wanted to rename the Peace Corps the Anti-Communist Freedom Corps, and insisted that all participants undergo a rigorous security check and be carefully indoctrinated in the principles of free enterprise. Campus ADA opposed any screening process based on political belief but supported one on screening for political maturity. ADA also horrified YAF by suggesting an International Peace Corps involving United Nations member nations.

During New York City's summer primaries in 1961, two

directors of YAF, David Frank and William Cotter, formed a group called Freedom Party, Inc. The Central Labor Council of New York City had planned a party with the same name, but YAF beat them to the listings. The young conservatives entered a candidate for mayor against liberal Republican Attorney General Lefkowitz. This was purely a protest vote, but in the City Council race, Manhattan YAF Chairman Edward Nash challenged liberal Republican incumbent Stanley Isaacs and got 42 percent of the vote.

When a new Conservative party was organized in New York State in 1962, YAF National Director Caddy opposed it as a splinter party, but most of YAF seemed to follow the *National Review*'s endorsement of the new party.

One of the prime targets of YAF has been the liberally oriented National Students Association, which is the closest thing in the United States to a congress of college campuses. By August of 1961, YAF felt confident in taking on its archenemy at the Madison conference. YAF headquarters occupied several rooms in expensive Madison Inn. A staff of several secretaries was led by Fulton Lewis, III. One source estimates that over $10,000 was spent by the conservatives for this operation. YAF delegates and observers were equipped with two-way walkie-talkie radios to provide constant communication with Madison Inn headquarters. They came to sessions with tape recorders and prepared texts duplicated in advance for press release and general circulation.

By never getting too far from a microphone, speaking up on all occasions, and holding press conferences. YAF was able to create the impression of strength beyond its numbers. While some of the uncommitted delegates were often miffed by the brashness of YAF enterprise, this was the first NSA conference to experience any genuine conservative opposition.

The most spectacular device YAF has hit upon is their Freedom Rally. Manhattan Center was the scene of their first endeavor in March, 1961. All 3,200 seats were filled and even more people were turned away. In his *National Review* account William Buckley was ecstatic. "The student band was first rate . . . flyers were exuberant. . . . The programs were well printed. . . . Tickets were in three colors." Senator Goldwater was the featured speaker (the senator delivered ten speeches to YAF during the year free of charge), and the following awards were bestowed: for International affairs—the Republic of China; for Business— Herbert Kohler; for Science—Lewis Strauss; and for Government Service—House Un-American Activities Committee.

The 1962 Conservative Rally for World Liberation from Communism filled all 18,000 seats of Madison Square Garden. Once again there was a turn-away crowd. Featured guest was to be Moïse Tshombe. When the State Department turned down his visa request, conservatives had a field day. This was better than getting him. Perhaps it was just as well. A week before the rally, Tshombe repeated his charge that the United Nations had intervened in Katanga "for the profit of United States capitalists."

Guests General Walker and Senator Dodd of Connecticut withdrew for political reasons. David Lawrence declined, saying he just didn't attend rallies like this. Herbert Hoover sent regrets from his Key Largo fishing lodge. John Wayne had to go on location in England, and Dr. Edward Teller was just A.W.O.L. This didn't prevent honored presentations *in absentia*. "The Chief," Hoover, was represented by Eugene Lyons. George Murphy substituted for John Wayne, who "will never forget the Alamo." Murray Kempton of the New York *Post* irreverently observed that "John Wayne forgot the Alamo after it petered out in the drive-ins."

Wild cheers greeted mention of Katanga, States' rights, victory over Communism, Bill Buckley, and St. John's College (Brooklyn). Boos went up for the United Nations, Washington, coexistence, *America* magazine, and Harvard.

Occasional audience apathy could be measured by the increase of paper airplanes fashioned from rally literature. Flights were appreciably strong during Brent Bozell's lecture on the danger of Gnosticism, a malady which had escaped the ken of most of his listeners. "Peace is inspiration only to those who want to surrender. . . . Nuclear tests should never have been stopped. . . . Tshombe should never have been ousted. . . . Is this extremism?" asked Bozell. Then he went on to suggest we tear down the Berlin wall, land in Havana, and have the C.I.A. foster revolution in Russia.

By the time Goldwater got up to speak, there wasn't much left except the balloons. But it was quite apparent that YAF's godfather was still its hero.

Conservatives made much of the fact that a counter-rally staged the same night by the young ADA at St. Nicholas Arena was poorly attended. ADA replied that the picket and rally were eleventh-hour decisions made primarily to steal the thunder of the Progressive Youth Organizing Committee. This affiliate of the Communist Party was planning the only organized protest. If liberals had not stepped into the picture at the last minute, it would have looked as if only Communists were protesting the Madison Square Garden rally.

The 1962 rally grossed $80,000 and an immeasurable harvest of conservative reassurance. In 1963 they hope to fill Yankee Stadium.

There have been a variety of campus enterprises. Twelve Yale YAF set out on a fifty-five-mile "victory walk" in December, 1961. They hiked from New Haven to Groton in support of the Polaris-firing submarine. In February, 1962, a group of University of Arizona YAF picketed the Mexican Consulate in Tucson, protesting Mexico's abstention in the Punta del Este voting to oust Cuba from the Organization of American States. A YAF campaign to purge overly liberal textbooks from campus paid off with the withdrawal of the Samuelson economic text at Oklahoma Christian College.

The campaign against the National Student Association has been a very bitter one. An extreme instance of this at the University of Oklahoma was reported in the *New York Times* of May 15, 1962. Two national officers of YAF converged on Rotary clubs and parent groups in Tulsa and Oklahoma City, warning them that NSA was a subversive organization. At a meeting with conservative students, one director was alleged to have said that "even though we know NSA is not Communist, we can use this as a whisper campaign to beat them." He also proposed that anti-NSA handbills be printed on pink paper. NSA was defeated by a student vote of 3 to 1. Similar charges have been made about YAF's vendetta against NSA at New York University.

But since conservatives insist this is primarily a war of ideas, what about YAF's publication the *New Guard?* In an editorial against a Federal Department of Urban Affairs (March, 1962), Lee Edwards criticized organizations that had supported the bill: the American Municipal Association, United States Conference of Mayors, American Institute of Architects, National Urban League, and the United Presbyterian Church. "These organizations do not appear to be concerned about anything but the short range gain for themselves." All they can think about is better cities.

A strange editorial (November, 1961) admitted the inefficacy of fallout shelters, claimed the bomb scare "seems to be the exclusive domain of hand wringing Liberals," and then concluded, "we think there is something indomitable about a nation of people who not only see an opportunity to make money by building shelters, but who make them attractive and liveable." Is this to be taken as sarcasm? A subsequent editorial calls fallout "essentially a phony issue." In the same issue Walter Trahan of the *Chicago Tribune* complains that ". . . for all its spending, the government can't and won't protect us in nuclear war."

"What the Well Dressed Girl Should Think" (March, 1962) objects to glamour magazines infusing liberal politics. They plug the peace campaign and push the idea that liberalism represents novelty and progressiveness. "Frontier dresses" and "frontier girls" reflect the "queenification" of Jackie Kennedy. "A whole group of Conservative Congressman are in Washington, and they have wives who are young, glamorous and charming. Why not a word about them?"

Getting back to the man's world, we have an article by William Schulz, YAF director and assistant to Fulton Lewis, Jr. "The Red Army: Myth or Menace?" (November, 1961) We are reassured that the Soviet army is dangerously unreliable. After all, didn't they desert in droves in World War II? There was singing in the streets of Moscow as the Germans approached. "Not a single satellite division can be counted upon to fight Western powers." But in the same issue Lee Edwards grudgingly admits the success of Herr Ulbricht's conversion of East German youngsters.

The April, 1962, issue has a "secret letter" from Khrushchev to Gus Hall telling how much the Communists fear the YAF. Richard Nixon's *Six Crises* is reviewed as "The Man Who Would Rather Be President." Nixon has long since fallen from grace. Recommended reading for the month includes Joseph de Maistre's *On God and Society* and Nietzsche's *Beyond Good and Evil.* Can't you see Nietzsche as a YAFer? Finally a New Jersey reader asks, "If I may express a pet idea, did anyone ever consider William F. Buckley, Jr., for President?"

Compared to the *New Individualist Review*, the *New Guard* is sort of a manual of arms. YAF's forte is action. They do not confine themselves to riverboat excursions to do homage to the city manager of Newburg or the writing of indignant letters. YAF has taken to political waters, has already captured the presidency of the Collegiate Young Republicans, and promises active participation in politics at all levels. The Young Americans for Democratic Action has met its match in the Young Americans for Freedom.

However, YAF's organization outdistances its ideas. Consistent anti-Communism is no guarantee of coherent conservatism. Anti-Communism is YAF's primary concern. The conservative indictment Editor Hamowy brought against Editor Buckley applies equally well to YAF, who are in effect Buckley's fieldmen.

Once reflection is subordinated to action, there is a danger of taking satisfaction in momentum itself. If YAF is going to do more than comfort the convinced, it must offer more than the pride of its commotion. Somehow YAF must demonstrate that conservatism can survive anti-Communism.

CHAPTER 10

Social Profile

*A*s an undergraduate at Boston University, I had a delightful statistics professor named Elmer Mode. I am sure his years have been made lighter by the thought that I never became a mathematics major. One of the things I thought I had carried away from the course was a proper respect for the hazards of statistical surveys. To prove that I had not even learned that lesson, I have launched my own survey.

With my random sample at best haphazard, I mailed about 2,000 questionnaires to 105 colleges and universities in forty-eight states. The forms were sent either to YAF campus chapters or to professors of political science who were asked to distribute them to professed conservatives and to a few liberals (to obtain a contrasting sample). The size of the sample appears a bit less appalling when you consider that less than 10 percent of the student body is politically active, and the poll was aimed at these people.

About 25 percent of the completed questionnaires were returned from forty-one different schools. There was a good

177

regional spread: fifteen from the West, thirteen from the East, and thirteen from the South. Results were tabulated with a dusty slide rule and without benefit of a Chi Square test for reliability. The survey was purely qualitative, trying to find out what conservatives were thinking, not how many there were.

Probably the chief value of such a poll lies in the scribbled comments you sometimes get. One question dealing with degrees of tolerance toward Communists asked if you would condone the boycotting of the soap product sponsoring an acknowledged Communist radio entertainer. One student responded, "We get our soap at the place where my uncle works." To the question of what is your parents' income, with choices ranging from $5,000 to over $20,000, a Princeton freshman asked, "monthly?" and added that he knew only his father's income and was not sure of his mother's.

Best of all was the reply of a wiseacre from the University of Chicago who had been piqued by some of my questions. To the final query, "Did any special event, issue, or personality influence your conservatism most?" he replied, "Yes, Doctor Cain."

Despite this, results of my poll will be used in this chapter in connection with existing surveys of some of the social-psychological factors determining conservatism among the young.

One of the standing fears of the family is that Junior is going to return from college an unwashed bohemian, the pride of the ADA, and the embarrassment of the neighborhood. The probability of this happening is so low that one wonders what myths thrive on. When asked to list ten ideas they had discarded since coming to college, most students in one study[1] had to use Santa Claus, Easter Bunny, Good Luck Charms, and Fairies to get their lists started. Less than 6 percent had lost their faith in the inspiration of the Bible or the inevitability of war. Most frequently discarded were superstitions, folklore, and factual ignorance. Few of the cherished beliefs were dropped. Another poll[2] showed more tolerance of debt and less alarm about socialism, but this was in keeping with national trends.

1. R. Bain, "Changed Beliefs of College Students," *Journal of Abnormal and Social Psychology*, 31, April, 1936.
2. W. Buck, "Changes in Attitudes and Interests," *ibid.*

SOCIAL PROFILE ⟩ 179

Father can still take comfort in the Mendelian Law of politics: most political loyalties are inherited. Professor Lane of Yale conducted depth interviews with fifteen young men of lower- and lower-middle-class origins.[3] Few could remember much political discussion in the home. Of those who had rebellious feelings against their fathers, almost none expressed rebellion in political form. Apparently the low interest in supper-table politics plus the grand opportunities for rebellion in other ways produced very little political revolt.

Lane did find that damaged father-son relations developed an authoritarian orientation that led to an enduring fear of expressing hostility toward authority figures and a reverence for power over other values. This left the feeling that it is useless to rebel or to petition authority and encouraged a cynical view of the political process. The domineering father is more apt to produce a political eunuch than a political Lothario.

The least degree of change comes when the parent is neither repressive nor permissive but moderately guides the youth, says a Harvard study.[4] Where parents have a high degree of political interest and a reasonable respect for their children's views, there is very little change in views between the generations. The more parental interference, the more likely a change of views, including a possible move toward apolitical attitudes. Friends are much more apt to exert influence if a young man is resentful of parental control.

The change while in college does tend to be toward the Democrats. This has been true since 1936. Samuel Lubell in the spring of 1962 claimed that one out of every six students with Republican parents was shifting to the Democrats. Only one out of ten was going the other way. However, when college graduates change, it is more often toward the Republicans.

The majority of conservative students share their parents' beliefs or are even less liberal (42 percent).[5] Once in college, two-thirds of the conservative students felt they became more

3. R. Lane, "Fathers and Sons: Foundations of Political Belief," *American Sociological Review*, Vol. 24, August, 1959.
4. E. Maccaby, "Youth and Political Change," *Public Opinion Quarterly*, Vol. 18, Spring, 1954.
5. Unidentified statistics refer to the author's poll.

conservative while in school. It is true that fewer liberal students share their parents' beliefs, and two-thirds of them felt they became more liberal in college. For both liberal and conservative, college seems to have merely reinforced their beliefs. Interestingly enough, the same percentage of liberal and conservative students indicated a slight change in the other direction: 14 percent.

At Sarah Lawrence College President Taylor found almost twice as many students sharing their parents' views as did the author's poll. This might be explained in part by the fact that the author's poll was directed more at the politically active who, apparently, are more willing to make up their own minds about political affairs. Once again, on President Taylor's survey, we see that exactly the same number (19 percent) became more liberal or more conservative. However, Dr. Taylor's poll had a neutralist alternative which the majority chose to explain the direction of their political change: "more thoughtful, more understanding, more aware of issues, less gullible, aware of complexities." I'm sure both liberals and conservatives would recognize this as their position.

There appears to be a decided difference between classes in college. A North Carolina study[6] showed each succeeding class more liberal and radical and less reactionary and conservative. The big difference here was between freshmen and sophomores. Seniors were held to be 10 percent more liberal than freshmen. A small group of freshmen reactionaries dissolved by the time they were seniors. But a plurality of students preferred to be called neutral rather than liberal or conservative. Liberal Bennington College turned up three times as many liberals among seniors.

Class differences in college are tempered somewhat by major fields. National Merit Scholars were asked "Should the government provide medical care for citizens who cannot afford such services?" The question was put at the end of their freshman year and again at the end of their senior year. Mathematics and humanities majors averaged a 56 percent Yes at the end of their first year and a 74 percent Yes at the close of their junior year.

6. G. Moore and K. Garrison, "A Comparative Study of Social and Political Attitudes of College Students," *Journal of Abnormal Psychology*, Vol. 27, 1932.

Engineering majors over the same period reduced their Yes by 9 percent. Math and humanities majors also reduced their Republican vote considerably, unlike the engineers.[7]

Nevitt Sanford in *The American College* claims that the most conservative groups are all in applied rather than academic fields. Psychologist George Stern comes to a similar conclusion in discussing students with authoritarian personalities. Two-thirds of these students chose "instrumental vocations" (engineering, medicine, business, and so on) as opposed to "consummatory" vocations (teaching, arts, social service, etcetera).[8]

All this clashes with a DePauw University study that assessed the liberalism of students in terms of their intended vocations. Agriculture ranked the most liberal on all social scales except censorship. Second place went to managerial and third to professional. The most conservative were clerical and commercial. The "instrumental vocations" fared rather well on this scale of liberalism.[9] This DePauw study is over twenty years old, but farmers couldn't have changed that much. Perhaps the liberal scale was weighted with New Deal farm issues.

The author's poll concludes that most conservatives are majoring in academic fields: 63 percent in social science and 12 percent in humanities. Liberals and conservatives have the same percentage of business majors (7.5 per cent). Vocationally, however, there is a difference, but it is not too great. Whereas 57 percent of the conservatives prefer instrumental vocations, only 48 percent of the liberals do. Yet more conservatives were going into teaching. Top preference in both camps went to law, and there did not seem to be any liberal engineers. Part of the new look of conservatives depends upon recruiting more from academic fields, and they are doing it.

While it is true that most parents look upon a college education as preparation for a better job for their children, this is not necessarily true of the offspring. *Fortune* could find only 15 per-

7. N. Sanford, *The American College*, John Wiley, 1962, p. 242.
8. G. Stern, *Studies in Personality Typologies*, speech to Midwest Psychological Association, Mimeographed paper, 1953.
9. P. Fay and W. Middleton, "Certain Factors Related to Liberal and Conservative Attitudes of College Students," *Journal of Social Psychology*, Vol. 11, February, 1940.

cent of parents who looked upon college primarily in terms of "knowledge and education." Yet only 26 percent of the conservative students recently polled looked upon college primarily as vocational training. Twenty percent of the liberals were vocationalists. Since it is "Non-U" to speak of vocational training, it is difficult to know how much this consideration influenced responses.

Parents have long taken a dim view of the liberal professor who corrupts the mind of conservative youth. The professors certainly give the old-school try. Back in the thirties, a comparison was done of radical and conservative teachers. It was found that radical teachers tend to make their pupils more liberal, while conservative teachers do not tend to cause greater conservatism in their pupils. Yet the last word was to be said at home. Parents rather than teachers, the study concluded, play the predominant role in determining the extent of liberalism and conservatism. The 1935 report observed, "This is striking and unexpected in view of the increase shown in the liberality of college students as a result of disturbed social conditions."[10]

Yet the professors still try, and the conservative student is well aware of the effort. When asked if they felt that any of their professors' courses reflected a liberal bias, 46 percent complained of a disturbing bias, while 42 percent felt a slight bias. Seventy percent found both lectures and readings to be prejudiced. A few who noticed a slight bias commented that some slanting was to be expected and that a course would be pretty dull without any at all.

As the classes go by, the conservative student either becomes inured to this liberal threat or magnanimous to the brink of liberalism. Michigan State students were asked to react to the statement "We are finding out today that liberals really are softheaded, guillible and potentially dangerous." Sixty-seven percent of the freshmen disagreed. Among the upper classmen, 83 percent disagreed. A similar response came from Colgate young men. They were told: "A lot of teachers these days have radical ideas which need to be carefully watched." Among the freshmen, 53 percent

10. C. Morgan and H. Kemmers, "Liberalism and Conservatism of College Students as Affected by Depression," *School and Society*, June 8, 1935.

agreed. Again 83 percent of the upperclassmen disagreed.[11] The faculty can almost always depend upon students to rally to the defense of academic freedom, and most of the conservatives go along unless it is a really hot anti-Communist issue.

So far we have been considering mostly external influences. How about the factor of personality itself? Are there significant personal characteristics of the young conservative?

Professor Newcomb suggested an interesting insight into how conservative attitudes were influenced at Bennington. He discovered that those not aware of their own relative conservatism, that is, who believed they were typical, were found to be timid and socially insecure, to have small groups of friends, and to come to college with almost no aspirations toward "social success." Those aware of their conservatism were less retiring and inhibited, more socially facile, and had high hopes of success. Those aware had considerable prestige; the unawares had almost none.

The unawares are plodding and conscientious and almost wholly swallowed up by family allegiances and concerns, and participate only superficially in college life. There was more of a divided allegiance among the awares. Newcomb says that those who are conservatives because they have avoided the community could scarcely have an opportunity to discover that they are conservative. Those who are conservative because they aimed at leadership, failed, and repudiated whatever the community stood for could scarcely fail to be aware of their own conservatism.[12] The unawares represent the majority of conservatives, and their apathy is one of the major concerns of the politically active conservative, who is very much aware of his role and mission.

Conservative personality was submitted to a very controversial dissection by Professor Herbert McClosky of the University of Minnesota's Laboratory for Research in Social Relations. Hundreds of conservative beliefs were drawn from theorists and commonplace remarks, sifted through pilot studies, and finally boiled down to a seven-point creed that was used to classify conservative respondents. Willmoore Kendall of Yale attacked the creed as being a distortion of the conservative position. McClosky

11. "Inventory of Beliefs 1950-56," American Council of Education.
12. T. Newcomb, "Community Roles in Attitude Formation," *American Sociological Review*, Vol. 7, 1942.

rejoined that the final items were not selected for specific face value but only for their ability to evoke responses from respondents.

The author used a rewording of one of these items in his poll and evoked some outraged comments. McClosky got 58 percent of the extreme conservatives to agree that "The heart is as good a guide as the head." My altered version, "Is intuition frequently as valuable as reason in arriving at decisions?" got only 26 percent to agree. It should be noted that McClosky was dealing with the general population. When you confine yourself to college groups, you are bound to affront more people with such a question. However, on the proposition "You can't change human nature," we both got 73 percent assenting.

Conservatives were found to believe that duties are more important than rights, that society is ruled by divine intent, that men are naturally unequal, that theory is to be distrusted, and that change is to be resisted unless absolutely necessary. Three-quarters of the conservatives agreed that "Few people really know what is in their best interest in the long run."

Responses are divided into Liberal, Moderate Liberal, Moderate Conservative, and Extreme Conservative. Professor Kendall wanted to know why not "Extreme Liberal" for balance? McClosky would have prevented considerable confusion if he had dropped the qualifier "extreme" and just referred to the conservative position as simply the opposite of liberal, which is what we shall do here.

Over three times as many liberals had a college education. Six times as many liberals scored higher in the awareness (actual knowledge) and intellectuality scores. "I was a slow learner in school" is answered Yes by one-third of the conservatives and one-seventh of the liberals. Even correcting for education, the differences on awareness and intellectuality remain large. "By every measure available to us," said McClosky, "conservative beliefs are found most frequently among the uninformed, the poorly educated, and so far as we can determine, the less intelligent."[13] This was only the first salvo.

13. H. McClosky, "Conservatism and Personality," *American Political Science Review*, Vol. 52, March, 1958.

On social personality traits, the conservative was four times as alienated, six times as bewildered, and over twice as pessimistic. They had only one-fifth the social responsibility of the liberal and only half his self confidence, plus three times as much guilt. Similar results followed from clinical considerations. Conservatives were the more hostile, suspicious, rigid, and compulsive. Seventy-one percent scored high on hostility as opposed to 18 percent of the liberals. About the same ratio applied to paranoid tendencies. "Uniformly, every increase in the degree of conservatism shows a corresponding increase in submissiveness, anomie, sense of alientation, etc."

McClosky concludes, "Far from being the elite or prime movers, conservatives tend on the whole to come from the more backward and frightened elements of the population, including the classes that are socially and psychologically depressed . . . people who lack a clear sense of direction and purpose, who are uncertain about their values and are generally bewildered by the alarming task of having to thread their way through a society which seems to them too complex to fathom."

How much of this applies to the young conservative? Let's examine the points made about intelligence and psychological instability.

Ever since Adorno and his colleagues published *The Authoritarian Personality* in 1950 (since called "monumental," "classic," and "a milestone"), social scientists have used his F Scale to measure the extent of authoritarianism in personality. The scale was used originally to determine anti-Semitism and ethnocentrism. It was found that some of the deeper needs of personality were being expressed by agreement with prejudiced statements. The F Scale checks for the following characteristics: conventionalism (rigid adherence to middle-class values), authoritarian submission, authoritarian aggression (urge to punish those violating conventionalism), anti-intraception (impatience with and opposition to feelings, fantasies, speculations, and other subjective or "tender-minded" phenomena), superstition, stereotypy (to shift responsibility onto forces outside one's control), power and toughness (accent on strong-weak dimension in human relations), cynicism and projectivity (plots, conspiracies, germs, sexual excesses).[14]

These qualities were found to correlate highly with strong conservatism but not with liberalism. Several other studies since *The Authoritarian Personality* have come to similar conclusions. Gordon Allport's *The Nature of Prejudice* (1954), George Stern *et al.*, *Methods in Personality Assessment* (1956), Daniel Funkenstein, *et al.*, *Mastery of Stress* (1957), and articles by others, plus the scores on the American Council of Education's Inventory of Beliefs, show authoritarian personality correlating with emotional instability, of which the highest incidence is found among extreme conservatives.

The ideal type, says Nevitt Sanford, one of the co-authors of *The Authoritarian Personality*, is the "genuine liberal" who is relatively free of stereotypy, ethically sensitive and independent.

The only break in the clouds for the conservatives seems to be a ray from a study done back in 1938 by McNamara and Darley which found correlations from .36 to .40 between general adjustment as measured by Bell Inventory and economic conservatism.[15] This means that between 36 percent and 40 percent of the time, the correlation applied.

A word of caution. To say that most authoritarians are also conservatives is *not* the same thing as saying that most conservatives are authoritarians. But it is safe to say that the authoritarian personality, as defined by Adorno, Sanford, and colleagues, is more of a problem for the young conservatives than for the liberals. The cultist anti-Communist presents the Right with a very special problem in this respect.

How about intelligence? Correlations as high as 58 percent between certain types of factual knowledge and liberalism have been reported among students.[16] A Princeton poll of adults showed that the type of information made a difference. Ques-

14. N. Sanford, "The Approach to Authoritarian Personality" in J. McCary, *The Psychology of Personality*, Logos Press, 1956.

15. W. McNamara and W. Darley, "A Factor Analysis on Attitude and Adjustment Tests," *Journal of Educational Psychology*, Vol. 29, 1938.

16. W. Kerr, "A Quantitative Study of Human Behavior," *Journal of Social Psychology*, Vol. 19, 1944.

tions regarding free press, bomb tests, immigration, and sexual equality found liberals more "enlightened" than the conservatives. On questions concerning workers' pay, labor's influence, unemployment compensation, and ownership of banks, conservatives had more formal schooling and knew more current events. Neither liberals nor conservatives were conclusively ahead when it came to United Nations' forces, anti-Semitism, price controls, or wage increases. Conservatives lead in areas dealing with financial return and class interests.[17]

It has been determined that on questions regarding labor and economic status, a respondent's economic level is more of a significant force than his education.[18]

George Smith's study for Public Opinion Research, Princeton, New Jersey, holds that areas of liberal superiority imply interclass values best recognized by educated people who discriminate and see relationships. "When issues pose no differential threat to the status of well-off people, and at the same time require a perception and comprehension of democratic values, liberals are apt to be recruited disproportionately from well-informed and well-educated voters." Liberals, continues Smith, are apt to be poorly informed and educated when the sample divides significantly along class and economic lines and likely to be well enlightened when a group of interclass democratic values is demanded (for example, civil liberties).

The McClosky study, which was also based on a general adult sample, gives no indication of these distinctions that are quite significant, especially if you consider a group of college-educated conservatives.

However, the bulk of literature on this subject gives the edge to the liberals. Gordon Allport found a positive correlation between conservatism and low scholarship.[19] Moore and Garrison claimed a positive relation between scholarship and radicalism.[20] Hartman discovered liberalism positively correlated with

17. George Smith, "Relation of Enlightenment to Liberal Conservative Opinions," *Journal of Social Psychology*, Vol. 28, August, 1948.
18. H. Cantril, *Gauging Public Opinion*, Princeton, 1944.
19. G. Allport, "The Composition of Political Attitudes," *American Journal of Sociology*, Vol. 35, 1929.
20. G. Moore and K. Garrison, "A Comparative Study of Social and

years of formal schooling.[21] Knowledge of current events and liberalism correlated six to two according to Pace.[22] Krout and Stranger held that radicals and liberals had more special aptitudes than conservatives.[23] Murphy and Newcomb obtained correlations from .40 to .50 between liberals and high college grades.[24] Theodore Lentz saw the conservatives as less active scholastically and intellectually but more active socially and athletically.[25]

In another book by Murphy, we find that liberalism correlates higher with scholarship than with intelligence. The conservatives were less "bookish."[26] Lentz reported 23 percent more conservatives having less than fifty books in their homes, while 25 percent more of the radicals had 151 or more books in their homes. Certainly the reputation for intellectuality clings more to the liberal.

The author's poll found only the slightest difference in grade points: 2.77 for the liberal and 2.75 for the conservative. Again it must be pointed out that this pool concentrated on the politically interested student. This does not always include the scholars. No attempt was made to gauge intelligence. Conversations with young conservative leaders would lead one to conclude that they can hold their own with the liberals. Of course, leaders are usually good verbalizers, and this may be deceiving. It may well be that the politically apathetic conservatives, especially the "unaware," are not so bright as their liberal counterparts.

Political Attitudes of College Students," *Journal of Social Psychology*, Vol. 27, 1932.

21. G. Hartman, "A Critical Appraisal of Teachers' Social Attitude and Information," *Harvard Educational Review*, Vol. 9, 1939.

22. C. Pace, "Relationship Between Liberalism and Knowledge of Current Affairs," *Journal of Social Psychology*, Vol. 10, 1939.

23. M. Krout and H. Stranger, "Personality Development in Radicals," *Sociometry*, Vol. 2, 1939.

24. G. Murphy and L. Newcomb, *Experimental Social Psychology*, Harper, 1937.

25. T. Lentz, "Personage Admiration and Other Correlates of Conservatism Radicalism," *Journal of Social Psychology*, Vol. 10, February, 1939.

26. G. Murphy and R. Likert, *Public Opinion and the Individual*, Harper, 1938.

In sum, it would seem that with the possible exception of questions regarding business, the young conservatives in general have not been so enlightened as the young liberals; however, the gap may be narrowed if the "New Conservatives" live up to their recently announced sophistication.

The past may be too much to live down. Back in 1939 Theodore Lentz compiled the names of 137 famous people living and dead. A sample of seventeen- to thirty-year-old students was asked to rate the names in terms of the most admired personages. There was a significant radical-conservative split. U. S. Grant was most admired by the young conservatives. Runner-up was Kate Smith. Also-rans, in order, were Huey Long (*sic*), Babe Ruth, Bing Crosby, and Edgar Guest. Radicals put Norman Thomas first and Steinmetz second. Third place for the radicals created perfect symmetry with the conservatives; it went to Lenin. Then came Kant, Eugene Debs, and Joseph Lister. In entertainers the conservatives went for Wayne King, Will Rogers, and Douglas Fairbanks. Radicals preferred Rosa Ponselle, Madame Schumann-Heink, and Isadora Duncan.

The top of the conservative list consited of religionists, military leaders, popular-type entertainers, and athletes. Radicals preferred scientists, inventors, authors, poets, and classical entertainers. The conservatives also marked more names unknown. When presented with fictitious names, the conservatives tried to bluff more often.

Lentz concluded his study, of which the personage data was but a part, by saying that young conservatives were more timid, inclined to moralize, more superstitious, less aesthetic and imaginative, less feministic, less tolerant, and more antagonistic toward science. This is pretty much what Herbert McClosky is saying twenty years later. The young conservative must prove that a quarter of a century has made some improvement. They can hardly claim intellectuality and Kate Smith too.

The young conservative's task is not just to prove that he is as bright and stable as the liberal. His major responsibility is to show how conservatism can help dispel the apathy the average American student inhales as inevitably as air. Even in the liberal 1930's Pearl Buck was asking "Where are The Young Rebels?"

(*Harper's*, September, 1935). She claimed American youths had a pseudosophistication that was touching in its shallowness. The young were docile not only to their parents or teachers, whom for the most part they ignored, but also to life. "They are vaguely rebellious not against their parents and teachers, their natural enemies, but against life itself." As Miss Buck pointed out, in rebellion we must find something of our own size against which to rebel—something less than life.

For those who could not scale down a target for rebellion, another alternative was possible. Merely choose those portions of life you find satisfying, and ignore the rest. We'll beat 'em with home rule. The average student of the post–World War II America did not retreat into a pleasure dome of indifference; he had never left one.

Ten years after World War II, Allport and Gillespie carried out a cross-national study of twelve countries to find out what young people were thinking about the future. It was learned that competitiveness, desire for success and personal ambition are higher in countries of newer nationalism, such as Egypt and Mexico. Americans want adjustment, security, sociability, pleasure. European youths were more concerned with the importance of forming character, a distinctive personality. Americans are less concerned about self-consistency and more interested in diversification.

Except for the French, no group mentioned social problems less than Harvard men. Even those American preferring social work thought of it more in terms of self-fulfillment. Only one in five American youths anticipated that a socially oriented activity (community, national, international, or religious) would be one of his three main sources of satisfaction in life, or considered helpfulness to others a highly important requirement for an ideal job.

The question was put, "If you should get a large sum of money five years from now, what would you do with it?" Only 2 per cent of the Americans would use part of it to alleviate social misery. The Italians were the most philanthropic. Asked "What two things could you accomplish in your lifetime that you would be most proud of?", only 3 percent of the Americans replied in terms of serving in national affairs or being a useful citizen. The Mexicans were highest on this one.

The privatism of these tight little American worlds is frightening. "I shall be a doctor, so I don't care what happens to the world; there'll always be work for me," boasted one American student. But the real divergence appears in the contrasting autobiographical statements of two women students, one from Mexico, the other from Radcliffe.

A Mexican student: ". . . In addition I should like to do something for my country—either as a teacher, as a psychologist, or as a mother. As a teacher to guide my pupils along the best path . . . in order in their future lives not to have so many frustrations as the youth of the present. As a psychologist, to make studies which in some way will serve humanity and my beloved country. As a mother to make my chlidren creatures who are useful to both their country and all humanity."

A Radcliffe student: ". . . Our summers will be spent lobster fishing on the Cape. Later we'll take a look at the rest of the country—California, the Southwest and the Chicago Stockyards. I want the children, when they get past the age of ten, to spend part of the summer away from home, either at camp, or as apprentices to whatever profession they may show an interest in. Finally, I hope we will all be able to take a trip to Europe, especially to Russia, to see what can be done about communism."[27]

The Cornell Values Survey is hardly more reassuring. It shows that only 12 percent of the students expect that activity toward national or international betterment would be among the three most satisfying activities in life. Also, five times as many students felt it was more important to learn to get along with people than to learn how to become good citizens.

American students, said Philip Jacob, are gloriously contented and unabashedly self-centered. They intend to look out for themselves and expect others to do likewise. Consequently the majority agreed, "It's only natural that a person should take advantage of every opportunity to promote his own welfare."

27. J. Gillespie and G. Allport, *Youth's Outlook on the Future*, Doubleday Papers in Psychology, 1955.

They also felt that one's first duty in our society is "to protect from harm himself and those dear to him."[28] Charity not only begins at home; it is lucky to get a night out.

How would conservatism help crack this shell of privatism? As long as the major force of conservatism is expended on the propagation of laissez-faire economic doctrines, it is difficult to see how it can do anything but harden the shell. It would seem that the last thing you would want to do is to make the socially isolated self-righteous, but this is precisely what conservatism would do. Not much apathy is going to be dispelled by asking, Is everybody comfortable?

One of the democratic by-products of this social malaise is looked upon by the conservatives as moral decay. Tolerance is bred of permissiveness. Conservatives look upon it as an absence of values. Students may be tolerant for the wrong reasons, but tolerant they are. Conventional moral virtues are esteemed by almost all students, but they are not inclined to censure those who retreat under fire from the canons of society.

There are almost no social sanctions taken against those who violate recognized student norms. Samuel Stauffer found that this was true of classroom cheating, which is admitted by 40 percent of the students. Sixty-six percent said they would not report a cheater if he were a personal friend. Only 16 percent would. If the cheating became public, only 27 percent would fail to report a friend. Friendship cannot withstand the possible wrath of the school administration. But it still pays to be friendly. Sixty-eight percent favor strong punitive action if the cheater is not a friend.[29]

The moral erosion here is obvious. There should be more than 16 percent seeing some intrinsic value in justice. Of course, the rather unsavory role of informer is involved, but this doesn't explain the willingness to turn in nonfriends. Conservatives would be justified in chastening this type of permissiveness.

But the Cornell Survey has turned up a brighter side to this alleged ethical nonchalance. Between 83 to 93 percent of the

28. P. Jacob, *Changing Values in College*, Harper, 1957, Chap. 1.
29. S. Stauffer, "Analysis of Conflicting Social Norms," *American Sociological Review*, December, 1949.

students would like to see more equality between the races within their lifetimes. (They are evenly divided as to whether the government should bring this about.) The charge that "Foreigners usually have peculiar and annoying habits" was repudiated by 72 to 90 percent.

Regionalism still makes a difference. "It's unwise to give people with dangerous social and economic viewpoints a chance to be elected" was accepted by 53 percent of the students at Texas but only 25 percent of those at Harvard. The national average was 41 percent agreeing. When given the proposition "If you refuse to support your country in a war you shouldn't continue to live in a country," only 32 percent agreed.[30] Even the majority of Texans disagreed. Sixty-six percent of all college seniors ended by being supporters of civil liberties. These responses show a high level of tolerance of nonconformity.

In spite of much talk about the softness of liberal education, today's conservative students reflect a great degree of this tolerance themselves even on the touchy issue of Communism. Only 38 percent go along with the ultra-Right's contention that Communism is more an internal than an external threat. Stauffer's series of questions on Communism were used on the author's poll with the following results:

Sixty percent of the conservatives would allow an admitted Communist to make a speech in their community (versus 89 percent of liberals). If someone suggested that a known Communist's book be removed from the local library, only 21 percent of the conservatives would go along with this action (only 6 percent of the liberals would). Half the conservatives felt that an admitted Communist entertainer should not be removed from a radio program (78 percent of liberals would oppose removal). Only a third wanted him fired. Whether the program's product should be boycotted brought an identical response (88 percent of liberals would not boycott).

The closest division was on whether a known Communist store clerk should be fired. Thirty-seven percent wanted him fired; 46 percent did not (77 percent of liberals would not).

If not by an absolute majority in each case, the conservatives

30. Cornell Values Survey, Social Science Research Center, 1952.

did manage at least a tolerant plurality for all questions. They were most favorably disposed toward the library. More respondents answered this question, also. This is in keeping with their general support of academic freedom. Support of free speech ranked second. Freedom to read and speak, both academic freedoms, enjoyed healthy support. Tolerant majorities dwindled when the economic factor entered, whereas they remained constant for the liberals.

Although 50 percent more of the liberals favored free speech for the Communist, it is very significant that such a large majority (60 percent) of conservatives went along. Whether this is a result of negative permissiveness or positive commitment is difficult to determine. However, given the gap in percentages and the fact that conservative tolerance runs low in the face of economic issues, one can say that tolerance per se has more of an intrinsic value for liberals than it does for conservatives.

The conservative might be tempted to reply that this is because the liberal is so naïve about Communism. A first rejoinder might be that conservatives have been traditionally less tolerant of nonconformist groups generally. As for naiveté and Communism, Rosalea Schonbar did a study on students' attitudes toward Communism in terms of the intensity of their attitude and the amount of information they possessed. Untrue propositions about Communism were stated, such as: "Most communists in this country are foreign-born," "The Communist Party in the U.S. is illegal," or "Most union leaders are communists," and so on. Students had been classified in terms of their intensity of anti-Communism. Then they were asked to identify the correct statements. Miss Schonbar's conclusion was that "among those with the greatest tested antipathy toward communism, we find a significant degree of lack of information in areas touching upon communists and communism, as compared with those whose antipathy is less intense."[31]

Anti-Communism cannot feed on intolerance alone without ulcerous consequences. Liberals are not prescribing the milk of human kindness, but they are asking the conservative to watch his diet.

31. R. Schonbar, "Students' Attitudes Toward Communism," *Journal of Psychology*, Vol. 27, January, 1949.

A somewhat cynical explanation of why just about everybody falls within the pale of permissiveness was suggested by Philip Jacob. "A liberal attitude in the sense that a student will not let fixed moral standards or ingrained prejudices govern his relations with other people is almost an imperative 'convention' of a society in which good business requires everyone to be treated with respect as a prospective customer."[32]

Then there are what used to be called the "Ivory Hunters," corporation agents who scout campuses for promising talent. As *Fortune* said on one occasion, students try to cut themselves to fit: the sloppy tie may be a sign of maladjustment. Why introduce unnecessary stresses and strains into the company? As corporations begin to recruit more from the liberal arts, it won't be only the business majors who are watching their school ties.

The undeniable liberal omnipresence must not be overestimated. Raymond Kuhlen has cautioned that so many of the early polls and studies reveal not so much a liberalism of character as a random collection of opinions that might be pure vogue. There is a vital difference between "a verbalized liberality of attitudes and a socially functioning personality."[33] Probably very few students experience a thoroughgoing transformation. If it is true that college socializes more than it liberalizes (Jacob), that it accommodates students to the *status quo*, then the moderate conservatives have very little to worry about.

Much of the student's liberalism consists of a personal sophistication in the arts and a tolerance of diversity. He may end up driving closer to the middle of the political road, but he always slows down going by family, class, vocation, religion, and other deeply seated values that were homegrown and for which he has a chronic nostalgia.

32. *Op. cit.*, p. 52.
33. R. Kuhlen, "Changes in Attitudes of Students," *School and Society*, Vol. 53, 1941.

CHAPTER **11**

Rally Day for Fundamentalists

WHEN the conservative Baptist weekly, the *Watchman Examiner*, called for those "who mean to do battle royal for the fundamentals" in a July 1st editorial in 1920, the word "fundamentalist," in this sense, was minted. It tried to provide a gold standard for Protestantism by reopening the Reformation issue of faith over works. Twentieth century heretics were suggesting that salvation might be achieved through humanitarian works and social reforms. These were viewed as arrogant indulgences.

The only road to salvation, maintained the fundamentalists, was through accepting the bodily resurrection of the Virgin-born Christ whose Second Coming is promised by the infallible Word of the Bible. As your life is lost in Christ, charitable acts will follow. You get no ultimate credit for good works without this previous commitment. Any Protestant who espouses a doctrine of works that jeopardizes the purity of this creed of faith is an apostate.

Modernists were not only asking needlessly academic questions about the Bible; too many of them were suggesting that good works produced faith. Trying to spawn faith out of good works is like trying to conceive a child with good intentions only. There is no faith and there is no life without the miracle of being born again in Christ. This is a personal, not a social, gospel.

To perpetrate these truths, the Reverend Carl McIntire, among others, has called for a Twentieth Century Reformation. The Reverend Mr. McIntire likes to conceive of himself as a contemporary Jeremiah who is attacking the scribes and their "false pens." Ever since he was drummed out of his denomination for doctrinal and pastoral conduct unbecoming a Presbyterian in 1936,[1] McIntire has tried to parlay his role of pariah into that of Pharaoh. First he made his loyal Collingswood, New Jersey, congregation the "mother church" of a new denomination, the Bible Presbyterian Church. To counteract the liberalism of the National Council of Churches and its ecumenical movement, McIntire championed the spirit of "separatism," and formed his own American Council of Christian Churches.

Although it boasts fifteen denominations, only two of the American Council's denominations are listed in the Yearbook of the Churches. Apparently such denominations as the Independent Baptist Bible Mission and the Tioga River Christian Conference have not yet made the grade. When the American Council released membership figures of a million and a quarter, the National Association of Evangelicals, whose ten million members represent the authentic voice of fundamentalism, challenged this claim. They offered McIntire $1,000 for any charity he might name, if he could prove to independent auditors 20 percent of the figure announced. Some charity is still out a thousand dollars.

In turn, McIntire has condemned his fellow fundamentalists in the NAE for co-existence with the enemy. The NAE has maintained that "evangelical" and "ecumenical" are not mutually

1. The Presbyterian Synod found McIntire guilty on three charges: (1.) disapproval, defiance, and acts in contravention of the government and discipline of the Presbyterian Church in the U.S.A.; (2.) not being zealous and faithful in maintaining the peace of the Church; (3.) violation of his ordination vows.

exclusive, and they have defended the World Council of Churches. This irritated McIntire no end. He was so furious about the convocation of the World Council of Churches in Amsterdam that he formed his own International Council of Christian Churches in the same city a few days before. As McIntire was to say later on in a pamphlet rebuking the NAE, " 'Let's get together' has become a widespread affliction not found exclusively in the NCC."

In the same pamphlet (Literature Item 120) McIntire chides the NAE for wanting to be numbered among the "intelligentsia" and for not defending the purity of the Church. "Them that sin rebuke before all, that others may fear." All adulterers are to McIntire's left. No criticism is directed at publications such as Dallas's "This Week in Prophecy" or "The Seventh Trumpet." Apparently he feels the NAE is getting snobbish about the Lakewood, Ohio, School of Soul Science and Divine Law.

The American Council's *Christian Beacon* has denied the Fatherhood of God or the brotherhood of man, except for true believers. Catholics, of course, are not acknowledged as Christians. Also condemned are Billy Graham, the Gideons, the Revised Standard Version of the Bible (McIntire applauded its burning in a North Carolina church), the International Court of Justice, the United Nations, and even NCC's "One Great Hour of Sharing" for missionary work ("cash to purchase . . . socialistic propaganda").

McIntire uses over two hundred radio stations and a continuous rain of pamphlets to comment on topics ranging from Mrs. Kennedy's papal audience (it took six minutes longer than Queen Elizabeth's) to the latest folly emanating from the Protestant Vatican, the NCC.

One of the most revealing remarks made by the Reverend Carl McIntire is to be found in his "Analysis and Refutation" of the NCC pamphlet "The Truth About the Churches." Here we find McIntire not an Isaiah calling Jerusalem "a people of Gomorrah," but a Luther indulging the secular princes.

Well-oiled J. Howard Pew, an ultraconservative layman, was commenting on the social policy of the NCC: "I would be just as much opposed to their making these [liberal] pronouncements if they were enunciating my philosophy. These people do not have the knowledge or the competence in these areas. They should stick to ecclesiastical subjects."

McIntire objected:

This is not sound, and it is too narrow. God is the author of liberty and the church of Jesus Christ does have a responsibility to defend freedom, to state the moral foundations for a free society. This involves a philosophy, a doctrine. The trouble with the NCC is that their philosophy is socialistic, basically materialistic. The church should not remain silent and have nothing to say. . . . The second table of the Decalogue is exceedingly social in its demands and concepts of man and his relations one to another.

. . . Freedom is indivisible. . . . Mr. Pew's weakness at this point places him in an untenable position. He would be in a much stronger place if he would call upon the church to enunciate a philosophy which presents the fullness of the revelation that God is the author of liberty.[2]

What it comes down to is, Whose "social gospel"? The theological argument over the primacy of faith and works has been drowned in an economic controversy. McIntire and his secular princes have made it quite clear that not only does democracy demand capitalism; so does Christianity.

Christian Economics, launched by Mr. Pew, agrees. Any economic system that is not capitalist is pagan or godless. "Would not we do well if we henceforth speak of the American Way as the Christian Way?"[3] The law of supply and demand turns out to be one of God's laws. Both Christianity and capitalism are in this together. "The church should be in this fight right up to the hilt. For no institution has more at stake."[4] Christianity, it appears, depends upon capitalism.

It used to be that the church judged social systems, and not vice versa. Evidently the Reverend Mr. McIntire and company do not gag on this heresy. There is no evidence to show that they even consider it a problem. If the McIntire–*Christian Eco-*

2. "The Truth . . . An Analysis and Refutation," Twentieth Century Reformation Hour, Collingswood, New Jersey.

3. *Christian Economics*, Sept. 26, 1950, p. 4.

4. *Ibid.*, Feb. 27, 1951.

nomics line is accepted as the fundamentalist position on religion and economics, they are guilty of idolatry,[5] which is much more serious than the charge of apostasy. Undoubtedly, there are many fundamentalists who do not condone this idolatry. But the McIntire–*Christian Economics* position has become the new social gospel for the most vocal activists among the fundamentalists.[6]

What bearing has this development had on young people? In the spring of 1961, the North American Ecumenical Youth Assembly announced an August conference of forty religious communions, mostly Protestant and orthodox, to be held at the University of Michigan under the auspices of the National Council of Churches and the Canadian Council of Churches. The first such conference had taken place the previous year in Lausanne, Switzerland. McIntire's American Council of Churches decided on battle royal, and dispatched its youth brigade: Intercollegiate Christian Youth. The American Council had long opposed the Evangelicals' Youth for Christ and Inter-Varsity Fellowship.

The ICY moved in on Ann Arbor, claiming that the Ecumenical Movement is non-Protestant in theology and that philosophically it is a chief promoter of Marxian programs, for example, seeking a one-world church and a one-world government. Among other things, ICY championed the divine right of property, individual responsibility, and the spiritual undergirding of the free-enterprise system.

Utilizing a four-page daily newspaper that showed more sophistication than the parent *Christian Beacon*, ICY tried to propagate its position. "Communist Accent on Youth," a Pepperdine College film, was shown at the first of their four programs. "Operation Abolition" followed, with a discussion on "Leftist Youth Activities in the Nation and Church." Whenever possible they would buttonhole youngsters for discussion.

The Reverend Mr. McIntire gave a speech on the vanity of

5. The contention that no man-made scheme or system can be given final and uncritical devotion without idolatry is made by Robert M. Brown in " 'Christian Economics' and Theology," *Union Seminary Quarterly Review*, June, 1951.

6. *Christian Economics*, Oct. 10, 1950. *N.B.:* R. Brown, "Is It 'Christian Economics'?" *Christianity and Crisis*, Nov. 27, 1950.

hopes for peaceful co-existence. He insists that co-existence with
an anti-Christian nation means no-existence for Christianity. This
might be rough news for Asia and Africa, but that's the way it
is. The "so-called" social gospel of the liberals was denounced as
travesty because all it produces is unchanged men in a changed
society. No points are given for changing society. Beware of co-
operating with liberals; you can't win. An *avant-garde* religious
play was called "lewd and offensive." He compared it to presenting an indecent picture as art.

Press releases were prepared during the day. One of them
warned that the NCC had advocated "the lawlessness of sit-ins
and freedom ride movements." Everyone was cautioned by the
ICY that "radical agitation and exploitation of racial differences
is a major program of leftist organizations." Some of the ICY
brochures were sophisticated in format and style if not in theology and politics.

At least you could not accuse the ICY of being ambiguous.
"We have started with the God of the Bible, the Author of
Liberty, and they [Ecumenicals] have started with a projection
of Karl Marx—the big brother welfare state. . . . The inclusive
church [NCC] must eventually lose its conscience as it has lost
its faith. Christ died to reconcile us to God—not to man."[7]

It was a curious performance. Nothing in the tone of their
newspaper, pamphlets, speeches, or conversation intimated any
grounds for compromise. In fact, McIntire believes the word
means surrender. No program of reconciliation was proposed by
ICY. It was in effect an elaborate picketing engagement under
the banner "Repent or Perish." One might have sensed more
comity if the Communist Party had shown up at the Republican
National Convention.

Besides denominational groups, young people were represented from the Boy Scouts, Girl Scouts, "Y's," Salvation Army,
the ministry to the Armed Forces, and others. How did they
react? Probably the sincerity of the ICY made an impression on
some. One NCC observer felt that indignation and laughter were
common reactions. New York GHQ of the American Council

7. Quotes are from Intercollegiate Youth's *Ann Arbor Views,* published
from Aug. 16-22, 1961.

was pleased with the splash made at the conference but lamented the lack of national publicity. One office assistant admitted with wounded candor that "students aren't very interested in fundamentalism." Perhaps, we should add, not as marketed by the American Council of Churches.

Carl McIntire is Ralph Roy's prime example of a clergyman engaged in the "ministry of disruption."[8] He is a separatist, not in the sense of a Roger Williams resigned to his Rhode Island exile, but more in the manner of a feudal lord aggrandizing his New Jersey fief.

Methodism has an intradenominational problem with the Circuit Riders, Inc., formed by thirty-three laymen in 1951. Its purpose is "to oppose all efforts to propagate Socialism and Communism and other anti-American teachings in the Methodist Church." The Riders also hoped to create goodwill for "Right-wingism" among Methodism's clergy, laity, and youth. They would like to see a chapter in every Methodist church to counteract the liberalism of the Church's Federation for Social Action. Some Riders want all liberals thrown out of the denomination.

Executive secretary is public-relations agent Myers Lowman of Cincinnati, who has been associated with several businesses, as well as having spent six months as a "secret researcher" for the Georgia Commission on Education upon the recommendation of Louisiana segregationists. Shortly after failing to secure a public-relations position with the Cincinnati Council of Churches, Lowman attacked it as subversive.

Professor Walter Steurman has called Lowman "a specialist in the statistics of suspicion."[9] The Circuit Rider's most notorious venture into this field came when his pamphlet, "30 of the 95 Men Who Gave us the Revised Standard Version," was revealed as the source of the Air Force Manual's claim that Communists had infiltrated the Protestant clergy. After quoting an anonymous editorial about the questionable sobriety of the politics of "a prominent Protestant church group," the Manual said:

8. R. Roy, *Apostles of Discord*, Beacon Press, 1953.
9. W. Steurman, " 'Crusaders' Go to School in Tulsa," *Presbyterian Life*, March 15, 1962.

The implications of this editorial are clear—Communists and Communist fellow-travellers and sympathizers have successfully infiltrated into our churches. The foregoing is not an isolated example, by any means; it is known that even the pastors of certain of our churches are card-carrying Communists! The extent of Communistic activities in religious groups is further detailed below.[10]

Then followed the charge that the National Council of Churches had officially sponsored the Revised Standard Version of the Bible. Of the ninety-five persons who served in this project, thirty have been affiliated with pro-Communist fronts, projects, and publications. The statistics were based upon Lowman's "investigations."

Among those who protested this charge was Senator John F. Kennedy, who called it "shocking . . . an unwarranted slur on the Protestant ministry in general and the National Council of Churches in particular."[11] Among the defenders of the charge was Congressman Francis E. Walter.

The editor of *Eternity*, a fundamentalist publication associated with the National Association of Evangelicals, decided on an impartial investigation. Contributing Editor Walter Martin inspected the files of NCC, the Senate Internal Security Committee, and HUAC. He interviewed Fulton Lewis, Jr., and officials of the Air Force. A complete job of research was done on the ninety-one (not ninety-five) men who had anything to do with the preparation of the RSV.

Of the thirty persons named in the Lowman pamphlet, only thirteen were on the Translation Committee. The rebuttals of two of the thirteen are cited. The Chairman of the Committee, Dr. Luther Weigle of Yale, stated that of the six organizations to which it was alleged that he was related, he had never heard of two and was not related to any of them. Dr. W. Russell Bowie said, "I have never taken part, nor would I take part in any movement which I had reason to believe would strengthen the communist cause." The remaining eleven had been members of friendship organizations during World War II when the U.S.S.R.

10. Air Force Center Training Manual 45-0050, 1960, Increment V, Vol. 7. For Reservists in Continental Air Command.
11. R. Roy, *Communism and the Churches*, Harcourt, 1960, p. 419.

was an ally, as had many prominent Americans, such as Eisenhower.

It should be noted that of the ninety organizations that Lowman lists as subversive, only eighteen are on the Attorney General's list. Thirty-six are on HUAC's list. The remaining fifty-four are not listed by any Federal agency. Thus, only eight translators had been associated with any group listed as subversive by the Federal Government.[12]

Philbrick's testimony to HUAC that he could not identify even one Communist clergyman in nine years' association with the Communist Party "comes as a refreshing surprise." The Manual had inferred the contrary.

Eternity maintained: "This guilt by association is religious McCarthyism in the extreme. Use of such methods of attack and slander by professing Christians, even if they bleat a creed that is orthodox in every part, is thoroughly unethical and thoroughly unchristian."[13] It was pointed out that this was only one more step to discredit the NCC, if not on theological, then on political grounds.

A further example mentioned was the furor created by the ultrafundamentalists when the NCC sponsored the tour of a delegation from the Russian Orthodox Church in 1956. Three years later *Life* magazine exposed one of the touring party, Metropolitan Nikolai, as a secret member of the Soviet security police. The ultras pointed to the earlier testimony of Rostvorov accusing the Russian Church of Communist infiltration. But he never named Nikolai. The charges about Nikolai were made by Peter Deriabin before HUAC, three years *after* the prelate's visit. If the NCC was duped, so was the United States Government.

"The cry of these groups," concluded *Eternity*, "was previously, 'Heresy! Modernism! Apostasy!' Currently it is, 'Subversion! Infiltration! Collectivism in the Churches!' The Air Force Manual itself drew heavily on these hostile sources, apart from which the Manual would have been virtually innocuous."

12. "Sowing Dissension in the Churches," Department of Christian Social Relations, Protestant Episcopal Church.
13. D. Barnhouse, "Communism and the National Council of Churches," *Eternity*, September, 1960.

It should be emphasized that the author of this article, the late Donald G. Barnhouse, was a moderate leader in the National Association of Evangelicals and had frequently denounced the McIntire-Hargis extremists.

Having alerted the young men of the Air Force to the dangerous infiltration of the churches, public-relations specialist Myers Lowman then turned his attention to the schools. Speaking at Tulsa, Oklahoma, in January, 1962, Lowman claimed that the colleges and universities of America generally are corrupted by liberalism; they are inclined to hire "mental prostitutes." He cited the pride of the Circuit Riders' research program: a 608-page volume called *6,000 Educators: College, University, Theological Seminary*, Volume I (1959), "A" to "L." It runs from James Luther Adams to Mary Ely Lyman, and alleges Communist and pro-Communist links of many of America's outstanding educators.

"If you are a heavy contributor to a liberal college, university, or church, you are about the most stupid person I know." He suggested that it was like giving support to Hitler. This jibes nicely with McIntire's objection to "One Great Hour of Sharing." The consolation of liberal-arts colleges and universities is that there couldn't have been many alumni in the audience. It was a vicious high in anti-intellectualism.

Lowman has not confined his services to Methodism. Besides *2109 Methodist Ministers*, he has contributed *1411 Protestant Episcopal Rectors, 42% of the Unitarian Ministers, 614 Presbyterian Ministers U.S.A.; and 450 Rabbis*. In the presses is *607 National Council of Churches Officers and Denominational Representatives*. At one time Lowman suggested there were 10,900 clergyman affiliation with pro-Communist activities. His surefire remedy, "Get some action in the churches at the dollar sign— and then we'll get some action at the cross." Where the pastor gets too liberal, congregations are urged to hold back on pledges.

How wild are Lowman's charges? Ralph L. Roy conducted at six-year study of Communism in the churches for the Fund for the Republic. He concludes that over the past fifty years only a small band of clergy ever joined the party, "possibly as few as fifty, perhaps as many as 200." Today Communist influence within American churches is "near the zero mark." Not more than twenty-five clergy were working with the Communists by 1953. This is a smaller percentage than for lawyers.[14]

The Circuit Riders were censured by the Methodist General Conference a year after they organized. In May, 1960, the General Conference read the riot act. "We regret that any Methodist contribute either money or leadership to such organizations as Circuit Riders Inc. which utilize the 'guilt by association' and 'fellow traveler' approaches as they stir up unjustifiable suspicions and develop unfounded fears. We direct attention to our general rules concerning uncharitable or unprofitable conversation, particularly speaking evil of magistrates and ministers."[15]

Any organization that has charges or accusations to make against any Methodist was urged to make them through Church courts so that a jury of peers of the accused might judge the truth or falsity of the accusation. No Circuit Rider has availed himself of the opportunity.

Outside of the South where the Riders hunt with the White Citizens' Councils, the movement has shown little growth. Without statistician Myers Lowman, the Riders might well be short-Circuited. Their attempt to influence Methodist youth groups has got almost nowhere. They do pose two real threats. By reaching conservative elders of the Church, they have, in isolated cases, exerted financial pressures that create difficulties. Second, the Air Force Manual episode showed how effective specious "documentation" can be in creating dissension, and this appears to be Lowman's specialty.

"The real issue," says Fundamentalist Donald Barnhouse, "is not Communism in the churches, for the NCC and its member denominations are clearly opposed to Communism. The real issue is theological conflict over the doctrine of the church. Splinter groups aided by vested business interests have been joined by certain patriotic and well-meaning persons who are ignorant of the underlying issue."

While the Circuit Riders function as a lay group obscuring

14. R. Roy, *Communism and the Churches*, p. 252.
15. "Attacks Upon Churches and Churchmen," General Conference of Methodist Church, May 6, 1960.

the issue within Methodism, the American Council of Christian Laymen work at it within all denominations. This peculiar stewardship was organized in 1949 by Verne R. Kaub of Madison, Wisconsin, who believes that "the top leadership of virtually every major Protestant church is controlled by clerics who cast aside the American system to accept basic Marxist doctrines. . . . only an organized movement of laymen can reverse this tragic trend."[16]

Kaub's obsession with capitalism led to a tract put out by his group called "Jesus: A Capitalist." It seems that "Jesus worked with his father in the construction business" in that glorious age when "there was no labor union to meddle with prices and wages." This is a crude follow-up of the *Christian Economics* line of identifying capitalism and Christianity. Atheists are not considered legitimate Right-wingers.

"An atheist can align himself with Rightists, echoing their protests against statism and professing love of freedom and individualism. But in so doing he does not in truth become a Rightist, because in his inner being he reserves no place to nurture the Christian concepts which are inseparable from the libertarian philosophy."[17]

Perhaps the most widely circulated pamphlet, and certainly a top contender for one of the most infamous pamphlets Kaub has circulated, is "How Red is the National Council of Churches?" In this "exposé" the Federal Council of Churches is accused of going "underground" when it merged with a dozen other agencies to become the National Council of Churches in 1950. You are urged to stop financial support to NCC, which "receives large sums from various Jewish and other non-Christian and anti-Christian groups." The anti-Semitic emphasis is quite deliberate, since Kaub is no stranger to anti-Semitic activities and has worked closely with racist Allen Zoll who founded American Patriots.[18]

Another good seller is Kaub's book *Communist-Socialist*

16. V. Kaub, "Shall Our Churches Teach Christianity or Communism?", a pamphlet.
17. V. Kaub, "Can a Man Be an Atheist and a Rightist at Same Time?", a pamphlet.
18. A. Forster and B. Epstein, *Cross-Currents*, Doubleday, 1956.

Propaganda in American Schools, published by his Council of Christian Laymen. Fortunately, these boys have their own presses, or things would really get frustrating. This is a book, says the ad, for "teachers who are misled by false prophets and school board members who are hoodwinked into purchase of poisonous textbooks." There would be no problem with alien ideologies if it were not for progressive education.

The remedy is to infiltrate the PTA's with parents who "know the score." To keep score, parents are urged to read *Progressive Education Is REDucation* by Jones-Olivier. Students should be primed with Noah Webster's *American Speller* (last copyright date 1908) and *McGuffey's Readers.* A set of seven is offered for $15.00. "(This well may be 'last call' for McGuffey Readers at this price.)"

Special target is a high-school textbook called *Democracy versus Communism* by Kenneth Colegrove, whose major sin lies in calling the United States a democracy. This would equate us "with the materialistic, decadent democracies of the Old World, including those with parliamentary systems of government." The article "Text Besmirches American Heritage"[19] insists that "democracy has no quarrel with either the aims or program of followers of Karl Marx." Obviously the United States is a federal republic, and "something special among republics, a government of law in which the basic law is the Ten Commandments, unchangeable, imperishable."

The whole book is seen as part of a plot to deceive each generation of citizens about the true nature of our government. It is quite clear that the professional educationists "wish to see America follow the road to destruction down which Britain and France have traveled so far."

One entire issue of Kaub's newsletter "Challenge" was devoted to this incredible attack on an innocuous textbook. Readers were desperately urged to get this book removed from school systems.

The American Council of Christian Laymen branched out into the educational field in 1954. Kaub wrote in a letter that

19. "Challenge," September, 1958, Council of Christian Layman, newsletter.

some of the Council's literature is "evidently read and appreciated by college students and high school students who have become interested in the type of brain washing being done under the pretense of educating which is prevalent in so many so-called institutions of learning."[20] Kaub's group worked closely with organizers of the Conservative Club at the University of Wisconsin. Students interested in the Council's ideological detergents are readily obliged. I wonder if the University of Wisconsin's Conservative Club is campaigning for *McGuffey Readers* in the Madison schools?

"Organized and chartered for religious and educational purposes only, the fields of action in which this Council may participate are limited," Kaub admits in a newsletter. He continues, "For example, we cannot urge rejection of the measure to abolish the House Committee on Un-American Activities which Congressman James Roosevelt proposes to offer in Congress. But Council members and co-workers can and must let their representatives at Washington know that they stand firmly in support of HUAC . . . we must act at once with all the vigor we can muster."

Patriots were urged to send petitions in support of HUAC. The same letter reaffirmed the Council's opposition to the United Nations and especially Philip Jessup's appointment as United States representative. "Spirit of 76" postcards are available to write your Congressmen. "For your information, the John Birch Society . . . is organizing a 'blitz' of letters to Congress . . . demanding impeachment of Chief Justice Earl Warren." This is clearly playing the political game, and represents a cavalier attitude toward the law that prohibits tax-exempt organizations from urging the adoption or rejection of any specific act of legislation.

A kindred organization, but comprising both clergy and laymen, is the Church League of America located in Wheaton, Illinois. It claims 6,000 clergymen and 50,000 laymen. The League was formed in 1937 but did not really get moving until Major Edgar Bundy took over in 1956. Bundy had been a sportswriter, public-relations agent for the Reverend Carl McIntire and a

20. Letter to author, May 4, 1962.

Southern Baptist clergyman. He also became president of Chicago's Abraham Lincoln Republican Club, which is dismissed by the state GOP as "strictly fringe."

"The greatest man alive," said Bundy of Senator McCarthy. "I like McCarthy and his methods."[21] Living up to his idol, Bundy led the Illinois American Legion to a new height of Americanism by persuading the national convention to condemn the Girl Scout Handbook as "un-American."[22] He followed this up by authoring the Legion resolution calling UNESCO subversive.

Collectivism in the Churches is Bundy's *chef d'œuvre*. When the Methodist publication *Church School* reviewed the book, first prize for silliness was given to Chapter Twelve, which makes a case for John Foster Dulles as a pro-Communist. Second prize went to Chapter Eleven, which "proved" that the United Church Women are Communist-oriented. Among the individuals condemned are Albert Schweitzer, Gandhi, Eisenhower, John D. Rockefeller, Jr., and three Methodist bishops. The competency of the translators of the Revised Standard Version of the Bible is also questioned.

The League stocks over 116 pamphlets and books. You could order *Marxist Brainwashing in the High Schools;* or, on the RVS, "Whose Unclean Fingers Have Been Tampering with The Holy Bible?"; or, on the United Nations, "The Hand That Needs To Be Restrained"; or the *Guide to Subversive Organizations and Publications*. Special monthly reports include "Social Progress or Socialist Progress—Which?" "Guilt by Collaboration" (Presbyterian), and "Treason or Dupery?"

"NOW! you can have a complete counter-subversive seminar in your town" announces one flyer. Ten tape recordings bring you this instant counterspy. No travel expenses or honorariums are necessary. The complete "seminar" may be purchased for $75.00 or individual tapes may be rented at $5.00 each. This is probably the ultimate perversion of the word "seminar": potted ideas on plastic tape.

In addition, personnel of the League will go on the road with

21. "The Truth . . . An Analysis and Refutation."
22. *Chicago Sun Times,* Oct. 14, 1954.

seminars. During 1961 these crusaders appeared on 189 occasions ranging from an address to the employees of Knot's Berry Farm to an appearance before the Empire State Society Sons of the American Revolution.

The League's newsletter of June, 1962, was devoted to the problem of Communism on the campus. Passages of J. Edgar Hoover's disputed report "Communist Target—Youth" were reproduced, and the question was asked "Could it be that some college or university presidents never learn, or do they not wish to?" Gus Hall's "triumphal tour" of West Coast campuses was decried and University of Oregon President Arthur S. Flemming (Eisenhower's Secretary of Health, Education and Welfare) was castigated for defending the right of a Communist to speak on campus.

Parents and taxpayers were urged to "investigate, protest, expose and oppose wherever the Red agents of the Kremlin appear in our educational institutions." The Church League said it agreed with the California Committee on Un-American Activities, which said in regard to the San Francisco riots:

> The contention that unless members of subversive groups are permitted to address students on the campus and unless faculty members are allowed to accomplish the same thing on university property, and unless any kind of subversive literature can be freely circulated, that freedom of speech and expression are being smothered, is to us merely an excuse to substitute license for freedom.

Edgar Bundy wants to protect the country from "National Socialism" and to preserve the spirit of "Christian Americanism." He boasts that the League maintains one of the largest files on Communist Party members, fellow travelers, and dupes in the United States. "It is, in fact, one of twelve such files in the entire country." This is a perfect come-on for whetting the appetite of the conspiracy-conscious. The League has had astonishing success in attracting supporters.

Bundy aims high when it comes to finances. In a slick brochure telling what you can do for the League, it is pointed out that for patriots with a $100,000 income, $720 can be saved on a $1,000 gift through the courtesy of the tax laws. This means it costs you only $280 for a gift of $1,000. If you care to exceed the 20 percent of allowable deductions, why not set up a "reversionary trust" lasting at least two years? Or you could give stock and avoid the capital-gains tax.

Deeding the "remainder interest" of property is another scheme. For example, Mr. X is in the 62 percent tax bracket and owns a $10,000 painting. He deeds the painting to the League with the transfer taking place only at his death. Mr. X gets a $4,100 income-tax savings the year he makes the deed. In addition the $10,000 painting will not be taxed in his estate. This also applies to homes.

Obviously, the Church League is not going to be content with coins in the plate. The back cover of the brochure lists forty-six companies that have supported the League. The honor roll includes United States Steel, Sears, Roebuck and Company, Monsanto, Greyhound Corporation, and Armour and Company.

A new $250,000 GHQ has been built at Wheaton. With his concern for buildings, wills, deeds, trusts, and corporate endowments, Bundy appears to be foundation-conscious. He loves "research" reports and organization and has a good eye for trimmings. Everything appears to be eminently respectable except his ideas. The caliber of his literature would preclude it from having much effect on college youth. Bundy's major threat seems to be in the much harassed PTA, where emotion runs high and conviction frequently doubles for reason.

Few men have contributed more commotion to the fundamentalist Right than the Reverend Carl McIntire. It was he who persuaded Dr. Fred Schwarz to come from Australia and launch his anti-Communist Crusade in the United States. Major Bundy was a McIntire protégé. When the American Council was looking for someone to head its campaign to balloon Bibles over the iron curtain, McIntire chose a young man called Billy James Hargis. It seems as if Billy has never let go of the strings. He has ascended steadily ever since and has become the envy of the ultra-fundamentalist Right.

Hargis's Christian Crusade has almost twice as many members as the Church League and a budget to match that of the Birch Society, of which Hargis is now a director. Two hundred radio stations and twelve TV outlets carry his message to forty-six states. In the fall of 1962, his programs were to be carried by the Mutual Network. This put an additional $39,000 on the budget. Mutual will monitor his broadcasts to see that his gospel doesn't become too political.

Mutual's apprehensions might have arisen with news of the rally for seventy-five Right-wing groups that Hargis convoked in Washington, D.C. Among the goals he announced to the conference was the election of conservative Congressmen. However, Hargis did make it clear that his tax-exempt Christian Crusade was not paying for the conference.

Hargis stole a march on Major Bundy by acquiring the files of Allen A. Zoll which he claims are "the largest and most extensive private anti-communist files in America today." The files were bought for $50,000 and contain the names of thousands of clergymen and educators who have affiliated with Communist fronts over the years. It is going to cost $2,400 to move the files from Washington to Tulsa. To cover the expense, a "File Fund" has been launched.

Anti-Semite Zoll has had a career harassing the public schools and used to run the American Intelligence Agency. In 1936 he founded American Patriots, Inc. which the Attorney General labeled fascist. The Anti-Defamation League of B'nai B'rith has run an excellent report which raises several damaging connections between Hargis and American Anti-Semites.[23]

Communist America: Must It Be? is Hargis's major effort in print. In it we learn that the unions, churches, and schools of America are about to be taken over by the Communists. "It is my contention that the majority of the American newspapers are actively promoting the Communist line" (page 32). Segregation and racism are dismissed as "the most artificial of all social crises instigated by the Communists" (page 102).

This extraordinary social blindness is understandable when we consider the equally incredible parochialism of Hargis's theology. "Brotherhood of Man—A Smoke Screen"[24] claims that

23. "Rev. Billy James Hargis: The Christian Crusade," *Facts*, April, 1962.
24. *Christian Crusade*, January, 1961.

the brotherhood of all men is a Modernist anti-Christian heresy. "Those who would water the Christian faith down into an all-inclusive religion of togetherness would destroy the truth of our Lord and Savior."

Hargis is exploiting the legitimate fundamentalist fear that liberal Christians will gloss over the importance of personal salvation and be contented with merely good works.

The Christian Crusade has finally zeroed in on youth. Writing to "Dear Fellow American Worried About the Future of Your Country," Hargis has announced his campaign to bring the Crusade to college campuses.

"Since I wrote about our plan to invade the campuses of our universities and colleges, a great American hero, Colonel John H. Glenn, has thrilled the world. . . . Here is a man who received his education before our colleges and high schools were shot through with the softening influence of liberalism and communism."

Only our young men and women can save us from the jaws of the Communist dragon. "That is why I consider our plan to have our Christian Crusade program carried on college radio stations the most urgent in my fourteen years of Christian, anti-Communist broadcasting. . . . These kind people who are helping us now—God bless them—know that Christian Crusade is the best equipped anti-Communist organization in America to do the titanic job of retrieving [sic] our college and high school students to paths of sound, decent, sane Christian-Americanism."

Then Hargis goes into his act about the desperate condition of the Crusade's treasury—that this is our darkest hour. "You" must bring the dawn. Every dollar will be "encircled with gold." He closes "with all the prayerful emphasis I can command . . . yours for God and our children." Then he goes back and underlines by pen and inscribes a pleading "P.S. Please answer today—we desperately need your help and prayers!"

The Crusade is wise in deciding upon the medium of radio. It saves the embarrassment of personal appearances. To the average student, Billy J. Hargis might well conjure up a composite of Oral Roberts and Robert Welch—an irresistible target for ridicule. Hargis also has the problem of living down three phony academic degrees. His Bachelor of Arts and Bachelor of

Theology degrees are from Burton College and Seminary in Colorado Springs. He has an honorary Doctor of Laws from Berlin Memorial University, Chillicothe, Missouri.

The U.S. Department of Health, Education and Welfare lists both these schools as "degree mills," organizations which "award degrees without requiring its students to meet educational standards for such degrees . . . receives fees from its so-called students on the basis of fraudulent misrepresentations, or it makes it possible for the recipients to perpetrate a fraud on the public."

In addition Hargis sports an honorary Doctor of Divinity degree from Defender Seminary in Puerto Rico. This school was founded by racist Gerald Winrod and directed by the anti-Catholic, anti-Jewish "cowboy evangelist" Harvey Springer. With such a background, it would take a brave man to face an impudent student audience and ask, "Are there any questions?"

No one could become as successful as Billy James Hargis without inspiring imitators. Out in the bush league of Kentucky, we find Youth for America founded by twenty-four-year-old Earl Atwell who calls himself a "Book and Movie Connoisseur." If Earl is ever going to get his organization off the ground, he will have to change its mailing address. He is from Horse Cave, Kentucky. At present the group is a little low on funds, but it hopes to expand nationally. It will concentrate on fifteen- to thirty-year-olds.

Their main theme is "a national return to God and a free way of life as He meant His Chosen (the Anglo-Saxon, Celtic, Nordic people) to enjoy. Our founding fathers set up our beloved country as a Republic not a mobocracy." Within a short time they hope to put on the road "a lively bunch of dramatic nationalist youth who will speak wherever and whenever the opportunity arises."

Plans are in the making for a monthly magazine, bulletins, leaflets, and so on. But right now Earl is distributing religious and patriotic pamphlets of fellow Rightists and sent on a fascinating sample. One is called "The Factological Story of America's 10-Billion Dollar Drug Trust" which includes the latest on the fluoridation plot, the hoax of Salk vaccine, and the case history of the author who was pronounced dead in 1950. Another is "The

World's Greatest Worry—Debt! Let's Make an Issue of It. Drag It Into the Open." We are told that "Karl Marx propounded his ratty theories just a hundred years ago. But the record of oppressed people under the debt system stretches back through scores of centuries. . . . At last, Karl Marx has met his master. His name is Lambert Schuyler."

The trouble is people have been blaming money instead of money *lending*. Lambert Schuyler has the whole thing explained in his book *To Hell on a Toboggan*, $3.00 cash, no credit. Avoiding shopworn conclusions, Mr. Schuyler suggests, as a starter, a six-month moratorium on all debts under capitalism the world around. There might be some difficulty clearing this with the boys in the front office.

For a straight anti-Communist leaflet, there is "Communism: Composite of All Crimes." Twenty, anyway, are mentioned, including rape, adultery, and tax evasion. "A Better World Begins With ME" serves as an inspirational tract. This is a sentimental plea for more love in the family and society. On the back of this pamphlet stamped in red ink is a picture of a soldier menacing two white girls with a drawn bayonet. This miniature is circumscribed with the motto "Remember Little Rock." Each piece of literature bears this stamp.

Earl is pretty good at mottos. He stamps his envelopes with "Fight CommUNism" and "A Christian who never makes enemies is no good to his Lord." At present he is trying to get more money for pamphlets by selling ball-point pens.

The credulity and naïveté of Youth for America is almost touching until you pause and realize that with a better letterhead and a bigger treasury, it might be difficult to tell the difference between this adolescent effort and that of big brother. If Earl got a secretary to take over the obviously painful job of typing, there is no telling what energies might be released. With its blatant racism, Youth for America might function as a Junior Citizens' Council in the South, but it is difficult to imagine such an organization surviving for long in the North, certainly not among college students.

The Roman Catholic Church has been relatively free of the charge of Communist infiltration, therefore there has not been a similar impetus for purgative organizations. When statistician of suspicion Myers Lowman made his wild charges about more than 10,000 Protestant clergymen being tainted with Communism, he put the figure for Catholic priests at only 200. Robert Welch suggested ½ of 1 percent, until Father Lally of the Boston *Pilot* offered to print the names of the first fifty that Welch would give him.

The offhand endorsement of the John Birch Society by Cardinal Cushing gave it a boost among Catholics, but Cushing has since condemned its excesses. Having Father Ginder, associate editor of the popular *Sunday Visitor* (c. one million circulation) and editor of *The Priest,* on the Council of the Birch Society has enhanced its Catholic appeal. In addition, support has come from the Brooklyn *Tablet* and a Catholic lay newspaper called *The Wanderer* which campaigns against "crypto-Socialism." This St. Paul paper has grown from a circulation of 8,000 to 19,000 in two years. The overwhelming bulk of the Catholic press has, of course, condemned the Birch Society.

Since the fading of Father Coughlin in Detroit and Father Feeney in Boston, you rarely find a Catholic fringe, anti-Communist organization. There is the Catholic Freedom Foundation which enjoys the anonymity of a post-office box in Grand Central Station. Professor Gargan of Loyola University, Chicago, reports that in November, 1960, this Foundation asked Catholic artists of America to prepare posters dramatizing the evils of Communism and suggested as suitable themes: "Red soldiers lined up (some with tunics removed) leering at a group of attractive young women being held for their choice (a nun among them) . . . possibly a screaming woman being dragged by a bestial soldier into an empty room."[25] The best thing that can be said of the Catholic Freedom Foundation is that it is awfully hard to find out anything about them.

Protestant ultrafringe groups do not have to worry about clearance. Condemnation by the National Council of Churches is a prerequisite. Catholic groups have to cope with the goodwill of the archdiocese. Cardinal Cushing, for example, considers

25. E. Gargan, "Radical Conservatism Among United States Catholics," National Catholic Social Action Conference, Aug. 1961.

Catholic political action groups anathema and would not even approve Catholic War Veterans for Boston. He feels such groups create needless divisiveness. Consequently, at present there is only one Catholic equivalent to the Church League of America —the Cardinal Mindszenty Foundation of St. Louis.

Founder and spiritual director of this organization is Father Stephen Dunker, for twenty years a missionary of the Vincentian Fathers in China. Father Dunker returned to the United States after the Communist take-over determined to do something about the world threat of Communism. "I never gave up the idea that a priest, who had heard and seen the things I had, should help others to hear and see these things."[26] Inspiration came after attending Dr. Fred Schwarz's Anti-Communist Crusade in a Baptist church in St. Louis in 1958.

When the sessions were over, the forty people attending decided to remain together as an anti-Communist group. It was mutually agreed that the Protestants and Catholics would be more effective working separately. Father Dunker and his coreligionists set out to establish their organization. The name Cardinal Mindszenty was chosen for the Foundation because it was both Catholic and anti-Communist while supposedly avoiding the negativism of "anti" and the exclusivist label of being Catholic. Three former bishops of China, the Bishop of Pusan, Korea, and ten Catholic priests make up the National Council. Executive Secretary is laywoman Eleanor Schlafly.

Despite the intimations of their literature, Cardinal Ritter has not endorsed the organization. The Archdiocese office makes it clear that the activities of the Foundation have been neither mandated nor prohibited. The bylaws of CMF try to court church favor. Cell leaders are advised to notify their local pastors of all activities. No public program should be held without clearance from the local Reverend Pastor. Any citywide program must be approved by the Bishop.

Press releases on Communism are sent to newspaper editors. One on January 15, 1961, was an attack on the Foreign Policy Association and its liberal director Vera M. Dean. Among other things, Miss Dean was condemned for quoting from the Soviet

26. "Cardinal Mindszenty Foundation," *St. Louis Review*, April 3, 1959.

Constitution in one of her articles. The FPA was also chastised for supporting coexistence, "a major Khrushchev propaganda tactic." Reprints from *Our Sunday Visitor* and familiar Right-wing literature is distributed.

But the Foundation's major effort is pushing a study course in Communism patterned after Fred Schwarz's program. "Seminars" are urged for groups of five to twenty-five. A ten-week course with specific readings (largely HUAC documents) and homework assignments is offered. Over 4,000 of these study groups have been organized. Seminars with over 10,000 participants each have been held in Houston and Milwaukee. A radio program, "Dangers of Apathy," is heard in thirty major cities.

The Foundation has had very little, if any, effect on collegiate Newman Clubs, which is not too surprising since the 18th Congress of Catholic College Students severely castigated HUAC, and the National Newman Club Federation in 1961 gave Bishop Hallinan of Charlestown, South Carolina, an ovation when he criticized Rightists for confusing issues.[27]

Dunker's group has been quite successful in reaching diocesan high schools through its anti-Communist film program. However, their offers to establish seminars in Communism in the Catholic high schools of St. Louis has been refused. The Foundation's office says it has supplied materials on Communism to 106 colleges and universities, 74 seminars, and 192 high schools.

The editor of the diocesan *St. Louis Review* has called the Foundation's approach to Communism "fearful, to say the least" and Father John F. Cronin of the National Catholic Welfare Conference has labeled the Cardinal Mindszenty Foundation "a racket."[28]

Fresh disputes over the new papal encyclical, *Christianity and Social Progress (Mater et Magistra)* calling for more understanding of the welfare state, may reveal a laissez-faire element as intransigent as the Protestant Right. But it does not appear that many Catholics are following the lead of the *National Review*.

27. *Pittsburgh Catholic*, Sept. 7, 1961.
28. Rev. J. Cronin, "Communism: A Threat to Freedom," Social Action Department of National Catholic Welfare Conference.

Cardinal Cushing might be an unrelenting anti-Communist, but he has not repudiated New Deal economics. Communism and liberal economics are seen as a double threat more by Protestant Fundamentalists who also have to worry more about religious heresy.

Just what influence does religion have in determining a young man's conservatism?

Granville Hicks maintains that ". . . Taken together, fundamentalists and modernists do not represent more than a fifth of the nominally Protestant population."[29] Even if this estimate is severe, it is difficult to deny that the majority of people are at best only nominally religious. A study has been done of the religious beliefs of nearly 2,000 YMCA members between the ages of eighteen and twenty-nine.[30] Three-quarters believed in a personal God, half thought Jesus divine, and 60 percent found "an essential connection between religion and the church." While 80 percent felt the Bible divinely inspired, barely half believed in immortality. Catholics were more orthodox than Protestants in each of these beliefs.

Religious practices showed sharp declines in percentages. Only 48 percent attended church once a week. Twenty-seven percent hardly ever go. Only 42 percent pray regularly; one-third hardly ever do. When it came to Bible reading 77 percent had not read the Bible during a past six-month period (62 percent of Catholics and 31 percent of Protestants had never read the Bible at all). Family worship was practiced by only 13 percent (same for Catholics and Protestants) and only 27 percent were used to hearing grace at meals. Less than half of those who "believe in God" regularly engage in traditional religious practices.

This gap between belief and practice has crimped youthful idealism. Asked if they would approve sending free goods to needy peoples abroad even though this meant higher taxes and fewer goods for us, only one in five agreed. Should displaced persons be helped even if this means sacrifices on our part such as housing and jobs? Less than 10 percent were willing so to sacrifice. Almost 60 percent supported some form of racial dis-

29. G. Hicks, *Small Town*, Macmillan, 1946, p. 123.
30. M. Ross, Religious Beliefs of Youth, Association Press, 1950.

crimination. While 44 percent of the agnostics felt whites and Negroes are equal, only 34 percent of those believing in a personal God shared this egalitarianism.

To be known as a religious person was one of the least desirable descriptions one could wish for oneself. Five times as many felt it was more important to resolve economic than religious problems. In "which great person do you most admire?" Christ finished fourth, after F.D.R., Lincoln, and parents.

The poll did show that Jews (a very small part of the sample) register the highest on questions of social idealism. The author's poll also showed that only 2 percent of the conservatives were Jewish.

Twice as many liberals as conservatives were found to be total abstainers from church by my poll, and conservatives do attend more regularly; but the total figures for those who attend regularly or occasionally is the same 77 percent for both camps.

Getting young people to church does not seem to be the problem. It's the gap between prayer and practice that has us stumped. Someone once referred to ours as a "cut flower culture," beautiful blossoms but no roots. Conservatives have long complained of our rootlessness and lack of values. But the values are still there. Young people are more religiously orthodox in belief than in practice. The failure is one of will, and ironically, it is the conservatives who benefit from the moral default.

Three-quarters of the conservatives on the author's poll were Protestants. Only 28 percent felt they were religious fundamentalists (versus 16 percent of liberals). The remaining 72 percent must be some variety of moderate-Conservative-Modernist, Liberal, or Neo-Orthodox. Given the theological complexion of this 72 percent, if there were a revival of religious will, the result would most likely be a revitalization of moral idealism, of the social gospel. This would be a setback for secular conservatism.

The fundamentalist prefers to resolve life into its simplest terms. This is true of his ethics as well as his theology. You can depend upon the bad cowboy being on a black horse. A fundamentalist knows what he likes and who his friends are; he is steadfast and loyal. But he faces two dangers. One is that the ultra thousands will speak more effectively than the moderate millions. A young fundamentalist brought up to fear Catholic domination of the local school board may be easily persuaded that there are Communists in the PTA.

The other danger is that fundamentalism will be used in a secularized form, that religious symbols will be used for political ends. The preference of the American Council of Churches for Billy Hargis over Billy Graham is a danger sign. Robert Welch has shown how this situation may be exploited. It is up to the young and old religious conservatives to show how it can be stopped.

CHAPTER 12

Other Decades on the Right

SOME liberals might not be willing to concede the legitimacy, but young conservatives of the 1960's do have ideological fathers as well as warmhearted mothers. The parents put in some fairly lean years before there was any prospect of salad days for the children. Let's consider the generation which led to Young Americans for Freedom. What were young conservatives up to in the last three decades?

Not much writing anyway. The *Readers' Guide to Periodical Literature* shows that there might have been a lot of conservatives out selling magazines, but not very many were contributing to them. From 1931 to 1940, there were only seven articles written on conservatism. During 1945-1947, no articles were done on conservatism. Forty-four were written on liberalism. For the forties the conservatives managed eleven articles, the liberals ninety-two. Progress was made in the fifties: eighty-eight conservative to 150 liberal contributions. The telltale years were 1959 to 1961. For the first time, conservatives pulled ahead of liberals: twenty-seven to twenty-six.

Of course, not everything written about liberalism in the thirties or conservatism in the sixties was favorablely disposed to these movements. The frequency of articles on each subject does indicate the relative importance of liberalism or conservatism as a public issue. The authors were writing up things that the people were talking about; and for the thirties, conservatism was not a very lively topic.

THREADBARE THIRTIES

Back in the twenties people were conservatives without even trying. Youngsters invoking the names of La Follette or Darrow were bucking for red pepper on their tongues. A typical conservative effort was Allied Youth which stood for "the liberation through education of the individual and society from the handicaps of beverage alcohol." They conducted "Show Me Tours" to places where the effects of drinking could be observed. Since the two major parties seldom ever got political, neither did the youth.

World War I had produced an appropriate issue of patriotic societies: the American Defense Society, the Military Order of the World War, United States Patriotic Society, and the United States Flag Association, to name a few. Celebrating its thirty-fifth anniversary, the Daughters of the American Revolution, ". . . in splendid cooperation with our own and thirty-two other patriotic societies," prepared a two-volume textbook on American history, *The Story of Our American People,* to salvage the public schools. This gesture was necessary because there were 8,000 disloyal teachers in our schools. Just to be sure, they advocated a special oath and pledge to the flag before any teachers' contracts were awarded.

A Southern town showed how lax the DAR was by administering the following oath to women teachers. ". . . I promise to abstain from all dancing, immodest dressing, and any other conduct unbecoming a teacher and a lady. I promise not to go out with any young men except in so far as it may be necessary to stimulate Sunday school work. I promise not to fall in love, to become engaged or secretly married. I promise to remain in the dormitory or on the school grounds when not actively engaged in school or church work elsewhere. I promise not to tolerate the least familiarity on the part of my boy pupils. I promise to sleep at least eight hours a nights, to eat carefully, and to take every precaution to keep in the best health and spirits in order that I may be better able to render efficient service to my pupils."[1]

And just in case you thought they were kidding, *The Nation* reported that "A girl was fired for singing 'It Ain't Gonna Rain No Mo'' soon after a rainmaker had come to town and prayed for a wet spring" (May 25, 1927). Young teachers hired under such circumstances seldom got around to campaigning for Socialist candidates.

If the teachers did not pass on the word, many of the textbooks did. Nationalism frequently reached a xenophobic pitch. Some were content to claim "The greatest thing that any man can say is that he is a citizen of the United States."[2] Others held that "While many of the European races present problems of assimilation,"[3] Greeks, Syrians, and Armenians were described as unassimilable. "They go at once to the quarter of their fellow countrymen where congestion, disease, and poverty abound."[4]

Bessie Pierce, historian at the University of Chicago, did a study of nearly 400 textbooks in 1930. She stressed the patriotic spirit that permeated all of the texts and concluded, "On the other hand, the attitudes engendered toward other peoples through a reading of these books must, in many cases, rebound to their ignominy in contrast with the glory of America."[5] College students who had been weaned on these texts would not generally be predisposed to question American institutions or the *status quo*.

1. E. W. Knight, *Education in the United States*, Ginn & Company, 1929, pp. 360-361.
2. W. Guitteau, *Preparing for Citizenship*, Houghton-Mifflin, 1918, p. 13.
3. E. Towne, *Social Problems*, Macmillan, 1924, p. 53.
4. M. Berry and S. Howe, *Actual Democracy*, Prentice-Hall, 1923, p. 163.
5. B. B. Pierce, *Civic Attitudes in American School Texts*, University of Chicago, 1930, p. 254.

Something earth-shattering would be required to persuade these students that America didn't have nearly all the answers. The depression almost did it.

A follow-up of the 1934 graduates of Minneapolis high schools showed that a third went on to college, and one-third was working. One-fifth of the boys was unemployed along with one-quarter of the girls. Seven percent of the boys had gone to Civil Conservation Corps camps. By 1936 there were to be 800,000 in the camps. At one point there were nine more CCC camps than there were colleges in the country.

Talk of federal interference with education was muted as the National Youth Administration provided part-time jobs for over a quarter of a million high school students, 121,517 college men and women, and 5,151 graduate fellows. Over 44,000 unemployed teachers were put to work by the Federal government. College enrollment dropped 14 percent from 1930 to 1934. Without Federal assistance, it probably would have declined twice as much. Ideological objections were suspended while students struggled with their life jackets.

In the spring of 1935 the *Literary Digest* carried an article called "College Rah-Rah Era Rapidly Passing into History" which quoted Doctor Walter Jessup as observing that the college student is no longer the blasé, sophisticated student of the twenties. He is more serious and demands more of the college library and laboratory than his brother of a decade ago.

The student editor of *The Daily Texan* claimed students were more interested in politics. ". . . Less emphasis on fraternity membership and athletics, greater independence of thought, less reverence for existing institutions show the college man is thinking more and playing less." The *Yale Daily News* added that "rah-rah" is now a term of derision.

The Psychology of Getting Good Grades ($1.00) became a best-seller at the bookstore while the sale of college banners declined. The intellectual was coming into his own. You could go to a concert instead of a football game and score points. When this intellectual curiosity reached politics some strong questions were asked of the *status quo*. The University of Chicago campus was somewhat in the vanguard of this political curiosity, but this editorial from their *Daily Maroon* was not too atypical of the times. ". . . We know that our social system rather than to be revered and its tenets memorialized, should be renovated and its principles rewritten." It then speaks of adopting some of the features of a planned economy and some of the ideals of Socialism, if not its methods.[6]

At Harvard the editors of the 1935-1936 *Lampoon* apologized to visiting Professor Harold Laski for the attacks made upon him by the 1919 editorial board in the days of the Boston police strike.

Student editors are generally to the left of the student body. But *Fortune* magazine admitted in June, 1936, that "Radicalism is ceasing to be a bar to respectability on campus." Vassar had its Daisy Chain Radicals who picketed factories and the state legislature. They helped kill New York state's Nunan bill which required a loyalty oath of those receiving state financial aid.

Conservative Brown University had the largest New England turnout for the famous student Peace Strike. On April 13, 1935, 175,000 students cut classes in a gigantic demonstration for peace. At many meetings the Oxford Oath against war was invoked. It was a rough day for the ROTC.

What were conservatives saying? That's what *Commonweal* asked in April, 1935. "There does not exist anywhere a journal of intelligent conservative opinion. Even the radio, which the conservatives own, is a weapon used against them." *Commonweal* editors feared what might be said if the silence were broken. "The impression one gets is that the conservatives are waiting for 'nature' to rescue them once more. . . . When the conservative ceases to believe in reasons—when in short he grows panicky—he is only a little bourgeois, fit for the scorn of poets and the stones of the mob."

The fears of *Commonweal* were realized a year later when the Bar Association and the Chamber of Commerce spoke. The Bar opposed the child-labor amendment, Social Security, WPA, and investigating abuses of civil liberties in strikes. In addition crop control, grants-in-aid, and collective bargaining were too much for the Chamber.

6. "College Youth Discusses Itself," *New Outlook*, Nov., 1932.

But students were not too attentive to such voices. Purdue University tested pre-New Deal liberalism among college students at 40 percent. A 1934 sampling put it at 50.8 percent, and after the 1936 election, students were two to one for the New Deal. Yet a University of Akron professor reported that whatever the trend in student opinion might be, it had not yet (1936) reached a point where many students had repudiated the party of their parents. It was a case of most Republican students just wanting a less liberal New Deal. The 1932 straw vote at Columbia University did not help out this theory. Norman Thomas was first choice followed by Hoover and then Roosevelt. A national student poll helped some: Hoover over F.D.R. by a large margin.

Actually conservative groups were more active than election returns indicated. The utilities lobby was effective in promoting economic orthodoxy in the schools. State committees of power companies scrutinized textbooks for economic heresy. The director of the Iowa Public Utility Information Bureau reported, "We believe we have this matter pretty much in hand here; after three years' work most of the really objectionable textbooks have been eliminated."[7] He was referring to economic textbooks used by high schools and colleges. Teachers frequently cooperated in this venture.

Professor Charles Lory of Colorado Agricultural College addressed a meeting of public utility men at Tulane University. "I thought I'd never live to see the day when the utilities would be providing educational material for our universities. Plainly a new day for the utility industry has arrived. I am certainly impressed with the progress you are making. If anything you are too modest in presenting the story of the utility business. Don't be afraid—tell us even more of your problems, hopes and ambitions. We believe you are truthful and sincere."[8] Few departments of business administration would need this special attention, but the power lobby wasn't taking any chances.

Most of the right-wing groups were preoccupied with problems of patriotism. There always seems to be somebody folding

7. Carl Thompson, *Confessions of the Power Trust*, Dutton, 1932, p. 380.
8. Ernst Gruening, *The Public Pays*, Vanguard, 1931, p. 39.

the flag wrong. The American Coalition of Patriotic Societies set itself two broad goals. First, to compile arguments made against Russia. Second, to list the names of organizations supporting and advocating recognition of Russia, "organizations to which certain prominent Americans belong." An incidental objective was to keep out radical immigrants. This pattern was followed by organizations such as Sentinels of the Republic, National Security League, Better America Federation, and the National Christian Family Defense League which spoke rather confusingly of pouring "an antidote into the poison of communistic individualism [sic] present at this hour."[9] That ought to keep the opposition guessing.

Everyone was trying to be helpful to the schools. The Masons thought it was dangerous to teach any foreign language before the eighth grade, and they weren't talking about the student's chances of passing. They even wanted a national law to prohibit any language but English in any assembly or gathering.[10] The American Legion avocated ten minutes per school day for patriotic exercises and suggested a roll call of the signers of the Declaration of Independence.

At Englewood, Colorado, the Ku Klux Klan gave a flag to the local school plus a flagpole topped with their initials: "KKK." The Klan was active in getting legislation requiring flags to be flown from all schoolhouses. To protect the public schools, the Klan opposed the hiring of Jewish or Catholic teachers: "National security can sanction no other course." A Junior Order of the Klan competed in age bracket with the Boy Scouts. It was for "native, white, Gentile, Protestant American boys who love the United States more than any other country in the world."

The boys were told that pacifists are "mollycoddles" and enemies of their country. The pillowcase brigade was also set straight on immigrants. ". . . This land of Liberty was to them a land of license. They were given the ballot almost before they

9. House Hearings "To Reconcile Naturalization Procedure with the Bill of Rights," 72nd Congress.

10. G. Thomas, "The Place of Masonry in the Renaissance of Democracy," *The Builder*, Vol. V, 1919, p. 105.

got rid of the vermin they brought over in their steerage passage. . . . Our American laws are trampled under the dirty hoofs
of swine with the ballot in their filthy jaws. . . ." But the boys
were rallied by heartening news. "Your Parent organization
(KKK) is becoming a Wizard Evangel proclaiming the 'coming
of the Lord' to America. This Evangel will cause multitudes to
'Flee from the wrath to come.' . . . Juniors—Awake—Up and
at Them—God Rules and Our Government Still Lives."[11]

I have always liked to think that the Klan was done in by
contour sheets.

Patriotism on the campus was championed by the National
Society of Scabbard and Blade. These young men believed that
military training was a necessity and an obligation. Their major
campus enemy was the score of flourishing peace organizations
which were calling for an end to ROTC. One of the most effective weapons the peace groups had was the War Department's
official manual on *Citizenship*, dated November, 1928. This is a
sample of what the Department thought should be taught in
training camps: "An impractical and destructive idealism called
internationalism is being propagated by many of the Nation's
'intellectuals.' Its efforts are to combat the spirit of patriotism.
. . . Pacifism is baneful in its influence. It promotes distrust of
country and debates the spirit of nationalism. . . ." It also denounced "collectivism" as that form of government which
stresses "equality of condition."

An assist came from the Intercollegiate Organizations of
America which were pledged to keep college youth from turning radical. They enjoyed the publicity of the Hearst press and
claimed a quarter of a million members. Liberals insisted that
IOA was lucky to have one-tenth that figure. A reporter at one
of its weekly meetings was told that a scrupulous effort is made
to see that "no radicals get to talk to our members."[12]

A combination of ROTC, Fraternity Row, and the athletic
associations provided the major reserves for Right-wing campus
activity according to James Wechsler in his *Revolt on the
Campus* (1935). These forces when combined with the pres-

11. *The Kourier Magazine*, Vol. III, Jan., 1927, pp. 19-21.
12. *New Republic*, Oct. 16, 1935.

sures of trustees made possible a startling amount of vigilante enterprise. A relatively innocent example was the debate which was to have taken place in August, 1934, between UCLA and Berkeley on the proposition: "Communism Is Fit for America." Just before the debate, the Berkeley team wired to Los Angeles:

"Rumored that Jingo press is making efforts to call off Monday's debate. We intend to debate and uphold Communism. We are not being financed by Moscow nor very much by anybody. We have yet to be propositioned by a Russian."

A nervous reply came back from Los Angeles:

"Telegram very indiscreet. Communism cannot now be discussed. We must debate: Resolved, that the power of the President shall be substantially increased as a settled policy, or cancel debate altogether."[13]

Berkeley refused to back down. The debate was cancelled.

Sometimes a college president went off the deep end when trying to prove to his trustees that there were no radicals on his campus. In the fall of 1934, the president of San Jose State College got alarmed about a Left-wing pamphlet circulated on campus. He asked that this "festering sore be eradicated. . . . Will all loyal groups, clubs, classes and societies act immediately. Make plans to get the necessary information. If you know members of the group, please feel quite free to take them to the edge of the campus and drop them off."[14]

At Michigan State University, a secret organization known as the Knights of Sherwood Forest set out to castigate the insufficiently patriotic and took an unfortunate anti-Semitic turn. They marched on the Jewish fraternity house and threatened those who had participated in the peace movement. Their triumph was breaking up a peace meeting and throwing the student leaders and a clergyman into the Red Cedar River.

As might be expected Harvard had to do things differently. Probably disdainful of the gaucherie of MIT "Patriots" who had shaved the heads of student peace leaders, Crimson Rightists decided on ridicule. Into a Harvard peace meeting trooped the Michael Mullins Marching and Chowder Club. They sported the

13. J. Wechsler, *Revolt on the Campus*, Covici, Friede, 1935, pp. 271-272.
14. *Op. cit.*, p. 275.

Nazi salute and a sign reading "Down with Peace." They really did it up brown. Besides the usual fruit and heckling some of them rode around in a car with a mounted machine gun stolen from a local armory.

Some of this, especially the tour de force at Harvard, represented a heavy dose of campus high jinks. In relating episodes like these, Wechsler probably did not make enough allowance for the student temptation to deflate self-righteous causes, however right they might be.

It is true that a frightened business community on occasion exerted unwarranted pressures on universities and that rightist fringe groups were quite active. We have not even mentioned the alarming popularity of Father Coughlin's Christian Front toward the end of the thirties. But aside from some unnecessary faculty dismissals, the usual minority intolerance, and considerable campus feuding, the ultra-Right did not make much of a splash. The Common Front linked the center with the far Left. Most moderates acquiesced in this alliance. In mid-decade Harold Seidman asked "How Radical Are College Students" in the *American Scholar* (summer, 1935). Not very, he concluded. There has been a movement to the Left. "But American students started so far right that they have hardly reached center." If *Literary Digest* polls are still admissible evidence, students had crossed well over the center line after the 1936 election.

The later GOP switch from Landon to Willkie was a reluctant tribute to the New Deal. Conservatism wore thin with the nap of one's coat sleeve. By the end of the decade, not only had the tables turned, but someone had started up a game of musical chairs, and the conservatives were convinced that the liberals were in cahoots with the pianist.

FERVENT FORTIES

Each of these three decades has a catastrophe which determines its character: depression, war, and Senator McCarthy. The Senator is one of the few phenomena which could come after a war and not be anticlimactic. The depression gave an earnestness to its young. There was a somber mood of people recovering from a blow. People were defensive about what they did possess and aggressive about what they felt they should possess. Class lines deepened. Adversity was not going to produce either a healthy conservatism or liberalism.

The forties brought war and pseudo prosperity. New energies released a fervor not found in the thirties. Instead of depressed withdrawal, you found enthusiastic involvement. For one thing everybody was patriotic. It must have been a shock to the American Coalition of Patriotic Societies to turn eyes left and find everyone in step. Patriotism was no longer the abstract preserve of any one group; it was being spelled out in concrete daily sacrifices by everyone. To the ultra-Right this was like gas rationing.

There was hardly any mileage in anti-Communism when Hollywood was turning out pro-Soviet war films and the American-Soviet Friendship Committee belonged almost as much as beer. Even the House Committee on Un-American Activities suspended operations. Until the shooting was over, everyone on our side was assumed to be at least 99 $44/100$ percent American. Those who felt they possessed the additional increment of grace had to kill time at the Legion hall or on the courthouse steps until the Hiss case broke.

Not everyone agreed as to why we were fighting the war. George B. Cutten wrote a "Credo of an Old-Fashioned Conservative" for *American Mercury* in November, 1942. He was talking about patterning his conservatism after the laws of nature and insisting that our instincts are surely conservative. "We are fighting this war to satisfy our pugnacious instinct and our instinct of self-assertion. When will it end? When we have fully satisfied our pugnacious instinct."

Cutten's explanation of the war was probably not widely shared among conservatives. This amoral attitude toward power is, however, typical of an element of the Right which became more prevalent in postwar years. This is the barroom bellicosity behind the foreign policy of Young Americans for Freedom. The young conservative of the forties was too involved in war not to long for an alternative. He needed the liberal's reassurance that something could be done. Even the American Legion had a brief interlude of internationalist idealism. Their 1946 convention pledged "Fidelity to the United Nations."

Some of the students going into the armed services were felt to be neither idealistic nor realistic by the conservative *American Mercury*. In the spring of 1941 they carried an article deploring the self-centered attitudes of some students facing the draft. A Princeton senior thought the draft might help his business career. A Stanford graduate felt learning to fly in the air corps would help to make him a well rounded sportsman. Some martyr at an Ivy League university believed the CCC and high school boys should go first.

The author feared that unless awakened, indifferent youngsters might soon become active appeasers. Almost without an exception, he felt, "their statements reveal a tragic mistrust of both the integrity and the purposes of their elders." This is a familiar parental lament. Things had not improved too much over that 1940 raid when a squad of New York City policemen and truant officers combed movie houses on two mornings and rounded up nearly two thousand children AWOL.

Conservative parents who had long lambasted modern education had a field day reading the *New York Times* report (April 4, 1943) on a United States history exam given 7,000 college freshmen. Only 16 percent of the freshmen offered anything very intelligible about Jefferson. Some thought he was President of the Confederacy; others knew he had originated the Monroe Doctrine. Thirty thought he had discovered electricity. Democrats would be delighted to hear that Teddy Roosevelt's greatest contribution to his country was his collection of animal heads. Roger Taney was a gangster, and Roger Williams turns out to be a movie star. The original thirteen states included Wisconsin, Kentucky, Utah, Nebraska, Michigan, and something called "East Virginia."

On campus the drafting of eighteen- and nineteen-year-olds brought some drastic changes. Fifty schools were forced to lock their doors. Schools exclusively for men began to admit women. Courses became so accelerated that half the boys didn't know whether they were sophomores or juniors. There were fewer and shorter vacations. Automobile rides were out. Dating was cut down. More students were marrying, and there was a general increase in seriousness.

Nation carried an article on "The Class of 1944" (July 22, 1944) which maintained that these students were realists and not glib verbalizers about their feelings. "In sheer honesty and straightforwardness they put the older generation to shame. . . . Give us this day our daily activities which make some sense to us, is their unsaid prayer." This crop of young people, said the article, possesses a surprising "psychic vigor." Why? Because we are getting beyond pure "book learning." In short, modern education has given our youth more resilience.

Liberals and conservatives will probably never agree on what is and what is not corrupting the youth in education. But modern education stood the test of World War II and demonstrated some effective lessons in social tolerance and world awareness.

Veterans returning to campus were sobersided. They were five years older than the average nonveteran and frequently outnumbered him three to one. College became less playful and more serious. Freshman caps were out and so was hazing. For the first time freshmen at the University of Missouri did not have to whitewash the huge stadium. Nonveterans at Lehigh University complained: "They study so hard we have to slave to keep up with them. . . . Those guys don't even know it's spring." Another undergrad at Lehigh criticized the vets for not coming out for sports. "If a vet can't be coach, he won't play . . . they can't take discipline."[15]

A further complaint was that veterans criticized freely but did not join. The conservative triumvirate of fraternities, athletics, and ROTC was temporarily broken. The power center on most campuses shifted to independents. Most of the direct action of these veterans was not the result of much formal organization. At Cornell veterans found that Ithaca as a nondefense area had no rent control, and rents had skyrocketed. They demanded a survey by the Bureau of Labor Statistics and got it. Controls followed shortly.

15. E. Efron, "The Two Joes Meet," *New York Times Magazine,* June 16, 1946.

In 1947 students at the University of Minnesota were responsible for politicking a three-million-dollar appropriation bill for the university through the state legislature. During the same year forty Michigan State students made 344 talks before 38,000 people. One of the most ambitious new liberal organizations was a veterans' group: the American Veterans Committee sponsored by young intellectuals like Charles Bolte, Norman Mailer, and Bill Mauldin. Its motto was "Citizens First, Veterans Second," and they came out against bonuses for veterans.

Before the postwar idealism wore off, AVC had as many as one thousand members in one chapter, 225 campus chapters, and a total membership of 20,000 (1947). Although only a year old, Wallace's Young Progressive Citizens had 3,000 members and American Youth for Democracy (replacing the Young Communist League) claimed a membership of 4,000.

Many veterans had enough of organization in the service and didn't join anything. Some of them as conservatives simply felt left out. The massed effect of these liberal postwar organizations might very well have completed the monolithic picture of what conservatives have come to call "the Liberal Establishment." There were no comparable national youth groups on the Right. Little conservative comfort was taken from campus straw votes going into the 1948 election. At Princeton, Stassen was first choice of Republican students. Taft placed fourth. Columbia University Law School chose Douglas over Dewey, and Truman had an edge at Temple University, Cornell, and the University of Chicago.

But 1946 had been a pivotal year for the conservatives. They gained control over Congress and forced President Truman into federal loyalty investigations and got the House Committee on Un-American Activities incorporated as a permanent committee under the Legislative Organization Act. The following year HUAC launched its futile but supercolossal investigation of Hollywood. Then came the allegations against our atomic scientists and the glorious Alger Hiss case. By 1949 the eleven Communist leaders had been convicted under the Smith Act, Judy Coplon was on trial, and one-eighth of an ounce of fissionable uranium was missing (later found).

Patriotism was restored as a conservative issue. It was getting harder and harder to claim your percentage of Americanism.

In 1949 Harold Laski was invited by the Sidney Hillman Foundation to speak at ten American campuses. At the last minute authorities at UCLA withdrew their invitation. At first they said no one could speak at Los Angeles without also speaking at Berkeley. There proved to be no such rule. Another university asked him to give one speech instead of the two scheduled. When the Harvard Law School Forum tried to rent a Cambridge high school auditorium for Professor Laski, the mayor turned them down claiming that Laski was a Communist and an enemy of the Roman Catholic Church.

In recounting these and other incidents of arbitrary action in American universities, Laski said, "The president and dean of a large Eastern university agreed that so long as they had any influence Justice Frankfurter, Professor Max Lerner, and I would never be invited to lecture because we were regarded as 'influences likely to disturb the students.' "[16]

The forties ended as the Right's appetite for retaliation was being whetted. The conservatism following World War I had been dissipated in a superficial social roar. After World War II, conservatism took a more serious turn. At home the liberal opposition was in power. Abroad was a well structured peace organization, not an amorphous peace movement. In less than a year, there were 137 campuses with Collegiate Councils for the United Nations.

Just in case either side was thinking of an extended morning at the movies, President Truman announced in October 1948, ". . . we have evidence that an atomic explosion occurred in the USSR."

FURTIVE FIFTIES

Both sides get edgy when foreign policy has to be played in terms of which side is inching closer to the atomic control but-

16. H. Laski, "Liberty on the American Campus," *Nation*, August 13, 1949.

ton. The Russians having the Bomb was bad enough, but many Americans were convinced that the only way they got it was by stealing it from us. After all, wasn't the government peppered with Reds? Ask Senator McCarthy.

The year 1951 began with the unraveling of the incredible imagination and cunning of Senator Joseph McCarthy. His first charge of subversion in the State Department ended up in three million words of testimony which proved to be only a modest appetizer for the Senator.

Real spies like the Rosenbergs were lumped together with fancied ones like Phillip Jessup. McCarthy outdid Hollywood and Detroit in promising that the next production would be more stupendous than the last—a real seller. In the fall of 1951, the *New York Post* came out with its brave seventeen-part series called "Smear, Inc.: Joe McCarthy's One-Man Mob." But it didn't daunt the Senator. He steamed ahead.

Although most students disapproved of McCarthyism, too many showed its effects by reflecting a climate of suspicion. In the spring of 1952, McCarthy was invited to keynote Northwestern University's mock presidential convention. His speech consisted of a blast at "our Moscow directed foreign policy." Student reaction was somewhat ambiguous. A motion was put to endorse Senator McCarthy's views. It won 543 to 387. The next afternoon the platform committee adopted a plank condemning McCarthy's methods. That evening there was an attempt to defeat this anti-McCarthy plank, but it was voted down. According to the *Nation*, this was the first formal test of McCarthy's strength on an American campus.

They also added that the only time in forty-four years that Northwestern students have agreed with the nation at large was in its choice of Calvin Coolidge in 1924. It is difficult to know how much they believed of Joe's foreign policy and how much they were influenced by his oratory. At least the controversial methods of McCarthyism were condemned.

Briefly sharing the limelight with Senator McCarthy was General Douglas MacArthur, Absent with Leave from Korea. His dismissal rallied all Right-thinking Americans. A psychology professor at the University of Colorado tested students' reaction to President Truman's dismissal of General MacArthur. First he administered an F-scale test. A high score on this test measures antidemocratic proclivities such as authoritarian submission, projectivity (a disposition to believe that wild things go on), and authoritarian aggression, especially against those who violate conventional values.

The majority of students against MacArthur's dismissal fell in the top quartile of antidemocratic scores. Those who supported Truman's action in dismissing MacArthur fell in the bottom quartile of antidemocratic scores.[17] Thus MacArthur ended up with the support of those students who had the highest authoritarian tendencies.

Authoritarian propensities or hero worship, however, can not explain very much of the conservatism on campus. An *American Mercury* article (April, 1957) by Patrick Riley suggested two factors which have contributed to the resurgence of conservatism: renewed interest in debate and a religious revival. The religious factor is discussed in another chapter of this book. Debate as an influence is an interesting idea.

Ever since 1953, says Mr. Riley, national debate topics have been designed to pit liberal versus conservative. "The student debater can gather facts on his own before they are varnished by the pink professors who patrol the classroom." Obviously a student who independently digs up his facts is more enthusiastic about them. A young conservative who goes into debate to sharpen up the case for his side would undoubtedly get quite a bit of satisfaction from the contest.

This still would involve only those articulate and eager enough to participate in debate. You can not extend this explanation to cover debate audiences, which generally are sparser than those at a chess tournament. No message would reach the masses through a debate, but it is an excellent training ground for leaders in student movements. Topics have become more controversial. There is more bite in "Resolved: The United States Should Recognize Red China" than there was in "Resolved: The Marines Should Get Out of Nicaragua."

To assure us that liberalism had not captured the heartlands,

17. P. Gump, "Anti-Democratic Trends and Student Reaction to President Truman's Dismissal of General MacArthur," *Journal of Psychology*, Vol. 38, Aug., 1953.

we have the word of a writer for *Flat Hat* at the College of William and Mary. He insisted that the vast majority of undergrads on campus were conservatives. "Political activity on the traditionally American campus—as opposed to the big-city campus which involves the many foreign elements and alien philosophies of Europe—is, here, practically nonexistent. These campuses are manned largely by conservatives, but no urgent need for standing up and 'being counted' exists." This was, of course, two years before the whistle was blown for Young Americans for Freedom.

Not that other conservatives weren't excited. J. B. Matthews claimed in April, 1955, that in the last twenty years the Communist party had enlisted the support of at least 3,500 professors. Many of them were dues-paying members, many fellow travelers, and some "outright espionage agents." He also sounded an alarm about the disease of "intellectualism" and the assumption that "the intellectual is tapped by God Almighty to 'bear rule.'"

Harvey Matusow, one of HUAC's most friendly witnesses, reported that 500 students at Antioch College "support Communist Party activities" and that seventy-two were members of the Young Progressives of America. Harvey had not talked to any Antioch Staff members, but he had spent two nights in a local tavern. President Douglas McGregor said the charges were too ridiculous for comment.[18]

But this was the year (1952) that Senator McCarran pontificated: "I can conceive of fewer greater crimes," when talking about Communist infiltration of the Boy Scouts. Nobody was taking any chances.

In the spring of 1953 Columbia's *Spectator* reported that the Dean's office not only furnished prospective employers with a student's grades but with a "loyalty report." At Harvard two law students who had invoked the Fifth Amendment before McCarthy's Senate Committee were berated by the president of the Massachusetts Bar Association as "unfit for admission to the bar in any of our states." He demanded their expulsion. Dean Griswold refused. However, the Alumni Association of the

18. "McCarran and the Boy Scouts," *Nation*, 23 Aug., 1952.

Law School did force them off the editorial board of the Harvard *Record*.

Four students in New York City who had protested the dismissal of professors who had used the Fifth Amendment were warned by a member of the New York Board of Higher Education: "Your names are being taken down. Some day you may want to apply for admission to the bar or to some other place. . . . Why don't you watch what you say?"[19]

Apparently by 1958 City College of New York felt it was time to save the students from themselves. Every campus organization was forced to file a membership list. Students feared that government investigators or prospective employers might be given the names. Since this ruling, Students for Democratic Action, the Young Democrats, and NAACP have virtually died on campus. "The kids feel any political action at all is 'communistic,' " lamented one campus activist.[20]

Wind had been taken out of the sails of a good many liberal groups. After the Wallace fiasco, the Young Progressives of America were down to a hard core of Communists. Only 150 members showed up on the roster of the Student League for Industrial Democracy. The American Veterans Committee withered as veterans left campus. Students for Democratic Action were fighting both student indifference and administration hostility.

Young conservatives had a great time razzing the World Assembly of Youth at Ithaca, New York. It was a low-powered affair sponsored by the "Y's" and Youth Hostelers. Unfortunately for their press, the obliging youngsters allowed a pretty Pakistani girl to dissuade them from passing a resolution against polygamy.[21]

Despite an increasingly favorable climate, young conservatives were slow to organize on a national level. The Intercollegiate Society of Individualists was launched in 1953 as a study group. But there was no national conservative campus group of an activist nature until Robert Munger of Los Angeles

19. "Now the Students," *Nation*, May 16, 1953.
20. "Atlas Shrugs at City College," *Nation*, May 3, 1958.
21. "Are Students Afraid of Politics?", *New Republic*, Oct. 29, 1951.

City College reworked his National Collegiate MacArthur Clubs. After the 1952 GOP convention, Munger decided it was time to rechristen his year-old organization. Retaining his monthly publication, *The American Student*, he called his new group Students for America. General MacArthur still served as honorary president.

There was to be a select hard-core membership, no constitution, and all officers were to be appointed, not elected. Local chapters would not seek recognition from college authorities but were to remain a "loyal underground." Its National Security Division claimed to have "direct liaison" with antisubversive government agencies. They were to get information on all leftish activity "by any means which may be deeded expedient." These security agents would not be known to the general membership.

They had not only a cloak but a dagger: the student handbook replete with an eagle on the cover. Munger wrote the *Students' Answer to the Marxist Challenge*. It offers the fraternal assurance that "almost all leftwing student organizations are merely the tools of groups like the Communist Party or other equally vicious outside adult agencies . . . a person does not have to call himself a communist or even be a communist to be an enemy of our country." The handbook disclaims any fascist label and insists that fascism is socialism.

You get "Nine Basic Tests of a Communist-Stalinist Organization" compiled by the California Senate's Un-American Activities Committee plus a list of fifty-two "subversive" student organizations based on the Attorney General's list and other state investigating groups.

Students for Freedom claimed 2,500 members on 160 high school and college campuses in thirty-five states. Material from the Foundation for Economic Education was circulated along with reprints of speeches of prominent Right-wingers including the Senator's own "McCarthyism—The Fight for America." They distributed 100,000 pieces of literature in one month, and their treasurer admitted that student contributions "don't even pay for postage."

Fulton Lewis, Jr., contributed a Washington column. His son organized a chapter at the University of Virginia, where the campus *Cavalier Daily* described SFA as "a kindergarten KKK." Endorsers included Walter Winchell, Senator Mundt, General Wedemeyer, John T. Flynn, Rupert Hughes, Martha Roundtree, and the American Legion.

Robert Munger moved on to the congenial climate of Pepperdine College in Los Angeles. Apparently the organization was a little too effectively structured on authoritarian lines. SFA never survived the drafting of Munger into military service.[22]

Few of the campus conservative groups reflected this extremism. At Harvard an anti-McCarthy Conservative Club was trying to replace the pro-McCarthy Conservative League on the argument that moderation was the essence of true conservatism. The Club said it could not approve of any extreme or arbitrary acts of coercion from any source. Senator Knowland, who voted for McCarthy's censure, was their model. The president of the League admitted that "it was the emotional element in politics that attracts me." But he also conceded that liberals outnumbered conservatives four to one at Harvard. In calling for a change of line, the New Conservative Club appeared to have a good talking point. (Both the League and the Club have been superseded by Young Americans for Freedom.)

Despite the strength of McCarthyism, there was remarkable resistance on the part of American students. Their activities might have been curtailed, but they retained considerable independence of judgment. During a vintage year for McCarthyism (1952), a poll was taken at Williams College where 96 percent of the students are sons of business or professional fathers.

When asked if members of the Communist party should be allowed to teach in colleges and universities in the United States, a bare plurality of the students said "yes." An absolute majority of the faculty said "no." In giving reasons for their answers, the students were more concerned about restricting basic freedoms. The faculty felt that Communists were not free agents.

On the question of whether American colleges should refuse

22. For SFA see: "Who Brought Sugar for the Gas Tanks," *American Mercury*, Jan., 1954; "The Undergraduate Underground," *Reporter*, March 2, 1954; "Students for America: Campus McCarthyism," *Nation*, March 20, 1954.

to sponsor visiting speakers known to be Communists, 81 percent of the students would allow the Communist speakers. Only 67 percent of the faculty agreed with this. Virtually every student felt the writings of Marx should be included in college courses. Despite the fact that most students agreed that the social atmosphere made it difficult to defend friends labeled as "subversive," 46 percent were willing, purely for the purposes of debate, to argue the affirmative of the resolution: "Communism is a better form of government than democracy." An absolute majority of the faculty refused to do this, mostly on the ground that they could not argue what they did not believe.

The most revealing question was this: "If, after examining the policies of an organization such as Americans for Democratic Action and deciding you wished to join, you learned that the organization was 'under suspicion' of acting 'subversively,' would this disclosure in itself deter you from joining?" Only 15 percent of the students said "no," versus 42 percent of the faculty.

Two-fifths of the students were on the fence with a "maybe," which is little more encouraging than the 12 percent of faculty who had "no opinion." A plurality of the students noted practical reasons such as job security and public opinion as explanations of their answers.[23] This was the question which hit them directly. They could be playful about debating and magnanimous about free speech, but they would not dare to join.

Why would only 8 percent of the students fear the "subversive" label in defending Communism in debate, while 54 percent would balk at joining ADA? The students' answers would appear to be that debating involves no commitment, whereas joining a liberal organization means taking the plunge. The contribution of McCarthyism lay in its persuading the beach chair liberals to continue hesitating at the edge of the pool of decision.

An associate editor of the *Harvard Crimson* pretty well summed up the mood. "The thing is *not* to be enthusiastic. It looks bad at cocktail parties. . . . Nobody wants to be identified with anything that is at all out of the way." This made young people of the fifties part of the "Silent Generation." Thorton

23. "Campus Poll #7, William College, 1952," a student poll filed at the Roper Public Opinion Research Center, Williamstown, Mass.

Wilder has taken a charitable view of this group. They are silent because they are busy fashioning Twentieth Century Man. "It holds its tongue because it cannot both explore itself and explain itself."

Because of this introspection which involves preoccupation with self and the "larger ranges of experience," says Wilder, they are indifferent toward middle relationships: current opinion, social usage, patriotism, morality, and so forth.[24]

To commemorate this indifference, Kerouac in his novel *The Town and the City* coined the sobriquet "Beat," which adds the element of resentment, at what and why, no one is too sure. The young novelist Clellon Holmes insists that unlike the Lost Generation which was occupied with the loss of faith, the Beat Generation is becoming more and more occupied with the need of it. "They are busily and haphazardly inventing totems for Him on all sides. The copywriter, just as drunk by midnight as his Lost Generation counterpart, probably reads *God and Man at Yale* during his Sunday afternoon hangover."[25] He sees a will to believe even in the face of an inability to do so.

Perhaps the liberal malaise has been an undue silence toward the middle relationships and a Beating off of too much of its intellectual talent. But the conservative's world consists of the middle relationships as Wilder defined them: current opinion, social usage, and the imperatives of traditional religion, patriotism, and morality. And the conservative despises the "Beat element."

As the fifties closed, the young conservative took heart and began to reap the harvest of a decade of liberal passivity. He was learning that you didn't have to have much to say to break your silence. New intellectuals were to appear to make him less self-conscious about his "middle" values. The young conservative felt a heady strength and was prepared to elbow the liberal in the ribs, smile, and stand his ground.

24. T. Wilder, "The Silent Generation," *Harper's*, April, 1953.
25. C. Holmes, "This Is the Beat Generation," *New York Times Magazine*, Nov. 16, 1952.

CHAPTER 13

Gentlemen of the Campus

RUSSELL KIRK hopes to see the conservative revival sustained by increasing waves of college-bred gentlemen.
Thoroughly grounded in the conserving values of our culture,
these young men will supply the mood of civility and purpose
which our wayward liberal society lacks. Wearing a white shirt,
tie, and jacket on a weekday is very likely an indication that a
student is about to be interviewed, has lost a bet, or is a young
conservative meeting his first responsibility of deportment: neat
grooming.

Nothing must offend middle-class propriety which has
treated them very well. Financially, nearly half their parents
are in the $10,000 to $20,000 bracket (versus one-third of the
liberals). Besides this economic security, they have enjoyed an
ethnic advantage. Fifty-eight percent of the young conservatives'
parents were native-born Americans (versus 47 percent of liberal
parents). While a quarter of the liberals had parents born in
Eastern Europe, only 4 percent of the conservatives did. Barely

2 percent of the conservatives were Jewish, and three-quarters were Protestant. This has meant less ethnic and religious friction for the conservative student and a readiness to identify with and champion American middle-class mores.

Defending such values makes the young conservative a community but not a campus conformist. Liberal permissiveness is the college norm, to the conservative's consternation. When Henry Miller's *Tropic of Cancer* was reviewed in the *Duke Chronicle*, three campus conservatives wrote in protesting the use of an obscene word. "Is the right to express oneself actually in question—or is it the license to use vulgarity?" The writers reported that in a telephone conversation with the Assistant News Editor of the *New York Times*, they were told that under no circumstances would the *Times* print the phrase in question. "The long tradition of student responsibility enjoyed by this University must not be broken down by acts of indiscrimination which render untenable the continuation of this privilege."[1]

What is different here is not the blush at obscenity but the stress on "the tradition of responsibility." One of the writers of this letter, Donald Gregory, turned out to be one of those engaging youths who probably cuts the lawn at home without being told. He insisted that conservatism was not something you got from reading; it was a way of looking at life and involved a rigid code of quiet decency. Donald appears to be approaching conservatism from both ends. The next morning I found him, nattily dressed, sitting on a campus curb reading Burke's *Reflections on the Revolution in France*.

A similar moral protest was voiced by conservatives at the University of Pennsylvania. In the spring of 1962 the *Daily Pennsylvanian* was suspended principally because of an intemperate and tasteless article on Billy Graham. Examples: "the total [of decisions for Christ] is rising almost as fast as the national crime rate," and "Is it true that Graham might be the illegitimate son of Norman Vincent Peale by Mary Baker Eddy?" If nothing else, the paper deserved to be chastised for its incredible ignorance of theology. Only plausible theology could have made this remotely humorous.

1. Letter to the *Duke Chronicle*, Oct. 13, 1961.

The suspended paper promptly received the support of the National Student Association and other college papers including the *Harvard Crimson*. Campus *Analysis* ("First Conservative College Magazine in the East"), which carries on a running war with the liberal *Pennsylvanian*, applauded the disciplinary action. They did admit that withdrawal of financial support probably would have been punishment enough.

Then they coupled their moralism with a homily on libertarian economics. "We can only hope that from this incident the *Daily Pennsylvanian* has learned that a relatively independent policy can only be followed through economic independence. We further hope that the new editorial board can relate this experience with federal aid to education, housing, *et al.*, in regard to the paper's content in the coming year."[2]

Just how much of campus conservatism is of the traditional variety, more evident in the Duke letter, and how much is economic libertarianism, which seemed to inspire the *Analysis* editorial?

Three questions on my poll attempted to register the response of conservative students to traditional versus economic conservatism. In each case, the choice was between a cultural and an economic value. One dealt with conservation. "Do you feel that parcels of government parkland should ever be sold for use as private economic enterprises or for private residences?" There was an even split: 50.5 percent said No (versus 74 percent of liberals who said No), and 86 percent of those willing to sell the land thought it should go for both residences and enterprises.

Cultural vulgarity was the next issue. "Some people consider advertising on TV objectionable, others do not. Do you find it objectionable?" Only 31 percent of the conservatives found it objectionable (versus 43 percent of liberals). Of the conservatives who did find it objectionable, only 9 percent would like to see the government do anything about it.

The third dealt with aesthetics. "Would you be willing to spend extra tax money to make new buildings architecturally beautiful? If yes, should this extra expenditure be made only if

2. Editorial, *Analysis*, March, 1962.

funds are available or even if it involves going into debt?" The split was even: 49 percent said Yes they would spend the money, but 82 percent added, only if the funds are available. On the other hand, 63 percent of the liberals would spend the money; and only 72 percent would hold out for available funds.

In each clash of alternatives, conservatives showed a much stronger willingness than did the liberals to sacrifice cultural to economic values. Stalwart defense of forest preserves, disgust at TV commercials, and a readiness to promote public architecture would seem to be attributes of a traditional conservative. These qualities are not a significant part of campus conservatism today.

One Northwestern conservative did comment on the architecture question: "We might as well have decent buildings. It engenders a respect for authority." He was willing to go into debt for the construction, but he felt the need of offering a strongly utilitarian rationalization.

A creditable respect for civil rights has been part of the American conservative's tradition—even though his conscience occasionally has to be elbowed. But on the poll, only 26 percent of the conservatives opposed the late Senator Joseph McCarthy. Sit-ins were supported by less than 14 percent, and the American Civil Liberties Union received an endorsement of a bare 8 percent. (Liberals supported the ACLU by only 42 percent. A remarkable 33 percent had no opinion.)

There were some outstanding exceptions. All of the University of Chicago returns endorsed the ACLU. In interviews many of the more sophisticated conservative leaders indicated their approval of ACLU, and a few said they might even join.

As we mentioned in an earlier chapter, the conservative position on civil liberties is often hopelessly intertangled with anti-Communism. The question which brought the highest conservative response on a Cornell poll was for retaining HUAC. Second highest was for aiding Chinese Nationalists on Matsu and Quemoy. Interestingly, the third highest conservative response was agreeing that the dress of students was too sloppy.[3] No canvassing was done of conservatives only.

The Chicago students who defended civil liberties demon-

3. Poll taken by Prof. Andrew Hacker's Behaviorial Studies Class, 1961.

strated their indifference to laissez-faire economics by going down the line for the New Deal. All but one would retain all nine of the New Deal economic measures cited. Generally conservatives split on these New Deal measures. Federal Deposit Insurance, Securities Exchange Commission, Minimum Wage, and Wagner Act were supported in that order. Most unpopular were farm subsidies, Reconstruction Finance Corporation, TVA, Federal Housing Administration, and Rural Electrification. These should all be dropped. Each part of the New Deal which they wanted to retain was a direct benefit to business. Three-quarters felt more businessmen should be in policy-making positions of government.

Only 28 percent of the conservatives endorse the Income Tax (versus 76 percent of liberals), a favorite Right-wing target. The Bureau will be relieved to learn that 43 percent are willing to tolerate it. Less than 18 percent would support federal aid for school construction (versus 83 percent of liberals). This question brought forth the highest degree of conservative protest among fourteen issue questions. It seems to epitomize his opposition to "statism."

Opposition to foreign economic aid (broken down almost evenly between oppose, tolerate, and endorse) was predictable, given the huge tax burden and charges of bungling and politics involved (yet liberals endorsed it by 80 percent). Also the coolness to coexistence comes as no surprise (15 percent endorse; 21 percent tolerate), although the liberal figures are only 46 percent endorse, 38 percent tolerate. The really alarming figures are on the United Nations.

Here you have a question that should not involve any economic dimension since costs are relatively insignificant. Anti-Communism seems to have dominated the picture. Only 21 percent of the conservative students endorse the UN; 23 percent will tolerate it. On the other hand, this issue brought forth the greatest liberal response: 87 percent endorsed it and 10 percent tolerated it.

Given these attitudes on foreign aid, coexistence, and the United Nations, it is not too difficult to predicate conservative foreign policy. It should be recalled that 60 percent of these students consider themselves moderate and 18 percent marginal conservatives. Although it is reassuring that only a 7 percent endorsement was given to Robert Welch, the ultraconservative implications for foreign policy are quite evident. When a Princeton senior said that we conservatives agree most on foreign policy, it was an understatement. Apparently when it comes to foreign policy, there is only one issue: anti-Communism; and all conservatives are ultraopposed. Hence foreign policy attitudes are spelled out in ultra-Right terms. The moderate-marginal brand of conservatism is not for export. It is restricted to the domestic free market.

The prospects for international idealism are considered grim to nonexistent, and the young conservative's reaction to the Peace Corps is illustrative. First Young Americans for Freedom (YAF) tried to hamstring it by demanding anti-Communist affidavits from the conscience-sensitive applicants. Then they labeled it the Kiddie Korps. A Princeton undergrad said his mother didn't object to him joining the Army, but what would she tell the neighbors if he joined the Peace Corps? Grove City Professor Hans Sennholz predicted that the Peace Corps would be no more effective than the Children's Crusade. These countries need businessmen, not students. The Corps is promoting socialism abroad.[4]

A glimmer of international idealism appears in the four goals listed by *Gentlemen of the Right*, a Cornell publication, second in caliber only to the University of Chicago's *New Individualist Review*. Editor William Grunbaum lists the publication's third goal as "national humility" which seeks modesty and caution in our world responsibilities. We should not try to impose our culture and institutions upon other institutions which have an equal claim to respect. Our highest obligation is to provide an example of a respectable, inwardly serene, prospering state.[5]

The October issue of 1961 sounded a warning against extremists. "It is time something was done by thinking conservatives to chastise the non-thinkers and denounce their activities, which have hindered the growth of an enlightened conservative movement in America. This publication has this denunciation as one

4. H. Sennholz, "The Peace Corps—Vegetable or Mineral?" *Analysis*, Nov., 1961.
5. Editorial, *Gentlemen of the Right*, May, 1961.

of its major goals. Excessive emotionality which is the most dominant characteristic in these people is to be condemned."

Editor Ronald Hamowy's criticism in the *New Individualist Review* of Buckley's policies has been mentioned earlier. Buckley's flamboyant style has been criticized by conservative leaders at Boston University and Columbia, and his attack on *America* didn't win many friends at Boston College or Fordham. A B.C. YAFer called Buckley's feud "foolish" and a Fordham conservative called it "rash and flippant."

Typical of a deep conservative commitment coupled with a rejection of the common extremism are the views of John Burnham, sophomore at Princeton. He doesn't want to set up "political gods or devils," and "Kirk's longing for the good old days does not move me . . . nor do I want to make a fetish out of economic liberalism." Burnham also supports the Peace Corps. However, he is a classics major and intends to take no courses in politics or sociology while at Princeton. John is an uncommon extremist. His strong views manage to avoid all of the ultrastereotypes making him a rugged intellectual individualist. His conservatism is just what the liberals need for jousting.

The vice-president of Princeton's Conservative Club, senior Bill Thom, is cut of the same cloth. The author was at Princeton during part of the Whig-Clio Colloquium on "The Reemergence of the Right Wing" in spring of 1962. Kent Courtney, chairman of the Conservative Society of America and editor of the New Orleans based *Independent American*, was holding forth on the plausibility of Robert Welch's foreign policy and maintaining that De Gaulle was indeed a Communist supporter.

I spoke to Thom outside the hall and asked him how many of the audience were with the speaker. "None," he replied. What he is saying is "intellectually ludicrous." People like Courtney, Walker, and Hargis may destroy the conservative movement, he added.

Thom reflected a very sophisticated conservatism. One of his major gripes was that the conservative point of view is never presented by a faculty member who believes in it. He feels a serious effort should be made to find a conservative faculty member for the Woodrow Wilson School of Public Affairs. If there aren't any, O.K., but first try.

This perspective of conservatism was also reflected by Edwin Blanchford, presiding Gentleman of the Right at Cornell. He said that Senator Goldwater sees things in blacks and whites while he sees them in grays. What the Cornell and Princeton conservative clubs fear from YAF is not only that the emphasis would be changed from intellectual discussion to political action but that the color scheme may exclude grays.

The most moderate voice of all is that of *Advance,* a Harvard publication which is really liberal Republican but prefers to speak of itself as "constructive conservative." They claim there are about sixty House GOP's from cities and suburbs who reject the unholy alliance with Dixie, and their appeal is geared to these men. "True conservatives are by nature suspicious of extreme solutions to complex problems."

Goldwater is criticized for not distinguishing between desirable and undesirable government. "The constructive conservative is distinguished from the liberal by his confidence that federal action is not inevitable if the problems of private enterprise and local government are detected and resolved early enough."[6] An article on British conservatism reminds Americans that in Britain tradition has been a source of flexibility and not an obstacle to change. The "hesitancy of the affluent" has been turned into a force for change. The GOP, on the other hand, has failed to recognize and accept "the conservative burden of anticipation."

Unfortunately, *Advance* is completely outside the pale of New Conservatism. It is referred to disparagingly as a Rockefeller publication. Conservatism has thus talked itself into the pathetic position of repudiating the very balance it must have to preserve it from wobbling ineffectually.

Given these limitations of Rightest ideology, why so many decisions for conservatism? For a variety of reasons these young men are irritated at liberalism. Here is a sample of some of their complaints. Harvard: Liberals are too complacent, have no new arguments, and tend to sloganize too easily. Boston University: Liberals do not look at both sides of the question and they are naïve in their attitudes toward Communism and the welfare state. Northeastern: There is no trust of the individual to choose his own economic path, and liberals are too defensive in foreign

6. "Ideology and the Party Split," *Advance,* March, 1962.

affairs. Boston College: Their view of men is all wrong, and they are always favoring the Left over the Right in foreign affairs.

Columbia: Smugness! They feel those in disagreement must have ulterior motives, be sexually frustrated, a hick, or unread. University of Virginia: Their educational permissiveness, especially in the education of children, also their bland equalitarianism. Duke: Liberals are too presumptuous and feel they have to speak out on all issues.

Frequently (70 percent of the time) you get charges of faculty bias. As one student put it, the Socratic manner is not a game at which two can play. Sometimes they complain about unfairness on term papers. One student felt he was getting a rough time because he had attempted to criticize relativism in Justice Holmes. These complaints are almost impossible to assay and actually are rather rare. It is the bias in classroom and readings that irritates most.

What conservative mentors have helped to crystallize this scattered opposition? The students have fairly consistently avoided extremes. Some interest in Ayn Rand has been sparked at Brooklyn College, University of North Carolina, Princeton, and even Boston College. But a Princeton senior said of Miss Rand's arguments, it is like giving a reasoned defense of monarchy. It is irrelevant. At most you hear reports of two or three Birchers on campus. Robert Welch was the most discredited figure in the entire poll (8 percent).

A sophomore girl from the University of Houston put it this way. "I don't know how to really classify myself exactly. I think that Robert Welch is an irrational nut. And I think the Kennedys are socialists. I think William Buckley is witty and charming. My parents are also conservatives."

But Buckley is only the number two persuader, followed by "friends," faculty, F.D.R. and the Mrs., Burke, and Kennedy. That's the way they were reported on an open-ended question on the poll. One student explained his conversion to conservatism as owing to "exposure to a real liberal," and another had read Father Coughlin somewhere. Number one, by several lengths, was Senator Goldwater.

M. Stanton Evans claims that Goldwater's *Conscience of a*

Conservative is the number one best-seller on the campus. Actually Mr. Russell Reynolds, General Manager of the National Association of College Stores, Inc., says there is no way of telling whether this is so or not since no central records have been kept. In my informal poll of fifteen college bookstores, only five considered it one of their best sellers. Seven said it was going slowly. State University of Louisiana reported that it had been one of their best sellers but is "slowly losing its attraction." Duke spoke of the drop-off in demand, and Barnes & Noble on Fifth Avenue said sales had "simmered down to a pretty slow trot."

But there is no denying the impact the book has had on the faithful. Almost 60 percent of the conservatives have read *Conscience of a Conservative*. A YAFer at Boston University said Goldwater's book sent him back to school. Critics, I am sure, wish it had had the same effect on Goldwater. While the Senator's simplicity and forthrightness had tremendous effect on students who were already conservative or conservative prone, there seems to have been no effect or even an adverse reaction on the part of the uncommitted student. When the conservative position was bared by Goldwater's candor, the majority of students were appalled by what they were offered.

This almost centripetal ideological force is excited by William Buckley also. A Northeastern student said of *God and Man at Yale*, the book "made me feel that others felt as I did. I felt that this side had been kept from me. . . . Liberals have always made things more complex than they are." Buckley has given tremendous assurance to the conservative activists who were looking for a galvanizer. But the young conservative sophisticate gives him strong second thoughts, and some can't take him at all. He has become such a controversial figure that on the liberal poll, his 4 percent endorsement ranks him between McCarthy (4.6 percent) and Robert Welch (2.5 percent).

Among the conservatives, Buckley ranks thirteen points behind Goldwater in popularity. This is remarkable given the briefness of his public career.

How are things going on campus? As one Harvard conservative said, "Conservatives are not as cowed as they were during Buckley's days." The editor of University of North Carolina's

Tar Heel found this out when he asked in an editorial, "If there are any conservatives around here I wish they would come out from behind the bushes." They did, he said. Certainly conservative clubs are increasing on campus. During the 1960-1961 season, 216 conservatively oriented clubs were formed. Liberals came up with 178 new ones.[7] The clubs average thirty-five to forty members. Young Americans for Freedom were overrepresented on my poll and almost equaled the number of Young Republicans.

At Hunter the YAF has displaced the Young Republicans who no longer have a campus chapter. YAF at Hunter claims that half its forty members turn out for meetings. Dues of $.75 per month are collected. This is very high. The usual political club is lucky to get $1.00 a year. (The Yale club charges only $.50 per year.) The Hunter *Arrow* opposes YAF editorially.

YAF does well on campuses where the economic libertarian spirit is strong and less well where traditionalism is strong. Three students at Duke considered themselves too conservative to join YAF. The Gentlemen of the Right at Cornell consider them crass, loud, and intruders on the turf. Despite this, YAF has taken a full-page $110-ad in the *Cornell Daily Sun* announcing its formation in the fall of 1962. A student at the University of Virginia merely commented that YAF was not "tweed" enough for campus.

A devastating attack against the YAF approach was published by *Insight and Outlook*, a conservative publication at the University of Wisconsin. The article was called "Mimeocracy" and asked why conservatives needed a national chairman. "The new conservative bureaucracy by mimeograph is not entirely unlike the Liberal bureaucracy to which these conservatives are presumably opposed. . . . If we claim the end justifies the means, what is going to justify the end we come to?" If this is a battle of ideas, why all the rallies and pickets? The writer preferred to fight fire with water. "Is there not an inherent danger . . . that in seeking amalgamation, coagulation, coalition, and company, the conservative cause is sowing the dragon's teeth—the Liberal dragon, I hasten to add—and will in time raise up the requisite crop of dead (or organization) men? . . . and what have we sold in exchange for

7. "Current Political Trends on American College and University Campuses," Ohio Wesleyan University Research Bulletin.

this particular National Young Conservative mess of pottage?"[8]

YAF leader Howie Philips got into hot water at Harvard. Philips, a prominent young conservative, had been elected president of the student council. This received great billing from *Time* and *Newsweek*. The insinuation that Harvard was going conservative infuriated those Cambridgemen who were not. Howie managed to overreach himself when he affixed his position as Council president on the letterhead of his latest front group, the Committee for an Effective Peace Corps (the anti-Communist affidavit, and so forth).

Miffed dissidents petitioned for a Council ruling which would bar the president and vice-president from holding office in or "acting as a spokesman for any partisan organization." This failed and Philips averted a censure move only by adjourning the meeting. The next meeting did pass a vote of "strong disapproval" of his actions. A move then developed to reexamine the entire student government organization to make it jibe more effectively with Harvard's house system.[9]

A law student at the University of North Carolina came up with a surprising piece of irony. Many students at the Law School, he confided, refuse to join YAF because they do not want the name of an extremist organization to appear on their law applications.

The conservative clubs attract a very determined crew. Boys from Villanova and the University of Pennsylvania helped the girls set up shop at Bryn Mawr, which for the first time has a conservative organization. This was not too difficult, said one young lady: "The average Bryn Mawr student always upholds at least one cause. She will arise and declaim anytime, anywhere." Girls generally have ignored the conservative revival. Only 15 percent of the conservatives polled were women, whereas 25 percent of the liberals were women.

The revealing part of the Bryn Mawr enterprise was this remark, "Many students who were interested in Republican politics per se came to us; but only the hard core conservatives

8. "Mimeocracy," *Insight and Outlook*, Jan., 1962.
9. *Harvard Crimson*, May 10, 1961.

remain."[10] If the campus conservative club is going to be merely the equivalent of a Marxist study group (a New Left Club has just formed at the University of North Carolina), this preference for the hard core is understandable. But Marxist study groups have been notoriously short of numbers and long on turnover when it comes to proselytizing. The young conservatives might keep this in mind.

The opposite approach might be the equivalent of a religious emphasis week where everyone is invited, if not shoved, into the act. This is precisely what occurred at Bob Jones University in Greenville, South Carolina. Bob Jones is a fundamentalist liberal arts school which does not belong to any "agnostic or materialist accrediting association." It was founded by evangelist Bob Jones, Sr., who claims that his university put "a red carpet on the sawdust trail."

Seven Right-wingers, including Billy J. Hargis, Dale Alford (Louisiana segregationist), and Dan Smoot, held forth for a week-long conference on Americanism. The seminar was to be part of the education program of the college. Students were held responsible in their courses for the content of the speeches. Students found no objections. "Everingham," said one student of a speaker, "had documented his speech with items from the *Congressional Record*, and still they call these men liars."

(The immediate credibility given any "public document" regardless of its context, sources, or content is one of the most exasperating hurdles one encounters in dealing with the credulous and poorly informed.)

Several students expressed shock at the facts they had learned. When asked if there were a minority opinion about the seminar, a student replied, "If there is a minority, it is definitely nil. . . . As Christians we believe the same thing: Principle, based on the Bible." Another added, "Why not appeal to the emotions if you are speaking the truth?"

President Bob Jones, Jr., put it on the line. "The Word of God is a conservative book and the man who believes the Word of God is by nature conservative." The reason for the unanimity of opinion became even clearer when President Jones added

10. "Breakthrough at Bryn Mawr," *Analysis*, Jan., 1962.

that no student who disagreed vocally with what was said at the seminar would be tolerated at the University.[11] At least not much time is wasted at Bob Jones University looking for the Truth.

This, of course, is an extreme case. However, if the Reverend Hargis is successful in bringing his Christian Crusade to more colleges, as he intends, the sideshow may remain as ridiculous as ever, but it will be heard. One is tempted to reply, it couldn't deserve a better fate; it is so absurd. But what is viewed as burlesque at Princeton is taken for tragedy at Bob Jones, and, most likely, Hargis's circuit will include more of the schools having "difficulties" with accrediting associations. He has never been bucking for Riverside Church, and he won't be after Columbia University. Much more is to be gained from unrolling his own Red carpet on the sawdust trail.

To return to recognizable conservatism, we do not have to proceed any further than the University of Virginia, where you encounter a hothouse of traditionalism. Everybody wears a jacket and tie here all the time. In a very conventional sense, the conservative rally is perpetual. There is quite a tradition to live up to. When I commented that the tiny whitewashed student rooms boxing the University's quadrangle looked like slave quarters, a student corrected me. "No, the slave quarters were in rooms below. Each student was once allowed to bring one slave to campus." And other colleges talk of traditions.

A transfer student from the University of Mississippi assured me that the University of Virginia was more conservative than either the University of Mississippi or the University of Alabama. The liberal editor of the *Mississippian* has been under attack from a *sub rosa* publication called *The Rebel Underground* because he soft-pedals segregation and favors the admission of Red China into the UN.

In contrast, the editor of Virginia's *Cavalier* is almost apolitical. "We have kept away from national issues ever since we gave up the wire services four years ago." He proved to be the only conservative student editor I was to meet. His conservatism, like

11. *Charlotte Observer*, Charlotte, N.C., Feb. 16, 1962.

that of the University's, was overwhelmingly social. The John Randolph Club includes members of both Intercollegiate Society of Individualists and YAF, but it is made apparent that YAFers had better toe the line. No formal affiliation with YAF's national organization exists. Instead of the Ivy League hazard of becoming an intellectual outcast, the YAFer at University of Virginia has to be worried about being a social pariah.

This social reserve can be stronger on Southern campuses than in Southern communities where economic expediency is a mitigating factor. Being "tweed" doesn't mean as much to young conservative businessmen. Young Americans for Freedom might well encounter on traditionalist Southern campuses some of the obstinancy which met the overtures of the CIO. However, it would not pay to generalize too much from the University of Virginia's unique example.

One final note on the gentlemen of Randolph. After some heady expositions on States' rights, the author stumbled across the following dusty plaque at the base of the imposing Jefferson Rotunda:

> Public Works Administration
> . . .
> Restoration of the University of
> Virginia Rotunda
> 1939

The devil which plagues both camps on every campus is still apathy. "Too bad you came to Duke," said a political science professor, "there isn't much student interest on this campus. You should try the University of North Carolina. They have a long history of student participation." Shortly after this a graduate student at Chapel Hill was lamenting the lack of student participation.

Student elections are usually hard hit by this. An editorial at Cornell reproached the senior class for electing its president with only 121 votes, 10 percent of the senior class.[12] Princeton had an even rougher time. At first try in the spring of 1962, there were

12. *Cornell Sun*, May 14, 1962.

not even enough candidates for senior office. One senior explained the apathy this way. Everyone who comes here was somebody. When they learn that they can't all be somebody, they do nothing. This paints a rather grim picture of future citizenship.

Given the apathy, what is the new conservatism doing to help dispel it? In the fall of 1961, one of the most vocal of Columbia's conservatives wrote a letter to the editor protesting "compulsory politics" as an activity of the student council. He accused the council of elitism and manipulation, of "claiming enthusiasm where there is only disillusionment." It was impertinent for the student council to take a political position in the name of the student body. "One's own conscience is burden enough."[13]

In reply *Spectator* editor Eric Levine agreed with the need for thought and voluntarism but felt the complaint was missing the essence of representative democracy by saying the Student Board should not take stands. These positions encourage rather than inhibit debate. A democratic government cannot wait for those not voting to participate. Finally, he asked, "Is the encouragement to think and debate a 'noneducative' purpose?"[14]

This exchange brings up the problem of what the conservative's attitude is going to be toward campus politics. If he chooses the Stoic alienation of a hard core in-group, or remains in individual isolation, he won't recruit many followers or change any campus policy. The conservative can hardly preach "community" and "responsibility" and then complain because students discuss national political issues and take stands.

Here we have the clue to YAF's appeal. These young conservatives insist on closing the gap between theory and practice. They agree that political issues should be discussed, but they want the conclusions to be theirs.

The *Spectator* exchange is a microcosm of the struggle going on in the National Student Association. This is a sort of congress representing nearly 400 student government associations and about 1.3 million students. Nearly all the major colleges

13. Letter to *Columbia Spectator*, Oct. 16, 1961.
14. Editorial Reply, *Spectator*, Oct. 20, 1961.

and universities belong. The group formed a few months after attending a world conference of students in Prague in 1946. At first the American group affiliated with (never joined) the International Union of Students. After the Czech coup of 1948 when the Communist orientation of the IUS became obvious, the non-Communist countries formed their own International Student Conference in Stockholm. "Unity" overtures with IUS were turned down with the comment, "There can be no unity of action when there is no unity of purpose."[15]

As members of the International Conference, Americans can participate in low-cost foreign travel and have students of other countries act as hosts. Student exchange, international tours, international sports, student relief, university reconstruction, and publications offer additional opportunities. NSA offers eighteen full summer scholarships in international relations for bringing foreign students to the U.S. This is arranged through a Ford Foundation grant.

NSA is the only student constituent member of the American Council on Education, the only student group in the National Education Association, and the only student representative on the U.S. National Commission for UNESCO.

The only library and research center devoted solely to student affairs is maintained by NSA in Philadelphia. Information and research data are supplied to student governments on every conceivable campus problem: cultural programs, radio and TV data, organizing of co-ops, housing, health, tutoring, political and social responsibilities, leadership training, course evaluation, and so on. Materials are sent to members upon request.

The organization was conceived by commendable idealism and has been characterized by extraordinary imagination, resourcefulness, and enterprise. It has received the acclaim of public figures ranging from President Kennedy to Russell Kirk.

Given such an admirable triumph over apathy, what is the complaint? Conservatives have objected to the consistently liberal policy positions in national and international affairs which NSA has taken since its inception. Particularly irritating has

15. P. Jones, *The History of NSA Relations with IUS*, Foreign Policy Research Institute, University of Pennsylvania, 1956.

been NSA's defense of Southern sit-ins and their call for the abolition of HUAC. Support of the UN in the Congo, the Nationalists in Algeria and the Indonesians in West New Guinea, and other groups has created further dissension.

NSA also believes in making a noise about student civil liberties. For example, a student named Charles Kamen heckled "Operation Abolition" at a showing by the Miami Rotary Club. The angered Rotarians pressured Kamen's draft board into opposing his draft deferment for the Peace Corps—since young Kamen was obviously not a suitable representative of Americanism. The Board obliged. NSA has championed Kamen's case.

Since conservative students are hopelessly outnumbered, they have taken a position similar to that of the *Columbia Spectator*'s letter. The charges are the same. First, NSA should not presume to speak for students, and, secondly, they should avoid off-campus politics. Much of the first objection could be removed if the organization would alter its preamble to read "we, *as* students . . ." rather than "We *the* students. . . ." This would seem to be a reasonable concession. But the major part of this first objection centers around an interpretation of those activities which do not affect students "in their role as students" (Constitution article X, section A).

An embarrassing weapon is used against NSA's penchant for standing on controversial questions. Section B of Article X says, "No substantial part of the activities . . . shall be devoted to carrying on propaganda or otherwise attempting to influence legislation."[16] This provision is necessary for tax-exempt status. Whether formal resolutions constitute lobbying is a technical point facing many educational organizations, including conservative ones. As an obstructionist minority, conservatives are insisting on a literal interpretation.

A further constitutional objection is that too many policy decisions are made between annual Congresses by the National Executive Committee. However, the only voting members of this committee are regional representatives, and the policies are valid only until the next Congress.

In January, 1962, the Young Republicans circulated a memo

16. *Codification of Policy* 1961-62, National Student Association.

to their campus chapters cautioning members about the liberal dangers of NSA. Besides the usual criticisms, this memo attacked the whole idea of "world student unity." Being a student is just a transitional phase. Political conditions in other countries give the student more importance. Anyway, their activities are generally against established government. This incredibly cavalier dismissal of the heroics of foreign students was coupled with a condemnation of Southern student sit-ins and the San Francisco demonstrations against HUAC—once again, protests against constituted authority.[17]

Students were urged to capture the NSA delegations, and if this failed to move for disaffiliation. The anti-NSA campaign has considerable force. An editorial in the *Daily Princetonian* advised calling off election of delegates to NSA until a vote was taken deciding whether Princeton should continue as a member.[18] The motion to withdraw failed by one vote in the student council.

At the University of North Carolina, selection of NSA delegates was put up to the entire student body for the first time. Generally delegates are chosen by the student governments, since technically these are the bodies represented. Conservatives went all out to corral votes. The results were surprising. The four-man delegation was split between two liberals and two conservatives. However, the two liberals were prominent campus personalities—the president and vice-president of the student government. The two conservatives were relatively unknown.

It is difficult to say how much of this vote was an expression of conservative strength and how much expressed dissatisfaction with NSA's "image," since the two conservatives were severely critical. Either way it was a jolt to the liberals.

YAF's opposition to NSA has been detailed in another chapter. Their overorganized efforts at the 1961 Madison Congress, where they wore suspenders to tell friends from

17. "The National Student Association," Program Issue Number Two, Jan., 1962, College Service Committee Young Republican National Federation, Washington.
18. Editorial, *The Daily Princetonian*, April 24, 1962.

enemies, brought forth the comment that Young Americans for Freedom was "the most pretentiously misnamed political alliance since the Holy Alliance."

There was no repeat performance at Columbus in 1962. Things were pretty quiet. "Most delegates said that last year's tactics had brought discredit on the noisier and more doctrinaire conservatives. The conservatives said they believed they could accomplish more by working quietly and persuasively."[19] Two controversial resolutions were passed. One condemned the McCarran Act for infringing civil liberties; the other condemned nuclear testing for military and political reasons.

Conservatives might have abandoned a frontal attack on NSA, but sniping operations will probably continue as long as conservatives consider themselves a continuing minority.

Where does this conservative minority find encouragement on campus? The faculty is overwhelmingly opposed. Perhaps their monolithic opposition is a kind of perverse encouragement. About one-third of the conservative clubs have encountered difficulties from the administration. Trying to get a faculty adviser can be a hopeless search, especially if the administration insists that the adviser come from one of the social science departments.

Grove City College (Pennsylvania) with Economist Hans Sennholz is a rare exception. Sometimes a faculty member will sponsor a conservative group just because he thinks the campus needs it. This might explain Andrew Hacker's sponsorship of Gentlemen of the Right at Cornell. The alumni have been a great help at Cornell. It is said that the conservative club operates on about $5,000 a year budget supplied by alumni contributors, some of whom have stopped giving to the regular alumni fund because they consider the University too liberal.

Bookstores are not very helpful. Most of the books, except in the larger stores, are there at the sufferance of professors' whims. Goldwater's *Conscience of a Conservative*, Buckley's *Up from Liberalism*, Viereck's *Conservatism*, and Rossiter's *Parties and Politics in America* sell. But students buy only paperbacks, and there are not too many conservative offerings. The Yale

19. "Students Parley Ends in Harmony," *New York Times*, Aug. 31, 1962.

Co-op did report that conservatives tend to buy more books to give away than liberals.

Kennedy, White, Galbraith, Schlesinger, Mills, Stevenson, Kissinger, Burns, and Lipset are the names most frequently mentioned by the bookstores as their dependable movers. Only one of the fifteen stores polled carried the *National Review*, the most popular of the conservative magazines. Yale reported that they sold about three copies of each issue. While mail subscriptions account for most of these magazines, stall sales might catch interested eyes.

Consequently, many of the student clubs have taken up writing for each other. *The Entrepreneur* at Grove City College is true to its name—straight economic libertarianism. More in the nature of a newsletter, the publication makes enough profit to bring in one heavy speaker a year. *The Campus Conservative* is edited by students at the University of Mississippi and the University of Virginia. It is distributed free to five Virginia colleges and all major schools in Mississippi. It gets as far as San Diego, claims thirty colleges in all, and circulates 15,000 copies per month. "Algerian Peace—Western Setback?" is a typical headline. Giving the liberals some of their own medicine, *The Campus Conservative* has pasted together Black Muslims, American Nazi Party, and Campus ADA as "ultra-Left." *Judgment at Nuremberg, The Rise and Fall of the Third Reich*, and the Eichmann trials are seen as unnecessary strains on our German alliance.[20]

When I wondered facetiously in an earlier chapter whether the Madison Conservative Club had taken to pushing McGuffey Readers, I had not read the January, 1962, issue of *Insight and Outlook*. They are. It must be admitted they give a persuasive case for dropping the "see spot run" readers. This well edited magazine has machine-tooled ads. Twelve of the seventeen ads in the January issue were for machine or steel products. There were none of the usual campus ads from service enterprises. The closest service ad was from a stockbroker.

The best of these young conservative efforts is probably the University of Chicago's *New Individualist Review*, which was discussed earlier. If young conservatives would only accept it as a conservative journal, first prize would easily go to Harvard's

20. *The Campus Conservative*, April, 1962.

Advance, spokesman for Modern Republicanism. Its maiden issue on the Republican Congress called "Revise and Dissent" was one of the best critiques of what is wrong with the GOP that I have read. It was reported to have caused a three-day stir on Capitol Hill.

"The Republican leadership," said *Advance,* "looks too much like the baseball team whose 'strategy' was to 'wear out' the opposition running them around all those bases."[21] The magazine claimed it was suicidal to keep Goldwater as head of the GOP Senate campaign committee, since he does not appreciate the importance of minority and urban interests. Why cozen up to Dixie when there are five marginal Democratic Congressional seats to be won in New York State?

Unfortunately for the young conservatives, such voices of sophisticated pragmatism appear to be the continuing minority of the conservatives.

What is the size of this overall minority? How many gentlemen have the conservatives managed to rally? At Yale where New Conservatism got an early start and the conservatives claim it is difficult to get liberals to debate, the politically active were estimated by undergraduate Peter Braun to number about 8 percent. Of this figure, 5 percent were conservatives, Peter maintained. University of Virginia conservative Jerry Reel (editor of *The Campus Conservative*) estimated overall participation at 2 to 3 percent giving his side less than half. Vice-president Bill Thom of Princeton's Conservative Club put participation at 5 percent, conceding each faction half. This is going to vary with each campus.

The Opinion Research Corporation of Princeton, New Jersey, sets conservative club membership in 36 colleges, with active memberships, at under 1 percent of the total student body. It is going to take a lot of fast talking and conspiracy to convert this into a decent insurrection, let alone a revolution.

Rick Ballard, editor of the *Harvard Crimson,* was asked if the liberal student group Tocsin ever debated the conservative club. "I don't think they would debate them, but they might play them in softball."

21. "Revise and Dissent," *Advance,* March, 1962.

CHAPTER 14

Young Men in Business and Politics

THE following case interviews were conducted with young men in business and politics. In selecting those for interviews, an attempt was made to keep the cutoff age at thirty-nine, which is the top limit for Young Republicans and Young Americans for Freedom. Young conservative congressmen were chosen on the basis of the lowest scorings on the ADA Congressional Index and their general conservative reputation. An attempt was made to obtain a regional spread.

The young men in business were recommended as being representative of conservative opinion by business or professional men in their respective communities. No other requirements than being young and conservative were asked. Each turned out to emphasize an individual viewpoint which reflects the multiform nature of conservatism. This chance selection turned up just about every variety.

Here is what they had to say.

HONORABLE BRUCE ALGER, TEXAS

As a former philosophy major at Princeton, Congressman Alger is very interested in the ideological dimension of conservatism and is rather conscience-stricken over what he has not been able to read. He not only knew of Ayn Rand but had read all her novels plus *For the New Intellectual.* Miss Rand's thoroughgoing individualism captivated him, but her emphasis upon self-reliance in the area of spiritual resourcefulness went too far. A person must be a steward to the Almighty, says Mr. Alger, and Ayn Rand's cul-de-sac of atheism ruins her title of philosophical champion of conservatism. He agrees that perhaps he might disagree with other aspects of objectivism upon deeper reading.

Walter Lippmann presents a "false version" of current events, says Mr. Alger. He feels himself on more solid ground reading *United States News* and "Human Events." *National Review* (sent gratis to all Congressmen) gets read occasionally. There are no major disagreements with Editor Buckley.

Goldwater could not be supported on his scheme of allowing college education funds to be tax deductible. Alger prefers to limit any federal assistance to multistate projects such as area resource development. In any question of public spending, two questions must be asked: (a) Is it constitutional? and (b) Can we afford it? We should never spend beyond our budget. Congressman Alger considers himself a student of taxation and pointed to a sixteen-inch pile of folders on a current tax bill.

Priding himself on his consistency, Congressman Alger declared that he had been the only member to vote against the school milk bill in the House. The government does not have the duty to feed and clothe people. It should never attempt to be more than an umpire.

In answering questions on degrees of tolerance toward Communists, Mr. Alger made it clear that he felt forced to answer with a low degree of tolerance because of the special nature of the Communist menace. Therefore, an admitted Communist should not be given permission to speak. If our people were more convincingly educated, he said, my answers would be different. He would also approve taking a book of an admitted Communist out of the local library for the same reason. It is too easy to mislead the people.

Congressman Alger regretted the necessity of such answers. Then he went on to say that a Communist entertainer should be removed from a television network, not for what he was doing, but because he was a Communist and hence a dedicated traitor. However, he would not go along with any boycott of the program's product. The Communist could be punished in other ways.

When asked if a clerk in a store should be fired for being a Communist, Mr. Alger replied that the law was wrong for allowing this man to be free. "I am a rebel against the law which permits Communists to operate. They should either be expelled or jailed." Other nonconformists such as atheists could be tolerated in these situations, but there can be no freedom for traitors.

Alger felt a leftish bias prevented the American Civil Liberties Union from being an effective watchdog of freedom. There was no protest from ACLU when Bernard Goldfine was tried by the press or when the House Rules Committee was packed and its functions distorted by the Kennedy Administration. As a result of taking these positions, Alger misses some of the former liberal courtesies such as being invited to union halls to speak or getting liberals to debate.

A major illusion of liberals, says Alger, is that life can be made to live up to our expectations. This naïveté is complicated by a liberal misunderstanding of the economics of capitalism, the limitation of government, and of what people are like. Liberals will not allow people to be people. President Kennedy illustrates this. He doesn't know his own or other people's limitations.

Alger sees this failure in Congress. "We are not honest and straightforward. . . . If Congress voted honestly, we would vote our convictions." No one ever complains about Alger not voting his. Although he bases these convictions firmly on the Bible, Alger does not consider himself a religious Fundamentalist. Personal tragedies in life have convinced him that his appraisal of men is basically sound. Alger realizes what a terrible press he is getting. But he also believes that the talks he is giving have never been given before, and he feels his constituents are solidly behind him.

Alger is conscious of a responsibility for his public image.

Although he will drink, he tries never to do so in public or at parties where it might be said that he was reveling with well oiled friends. This is not done through hypocrisy but out of a sense of propriety, part of the self-discipline a public representative should be willing to assume.

As the only Republican member of the House from Texas, Congressman Alger could be expected to be a maverick. Many of his conservative colleagues consider him long on philosophical conviction while sometimes short on political discretion. But Bruce Alger would probably rather consider himself a militant in conservatism's Defense Department rather than a negotiator in its Diplomatic Corps.

HONORABLE WILLIAM JENNINGS
BRYAN DORN, SOUTH CAROLINA

Congressman Dorn was not named after William Jennings Bryan because of the crusader's easy money policy. The Congressman's father had opposed our entry into World War I. When Bryan finally broke with President Wilson over foreign policy, the rupture was memorialized by giving junior the full treatment. Evidently not self-conscious of the honor, Congressman W. J. B. Dorn uses just about the entire lower third fold of a business letter for his signature.

It is made clear that Mr. Dorn considers himself a representative of South Carolina *to* the United States government. The emphasis is understandable. South Carolina has been considerate of Mr. Dorn. When elected at twenty-four, he was the youngest member sent to South Carolina's state senate and had to be seated by a special vote. Localism cannot be stressed enough. For example, Mr. Dorn favors local civil rights but not federal on the theory that no race can ever be persecuted on a nationwide basis as long as the fifty state constitutions are as strong as possible. As an example of South Carolina's tolerance, Dorn points out that for twenty-two years the speaker of the legislature has been a Jew.

After the Civil War Calhoun's theory of state compact ceases to remain a matter of debate. It becomes a matter of apologetics. Mr. Dorn's grandfather came home from the Civil War with five dollars in his pocket. He gave the five dollars to the preacher to get married, went to work on the land, and died a wealthy man. South Carolina was in a worse state after the Civil War than France or Germany was after World War II. But she pulled herself up by her own bootstraps without looking to Washington for help.

This is the spirit of self-reliance which motives Congressman Dorn. "I could start out anew with a false name and a moustache . . . and I could go up the ladder. . . . Try me for a week, and then pay me!" Young men who apply to him for work in terms of how much pay and vacation time they can command disgust him. He said he gave twice the salary originally intended to a deserving young man who didn't even bring up the subject.

You get the feeling that Mr. Dorn is more alarmed about the real decreasing number of Horatio Algers than the potential increase of Alger Hisses. Although safely anti-Communist, Dorn scores rather high on the question of tolerating individual Communists. He would allow a confirmed Communist to speak in public, have his book in a public library, and perform as a singer on television. Boycotting the sponsoring product of the Communist entertainer should be up to the individual. Citizens of the Congressman's home town have in the past boycotted the products of G. Mennon Williams's company on the belief that his extreme Left views outraged the theory of free enterprise upon which his fortune was based.

"I never speak against Communism because psychologically it is bad. It is advertising the subject," says Mr. Dorn. "It's like lecturing girls on the evils of sin." It's much better to emphasize something positive. After addressing a Right-wing group in Chicago, someone came up after his speech and asked him why he failed to mention Communism. Dorn reminded him that in presenting a program of positive Americanism, he was talking against Communism.

The race issue is handled in the same way. Dorn, who hails from strongly segregationist west South Carolina, says he never mentions the race issue in a campaign. He doesn't want to play this up any more than Communism. Living up to his words of moderation, Congressman Dorn has never joined the KKK or a Citizens Council. He feels that the United States has handled the race problem more smoothly than any other country in the world.

"I am as conservative as anybody you can find," insists Dorn, and one of the things that keeps him so is liberal hypocrisy. The liberal in America, he claims, is the most intolerant person in the world. Look how they hounded Lindbergh, Wheeler, and Nye. On the other hand, "I don't care if Henry Wallace was backed by Stalin, he deserved to be heard." Similarly people should be willing to listen to Robert Welch. "Liberals never come to hear us. . . . We hear them all the time." Dorn also criticizes the liberals for their conformity. If you have seen one, you have seen them all. And what the nonacademically oriented Dorn especially resents is that every time he brings up a point, the liberals want to know what book he got it from. "I got it from the farm, knowing people, etc.!"

Of the six Congressmen interviewed, Dorn showed the keenest interest in the aesthetic responsibility of government. Personally gracious, Dorn feels the government should encourage beauty in public buildings whenever it can. "Beauty is important for making people feel good." South Carolina's state capitol building is an architectural gem, boasts Dorn. Also he does not begrudge expenditures for beautification on his farm. A Southerner's pride in region and family evidently explains some of this aesthetic concern.

But even these expenditures should not be made if it involves getting into debt. Debt is bad morally and educationally. The government must set a good example. "I take better care of the people's money than my own." And he is proud of turning money back to the Treasury. Admitting that there is tremendous political mileage in the saw: "the more money you roll, the more people get it," Congressman W. J. B. Dorn would prefer to reduce the rolls and encourage self-reliance. Far from throwing in a towel in this fight, Mr. Dorn has given us a William Jennings Bryan Dorn II.

HONORABLE EDWARD J. DERWINSKI, ILLINOIS

When the neighborhood boy emerges from a creditable Catholic college lauding its conservative professors and joins the Moose, Eagles, and five veterans' groups, he shows signs of becoming a dependable citizen. When he joins Kiwanis and becomes president of a savings and loan association, he becomes a "J.C." dream. Accordingly in 1959 and 1961, the Chicago Junior Association of Commerce and Industry voted Edward Derwinski one of the city's ten outstanding young men.

Congressman Derwinski reflects the confidence of the solid blocks he has used in building his career. Taciturn, he does not believe in speaking too soon or too often on the floor. He says he prefers to hold his fire until he sees the whites of their eyes and criticizes some of his more volatile colleagues to his right for not being more temperate. The important thing is not to make a fuss but "to see what you can salvage from a principle." For example, which one of the education bills is *least* objectionable?

A similar realism is applied to the far Right. Their "nutty schemes" such as the impeachment of Earl Warren are described as sheer stupidity. It is much more important to concentrate energies on electing conservative candidates and supporting or opposing specific legislation.

But the Chamber of Commerce need not fear that its principles are being unduly compromised. Derwinski is against all foreign aid (with its "roads to nowhere") and has introduced a House resolution to reduce nonessential expenditures in the Federal Government through an orderly 10 percent reduction in personnel by not filling more than one out of four vacancies in Federal agencies until a reduction of 10 percent is reached.

The far Right was also pleased by Derwinski's threat to introduce legislation to prohibit any purchase of the United Nations bond issue.

"Liberals as I see them here in Washington are socialists," says Derwinski. When asked to suggest some of the things that irritated him about the liberals, he said, "Liberals don't irritate me. They scare me." Their economic and foreign policy is viewed as disastrous. To shore up the administration's soft foreign policy line, Mr. Derwinski introduced a bill to create a special House Committee on Captive Nations. This is an understandable gesture on behalf of a Congressman who belongs to five Polish-American organizations. So far Dean Rusk has not warmed up to the idea.

This ethnic preoccupation explains one break with Senator Goldwater. The Arizona Senator wants to restrict immigration. The Chicago Congressman wants to expand it. Apparently the usual conservative economic arguments can not be heard against the Baltic sea of voters.

But we are back guarding the Treasury when it comes to the question of spending additional funds to enhance the architecture of new public buildings. This doesn't make very good business sense. It is all right to incorporate a regional style in the architecture, but not at additional expense. Nor should we hesitate to turn over portions of public lands for the development of private enterprises. Derwinski shows as little sympathy for the conservationist who tends to get "dogmatic and emotional" as he does for the aristocratic conservative whose sense of "good form" contains more "frills" than the business community's.

On the tolerance scale toward individual Communists in the community, Derwinski rates high. He would allow the acknowledged Communist to speak in public, have his books in the public library, and sing on television. And he sees no reason for a boycott of a sponsoring product. But he does not endorse the objectives of the American Civil Liberties Union. This organization, says Derwinski, is a typical case of the liberal's attempt to "regiment minds." When they oppose nativity scenes in the public schools, they are being just as dogmatic as the John Birch Society.

This is refreshing realism and reflects the image of judicious balance which Congressman Derwinski is trying to cultivate. He prefers to wait until the problem has come before his jurisdiction and *then* he will give an opinion on the facts he has. This is to avoid the appearance of generalization. Derwinski's wild generalizations about foreign aid perhaps indicate that his carefully contrived posture is fine for a judge who can circumvent political realities but impossible for a legislator who has to face them every day.

HONORABLE JOHN H. ROUSSELOT, CALIFORNIA

Richard Nixon wasn't the only enterprising young man that Whittier, California, sent to Washington. The president and owner of John H. Rousselot and Associates, Public Relations Consultants, also made it. Becoming a freshman Congressman at thirty-three was quite an achievement for a young ad man. Admitting that he was one of the two members of the John Birch Society in the House of Representatives (Hiestand of California is the other) seemed to violate every tenet of his profession. Rousselot's hard sell approach proves that Madison Avenue can't be right all the time. In an interview the Congressman sounded much less extreme than many of his public pronouncements.

When asked if an admitted Communist should be granted permission to speak in his community, Rousselot hesitated and then said it would be all right if the group were reasonably mature. He should not be allowed to speak before a high school group, for example. Also certain civic platforms may be justifiably limited by local law. Otherwise, let him speak. What if this professed Communist had a book in the local library, and someone suggested it should be removed, would you favor removal? Quite readily, the Congressman said no, as long as the library wants to keep the book, let it. After all, libraries have many books by Marx, and he is a pretty devoted Communist. It might help, however, to have Communist books so labeled.

What if the avowed Communist were a television entertainer? Should he be fired from his position? No, affirmed Rousselot, not unless there was a violation of some provision of the Federal Communications Act. Leave it up to the viewers. If they feel his Communist beliefs are becoming obtrusive and demand his removal, then it is something else. Should his sponsor's product be boycotted? Here Rousselot was uncertain. First he said he probably would. Then he confessed he wasn't sure. Preferring to stress the positive, Rousselot admitted that he admired sponsoring companies which did a yeoman's job in the ideological battle. He said he was more interested in encouraging those sponsors who were doing a good job. For example, he wrote letters commending Richfield Oil and Union Oil for television programs they had sponsored in California, and he tries to favor their products.

The extent to which Congressman Rousselot carried his aversion to centralization was surprising. He was asked if there were any public position taken by Senator Goldwater with which he disagreed. After considerable thought, the Congressman said he opposed Goldwater's metropolitan government concept. Actually this is a project of more interest to Barry Goldwater's brother in Phoenix, but the Senator is on the board. It is a group favoring more amalgamation around a metropolitan nucleus and some urban planning. The pull of localism is so strong for Rousselot that even metropolitan organization appears undesirable.

Goldwater's scheme providing federal income tax write-offs for education got no encouragement from Rousselot. The only time federal aid to education is justified is when the Federal government moves a defense plant or some installation into an area and puts an extraordinary strain on the locality's school system.

Treading lightly on the segregation problem, "My state has not faced a massive Negro problem . . . ," Rousselot ended up a bit to the left of William Buckley, Jr., who favors peaceful sit-ins. According to the Congressman, restaurants open to the public should have a responsibility to serve the public. This is all a part of being in business. However, no law should be passed requiring restaurants to live up to this responsibility. This has generally been the approach of non-Southern conservatives to segregation. Even when they admit its injustice, they propose nothing stronger than local option for a remedy.

The leitmotiv of the interview was Mr. Rousselot's recurring emphasis on individualism. Ayn Rand was extolled for her admittedly erratic individualism. The important thing is to think out your own solutions and stick with them. Never be afraid to voice them. Franklin D. Roosevelt was admired by Mr. Rousselot for the outspoken positions he would take on issues. Too many people keep silent. Perhaps Mr. Rousselot's Christian Science background in part helps explain his willingness to stand on unpopular issues and his generous supply of self-reliance. Some of Mr. Rousselot's conservative colleagues consider his inability to keep silent on some issues a major liability.

One of the most irritating things about liberals, said Congressman Rousselot, was their very claim to the word "liberal."

Today's "liberal" is far too much of a collectivist to have any right to the designation "liberal." This is a common irritation among conservatives. Consequently many of them like to style themselves "libertarians," meaning a belief in nineteenth century liberalism. Also the liberal is too willing to spend tax money as if it didn't belong to anybody. When asked to suggest a third gripe against the liberals, Rousselot came up with another favorite, "their arrogance." This is in keeping with the conservative's view of the Liberal Establishment which has wallowed in its own conceit far too long.

On the Birch Society, Rousselot loyally defended Robert Welch's leadership as necessary and inoffensive. He admitted that the International Communism Score Board published in *American Opinion* might be inaccurate here and there. How about the listing of the United States as being 40-60 percent under Communist domination? "The 40 percent score is probably true," claimed Rousselot. You see this especially in government, education, journalism, communications, and business. How about Welch's suggestion that citizens cash in their government bonds in protest against administration policies? Rousselot thought this was perfectly all right, but he would not personally do it. It might, after all, be questionable form for a Congressman.

Mr. Rousselot's stand on the American Civil Liberties Union was a bit confused. He said their original principles of defending the right of anyone to speak were fine, but their current programs render conservative support impossible. By current programs, he meant support of entry of Red China into the United Nations. But the ACLU has never taken this position. Their by-laws prohibit policy declarations outside the civil liberties field.

Much of John Rousselot's reputation has been prejudged because of his membership in the Birch Society. But this membership is just an occasion of his conservatism. It is worn as casually as his Kiwanis pin.

HONORABLE JAMES F. BATTIN, MONTANA

The Congressional team of Montana is perfectly balanced as far as the ADA scoreboard of the 78th Congress is concerned.

Democrat Olsen has a perfect 100 percent, and Republican James Battin has a neat "0."

James Battin's conservatism is probably the most conventional of those of the Congressmen interviewed. He answers to a wealth of social stereotypes normally associated with the middle-class conservative. A Kansas-born Congregationalist who becomes a Mason, Shriner, and member of Demolay would arouse few suspicions of radicalism. As an Elk, Moose, American Legionnaire, and member of the Junior and Senior Chambers of Commerce, Battin seems to have satisfied the most demanding Americanist prerequisites. He is not a vogueish conservative like Derwinski who exploits his efficient anti-Communism, nor a militant causist like Rousselot. Neither could he be considered a conservative intellectual like Alger or Goodell. He is closer to being a sincere Babbitt who has yet to be disillusioned by Main Street.

While both Congressmen Dorn and Rousselot would favor the government spending extra funds to make civic buildings more beautiful, Congressman Battin would rather save taxpayers the money. And unlike his two colleagues, Battin does not find the advertising on television objectionable. It is accepted as an economic fact of life. Very little conflicts with Congressman Battin's theory of economic self-reliance. Yet he insisted that he is not as conservative as Senator Goldwater. "I will support a program that is good regardless of party." As an example, he offered his support of legislation for educational television. This is a pretty safe federal program for a Montana conservative to support.

Montana is very conscious of its unique space problems. Battin claims to represent the largest territory for a Congressional district outside Alaska. There are great difficulties in getting qualified teachers to staff the tremendously dispersed school system. Even centralized schools cannot draw from too great a distance. Educational television seems an ideal answer to the problem of getting good teaching into remote areas. In this instance federal assistance could be used to further the interest of localism.

Mr. Battin has two constructive suggestions for aiding education. Both of them, he felt, would strengthen rather than weaken local authority. First he favors a "pass back" system of federal assistance. For example, 2 percent of the federal income tax could be paid directly to the education agency of the state. This is a stronger plan than Goldwater's tax rebate scheme which would make state use of the money for education optional, not mandatory. Another suggestion is to have a program of federal assistance to education, but first require all states to live up to a tolerable level of state taxation. One of the things conservatives especially resent is the free-loader. If states are not willing to pull hard on their own bootstraps first, there is no reason why they should receive federal help. Given such an alternative, lethargic state legislatures would take the necessary action.

In speaking of the differences between liberals and conservatives, Congressman Battin held to a moderate position by insisting that the goals of both groups are the same; the difference comes in methods. The major difference in means is the issue of the centralization of power in the federal government. By its sheer physical remoteness, says Battin, the federal government is bound to be insensitive to local differences. In planning for government housing programs, how is the federal government going to know how much snow load to expect on the roofs or what the special problems of heating might be? There is too much danger that a federal administration of housing would not appreciate the importance of these problems.

This business of playing means against ends can be very handy politically. Battin insisted that he approved of the principle of foreign aid, but because there was such a lack of proper administration of funds, he had to oppose the current program. If we ran specific, closely controlled projects, that would be a different matter. Consequently, Battin voted against the administration's foreign aid bill in the 78th Congress. The same is true of the United Nations. It can be an excellent political forum, but, after all, nothing was done about India taking Goa. Incidentally, Congressman Battin disapproves of military action on the part of the United Nations. Liberals have long accused conservatives of indulging in far too convenient a perfectionism in foreign affairs.

Congressman Battin's moderation is highly in evidence on the question of political tolerance. Should a Communist be allowed to speak in the community? As long as he is an acknowledged Communist and not trying to pass as a liberal, this is perfectly all right. There were no other qualifications. No books should be removed from community libraries merely because they were written by Communists. Let the Communist entertainer sing on television, Battin would not have him removed. Would you favor a boycott of his sponsor's product? "I am not a boycotter." Unlike Congressman Rousselot's answers, which were products of considerable agonizing, Battin's answers were immediate and direct. His tolerance was never in doubt.

However, he did share Rousselot's misconception about the American Civil Liberties Union. He too believed that the ACLU favored admitting Red China into the United Nations. Battin's tolerance seemed to reach the straining point with the Civil Liberties Union. He objected to it because it had become too much of a pressure group. A bit ambiguous on this, what he apparently meant was that the Union had been supporting too many liberal causes, and frequently picayune ones such as opposing Christmas carols in public schools.

Congressman Battin had not heard of Ayn Rand and considers William Buckley, Jr., too conservative. Proud of the fact that "50 percent of the time I voted on the prevailing side," Battin is typical of the meat and potato variety of conservatives who usually dominate the House of Representatives.

HONORABLE CHARLES E. GOODELL, NEW YORK

When the voters of the Jamestown area in western New York replaced Daniel A. Reed with Charles Goodell, they were still represented by a dependable Republican, but they were in for a new species of conservative. Goodell is Phi Beta Kappa from Williams College and has both an LL.B. and a Master's degree in Government from Yale University. This impressive academic record was tempered by a brief career in semipro baseball and time out for four sons.

In an interview Goodell played it cagey. He wouldn't take

just any question coming over the plate. The issue that did especially interest him was the difference between the contemporary liberal and conservative. "I am a liberal in Mill's sense," claimed Goodell. This, of course, refers to the early John Stuart Mill, not to his later years when he favored Socialism. Today, said the Congressman, it is the conservative who talks about the individual. Liberals are not sufficiently excited about the quality and the potential of the individual. They have dropped the ball of individualism and the conservatives have picked it up. The skepticism of the liberal regarding free economic enterprise would be one example of this. Goodell implies that in this area the liberal has no taste for innovation, experimentation, and risk-taking.

Even more dangerous is the liberal's inability to fathom the nature of Communism. They are far too trusting of professed good intentions. Obviously Mr. Goodell wishes the liberal had not expended quite so much of his skepticism on economic individualism; more could be used on Communist professions of good faith. Because the liberal is so trusting, he is susceptible to being used for Communist purposes.

There are two further objections to liberals, which especially annoy the Congressman. The liberal is generally ignorant regarding money matters. And he has too facile an approach to politics, forcing issues into arbitrary molds. This first charge might be translated to mean that Congressman Goodell cannot agree with very many liberals on economics. Resentment of the arbitrary categorization or labeling of issues is largely a reflection of Goodell's academic background and is a healthy resentment wherever it truly applies. Unfortunately, it is a charge which could apply to either side. This is a complaint about over-simple thinking, the temptation to resolve a problem with a hastily moistened label or an overworked cliché. Nothing can quicken tempers faster, harden positions, and deaden the prospects of compromise more readily than this misplaced sense of logical neatness. It is heartening to hear a Congressman complain about it, but you can hardly expect liberals to dispel clichés about "profit-hungry corporations" until the conservatives have exorcized the specter of "creeping socialism."

Unlike Congressmen Derwinski and Battin, Goodell does

favor appropriating extra public funds for building architecturally beautiful buildings. Merely being utilitarian is not enough for a public building. Soviet society, said Goodell, suffers from being too dull and utilitarian. People should be willing to pay the extra revenue required for this deference to beauty. This curtsey to cultural values is rare among today's conservatives who, like Congressman Battin, would generally rather save the money.

Goodell would not say whom he considered to be a good conservative. He did say that he disagreed with Senator Goldwater on some points, one of them being the United Nations. Goodell feels too many people are asking too much of the United Nations and are not being realistic about its limitations. He voted for the Kennedy foreign aid bill, which gave him one plus on his ADA rating, but he has been very critical of its administration and feels that there is a real danger that we might overextend ourselves in trying to provide foreign economic aid. Goldwater's plans for returning money to the states for education was generally backed. Actually Goodell's position was closer to Congressman Battin's. The failure of the administration to propose this or a similar remedy has been especially frustrating, since Goodell feels the localities do need some kind of assistance.

One Kennedy bill which Goodell was enthusiastic about was the measure to provide for the retraining of men displaced by automation or economic relocation. This kind of self-help he considered sound legislation.

On the tolerance scale, Goodell gave carefully measured and qualified answers. The admitted Communist may speak but not to urge violence. His books should not be removed from the public library, but the library should inform the public that they are by a Communist author. He did suggest the red labels pushed by the Birch Society for this purpose. The Communist television singer may remain on the network but the network should be alert for any abuse of his privilege. No boycott of a product is favored. Most of the conservatives are living up to the broad objectives of the American Civil Liberties Union, whether they formally endorse them or not.

Welch and his Birch Society are unduly berated and overrated, says Goodell. One of their chief values has been to demonstrate how eagerly liberals will resort to guilt by association if it serves their purpose. After all, the Congressman reminds us, there are more extreme Left-wingers in government than Right-wingers. What we are really witnessing is the liberal counterpart to the McCarthy era. Now the Right is being intimidated.

Congressman Goodell is fond of a local country adage: "Spraying the orchard is not merely to kill worms." He used it to explain what appears to be such a negative record on the part of Congressional conservatives. Our objections, he affirms, although negative per se, are also taken to allow the survival of other ideas and practices.

DERWOOD CHASE,
CHARLOTTESVILLE, VIRGINIA

During the 1960 presidential campaign, the Republicans of Charlottesville approached Derwood Chase, who owns his own investment counseling firm, and asked him to lead a group of young professionals for Nixon. Feeling little enthusiasm for Nixon but less for Kennedy, Mr. Chase took on the assignment. The experience whetted his appetite for political contest. After the campaign, he and several co-workers decided that what the community and the political parties needed was an organization which would sharpen up the political issues and emphasize the clarity and importance of the conservative position.

The intention of forming such a group was announced. A meeting produced about seventy-five interested citizens. They called themselves Virginians for Conservative Government. Mr. Chase became a director and chairman of the education committee. Today there are 250 members; some are in other states. Along with seven other local conservative groups, the Virginians for Conservative Government are represented in the Virginia Conservative Council, a state coordinating agency. The VCG is primarily an educational effort. Speeches and articles are screened for sound conservative material and sent out to members. Frequently, reprints of "Human Events" articles are mailed. Speeches by T. Coleman Andrews, Clarence Manion, and

Senator Goldwater are also distributed. The group now plans to send their material to nonmember teachers in the state's high schools.

An address Mr. Chase made before the Charlottesville Rotary Club has been prepared as a pamphlet for distribution. Although a graduate of the University of Virginia and the Harvard Business School, Mr. Chase did not gear "Citizenship Challenges of the Sixties" for the academic community. Businessmen were familiar with the sources quoted: *U.S. News & World Report, Christian Economics,* and *Business Week;* and certainly with the authorities: Congressman Judd, Senators Goldwater, Dodd, and Thurmond—even a quote from George Washington. Page one warns that capitalism is "under attack from some political, labor, religious, and educational leaders." The major difficulty is that these people either do not understand or deliberately misrepresent the nature of the profit motive.

Mr. Chase also sees a little radical arsenic in each federal legislative proposal which is bringing us closer to socialism. What hurts is that "we are being bought with our own money." People are being continuously deceived by public welfare programs. "The Federal government cannot give the people anything it does not first take away from them by taxation, inflation, or expropriation." The really despairing thought, says Mr. Chase, is that neither the public schools nor the universities are doing an adequate job of grounding students in economics. This is why his group is so interested in reaching high schools.

Economic self-reliance is paramount with Mr. Chase who had even prepared a chart for his maid showing how much better off she would be if an amount equal to her Social Security deductions were privately invested. The failure of people to respond to the opportunities of investment is a source of both ideological and professional despair to Mr. Chase. Ayn Rand is extolled because she is excellent for reminding people of the value of profits. "We need a high-leveled far-Right exposition to soften up intellectuals." By this, Mr. Chase meant that Ayn Rand is very effective because she is so extreme. She shapes up the Left-wing intellectuals and deals with them on equal terms. This is precisely the way Miss Rand would prefer to picture herself operating—as a fermenting force consternating the Left.

Strategic considerations were strong with Mr. Chase. Just as Miss Rand is admired for her gadfly activities, "Human Events" is valued for its common-sense approach, and *National Review* is condemned as "a smug workshop of conservatives." Buckley's publication has too many intellectual pretentions, and this restricts its potential readership. These pretentions also deprive *National Review* of a proper perspective. It gets too wound up in itself. Somehow, says Mr. Chase, Buckley is going to have to strike a balance and stop pretending to be Kirk's *Modern Age*.

The one person who seems to have struck the balance Mr. Chase is looking for is Senator Goldwater. His only criticism of the Senator's policy positions is Goldwater's support of the Peace Corps.

On the community level, Mr. Chase is more interested in getting Right publications *in* the library than in getting Left-wing material out. Public libraries have a responsibility not only to stock Right-wing books but to display them. One difficulty with librarians, said Mr. Chase, is that they place too much faith in the book review section of the *New York Times* which is biased when it does get around to reviewing conservative authors.

Should the products of offending radio and television entertainers and commentators be boycotted? Mr. Chase said he always avoids Listerine products because of their sponsorship of liberal programs. "I believe in writing sponsors." This is to praise them for good programming and not merely to condemn. Mr. Chase would not fire a store clerk merely because he was a Communist. But he would not hire one.

Conservatives seem to be harder-working people, confided Mr. Chase. The trouble is they are too busy to take their place in public life. Consequently, too many of the lawyers who do run for office are not successful to begin with. Successful conservatives do not want to rock the boat by taking stands to the right of the public. This deplorable reluctance to take a firm position is true of presidents of corporations who are frequently uninformed about what their policy researchers are doing. It hurts to see these positions of conservative power unexploited.

Derwood Chase, who could talk of the advantages of investing in conservatism by the hour, is hopeful that Virginians for Conservative Government will continue to alert the faithful and convert the faithless to a turn to the Right.

G. F. FITZGERALD, ROCHESTER, NEW YORK

The local Young Republican chapter has never been conservative enough for Mr. G. F. Fitzgerald, so he never joined. He would rather stay home with his hi-fi jazz collection and read. Mr. Fitzgerald seems to fit the pattern of the "silent American" conservative voter for whom Senator Taft used to yearn. After a business degree from the University of Rochester, Fitzgerald settled into a suburb and the Credit Department of Eastman Kodak Company, which has avoided unionization by outpatronizing labor's demands. Given their profit-sharing plan, Kodak employees may well wonder what all the noise is about over at the Amalgamated Clothing Workers' Union hall.

It isn't that Fitzgerald keeps his views to himself. He doesn't hesitate to sound off at the office or "J.C." meeting, but his beliefs seldom kindle action. Somewhat chagrined, he admitted that he has written his congressman only twice. A poor joiner, Fitzgerald is not a member of any veterans', service, or civic group. If the new Conservative party in New York state becomes significant, he might join up, but he showed little enthusiasm for helping organize it. Although he styles himself "a bit more than moderately conservative," Fitzgerald has a relatively dispassionate approach to politics. This may be a result of his detachment from the heat of partisan battle.

"Human Events" was first given to him by a friend, and he has since sent a subscription to another friend. He admits that some of their articles have to be taken with a grain of salt, especially their buildup of General Walker. People like General Walker and Robert Welch represent conservatism's single biggest problem, he feels. They are the loudest propagandizers of Conservatism and give the impression that all conservatives are extremists. The "Kiplinger Newsletter" and the *Wall Street Jour-*

nal are read regularly. William Buckley, Jr., and the *National Review* were totally unknown to Mr. Fitzgerald. None of his conservative friends subscribed to *National Review*, as far as he knows, and Buckley's name never comes up. "Our conversation is mostly in terms of issues . . . we don't get too intellectual."

Yet Mr. Fitzgerald does read beyond newsletters. All of the enthusiasm not expended upon Welch or Buckley is showered upon Ayn Rand. He has read three of her novels and considers them "stimulating and forthright." Miss Rand's appeal, he admits, is not shared by all of his conservative friends. The stumbling block seems to be her atheism. Since Fitzgerald admits that he is generally lukewarm about religion, this does not trouble him. He does concede that Miss Rand tends to overidealize her characters. "Not enough people would be good enough at being complete egotists." Ayn Rand's major error is in believing that too many men are too perfect. But her emphasis on individual responsibility is refreshing. President Kennedy, he says, might well heed Miss Rand's warnings about catering to the masses. We are far too oriented toward Communism; our government already accepts the Marxian admonition "to each according to his needs." This is one of the major themes of *Atlas Shrugged*.

On civil rights, Mr. Fitzgerald reveals considerable tolerance which is often typical of the northern conservative. The federal government has a duty to guarantee the right to vote in national elections. Sit-ins are O.K. as long as they are peaceful. Not only do public restaurants have a responsibility to serve all orderly customers, says Fitzgerald, but it might be in order to pass state or local legislation to enforce this responsibility. This tolerance was not limited only to the race question.

The county district attorney had recently brought charges against a Rochester bookseller for stocking Henry Miller's *Tropic of Cancer*. The University of Rochester rallied to the bookseller's defense. Mr. Fitzgerald criticized the district attorney, whom he knew and admired as a former teacher, and backed the University on this issue. He felt the book should be available until a court had ruled it obscene. When asked about boycotting a product or business, he was undecided. Mr. Fitzgerald was not familiar with the activities of the American Civil Liberties Union. When told about them, the only objection he had was to the Union's call for abolition of the House Committee on Un-American Activities.

A friend had bought a copy of "Operation Abolition." "I borrowed it and showed it at a Friday noon presentation at Kodak." No one spoke against it at the time, and no formal provision had been made for rebuttal. He thought it was a good film. This seems to have been one of Mr. Fitzgerald's rare ventures into political activity, or perhaps he considered this more in the category of passing on a good book.

The most annoying thing about the liberals to Mr. Fitzgerald is their feeling that man owes his fellowmen a portion of his productive effort. Miss Rand's prompting has seldom been more obvious. But this self-regarding premise softened before the plight of the aging employee. A friend had suggested that aging employees losing their productivity should be dropped as a matter of cold efficiency. Fitzgerald objected. He would carry them along. "I can see the importance of the social question," he said. But in light of his Randian premise, such indulgence can never be a matter of right.

The importance of the social question is not merely whether the afflicted should get aid, but why. This is a basic question dividing liberals and conservatives. Why should the needy be helped? Fortified with the ethic of egotism, Mr. Fitzgerald can at least say, Because I feel like it! Economic conservatives looking for a less patronizing answer might find themselves hard pressed.

HERBERT S. RICHEY, CLEVELAND, OHIO

As the energetic president of a coal company, Herbert Richey performs the role of conscientious steward to both his church and his business. It is important to him to do a thorough job. Efficiency is crucial, whether he is installing a new machine at a mine or a retaining wall at his lake front home. He deliberately chose engineering as a background at Case Institute and the University of Michigan to prepare himself for business.

Government should reflect businesslike efficiency, too. He feels that the presidency is primarily a job for an administrator. Senator Goldwater may be an excellent administrator, but has yet to prove himself in this respect. He must be able to convince conservatives that he can do more than make good speeches. George Humphrey, Eisenhower's Secretary of the Treasury, would have made a fine President. So would Tom Dewey. The coupling of Humphrey and Dewey emphasizes that their important common quality is their proved administrative skill. Poor management policies have ruined many businesses, says Mr. Richey; it should be obvious what can happen to government.

A very solicitous regard for property rights came out in a discussion of sit-ins. Mr. Richey considers sit-ins immoral as well as illegal. When his church appealed for support of ministers arrested in sit-in demonstrations, Mr. Richey was a vocal dissenter in his Bay Village church. The clergy, he felt, had no right to sanction this violation of state law. Mr. Richey is of the firm conservative belief that those who own property are entitled to the right to develop their property as they see fit, so long as it is not made into a public nuisance, and that property owners should at least be equal under the laws to nonproperty owners.

Although not too familiar with the American Civil Liberties Union, Mr. Richey has no strong objection to its purposes as they were explained to him by the author. His main gripe with the so-called "liberals" is that they seem to be largely ignorant of American business—the fact that business creates jobs, pays wages, develops new products, pays taxes, and has contributed so much to the growth and development of the United States. He feels that business is losing its ability to do this through unreasonable taxes, some of the proceeds of which seem to be used for the support of inexperienced egghead liberals who think up new ways to destroy business through taxation. Mr. Richey would like to ask every liberal, "At what point do you stop taxing incentive?"

The cultural conservative's concern about civic beautification does not especially move Mr. Richey. The millions that the Cleveland Museum was spending on paintings could be put to better use. "Those paintings would be just as happy in Paris or

London." Public buildings should be functional. There is no need for frills and extras. The work on a new water processing plant on the city's outskirts annoyed Mr. Richey. He alleged that the local politicians were using marble to memorialize themselves architecturally. One wondered what Athenian coal merchants said about the local politician, Pericles, hauling all that marble up on the hill. Mr. Richey's comment was that Pericles and his group frittered away Greece's assets, building monuments instead of developing resources, business, and trade. This policy contributed to Greece's financial ruin and eventual domination by Rome. The Romans became monument builders, destroyed their economy and went broke. The United States seems to be following the ancients' policies to economic ruin.

One of the frills that disturbs Mr. Richey and a good many other people is Ohio's emphasis on band music in the public schools. In Ohio a high school is not fully accredited unless it has a band room. Seldom has progressive education left itself more vulnerable to ridicule.

Anti-Communism does not play a prominent part in Herbert Richey's conservatism. "Communist," he believes, has become too convenient a dirty word. The John Birch Society has gone overboard in exaggerating the threat of Communists in our government by its failure to prove specific cases. The more the Communists speak, the better they will be known. To hear them out is to expose their follies and failures. Nor should their books be censored. When pressed about an economic boycott of Communists, Mr. Richey quickly moved from an ideological to an economic justification. He had no objection to trading with them on a gold or dollar, paid-in-advance, basis.

Mr. Richey was not familiar with the Young Americans for Freedom and is generally skeptical about any splinter movement. He was also not familiar with William Buckley and his *National Review*, and as far as he knew none of his friends read it. So far no one has sent him a subscription to "Human Events," which he has not read. Someone did send him the *Manion Letter* for a year; "but I did not contribute, and it stopped." He does contribute to the Committee on Economic Development and receives their literature regularly.

Although he had not read Ayn Rand's *Atlas Shrugged*, he

sounded intrigued by the plot and jotted down the title. Mr. Richey prefers *Time, Life,* and the *Wall Street Journal* for news, relaxes with *Antiques* magazine, *The National Fisherman,* and *The New Yorker.* He also reads periodicals relating to his business, including the United Mine Workers' *Journal.*

Other than his church, the only organization in which Mr. Richey considers himself active is the Young Presidents Organization. Members must have become presidents under the age of forty in businesses with gross sales of at least one million dollars annually. Occasionally a chapter will sponsor lectures on politics. One evening "Operation Abolition" was shown back-stopped by HUA Committeeman Scherer from Cincinnati. This was balanced by the appearance of a State Department specialist who is the United States Information Agency's answer to Doctor Fred Schwarz and gives a very sane picture of Communism.

Except for sending opinions and clippings to his Congressman, minister, and friends, Herbert Richey remains politically passive. He contributes money to his party but not time. Somehow political conservatism has to think of a way of enlisting men with the ability and moderation of Mr. Richey.

FREDERICK J. WALKER,
READING, PENNSYLVANIA

Mr. Walker was the youngest and probably the most angry of the young businessmen interviewed. He is just setting up his own photography studio, but business does not appear to be his primary concern. His major criticism of conservatism today is that it tends to emphasize economics too much. "Creeping socialism" he considers to be a tired phrase. Ayn Rand's capitalistic egotist he feels is as bad as complete collectivism. Sidney Hook was quoted with favor for saying that there can be many ways to solve economic problems. We have no monopoly on solutions.

"My sympathy for big business has declined," he admitted. The price-fixing episodes unsettled him. Frederick now suggests that the righteous articles businessmen are fond of publishing in national magazines will have to be taken with a grain of salt. But the major difficulty with businessmen is that they do not fully understand the nature of the Communist threat. This is demonstrated by their willingness to support party candidates and issues but their reluctance to contribute to anti-Communist organizations and causes. The central issue is Communism.

This does not mean that Mr. Walker favors extremist organizations. He has no use for the Birch Society. "Conservatism will not prosper by secret cells or fronts, only by open debate . . . Welch confuses *his* enemy with *the* enemy." The last remark apparently refers to Welch's tending to make the New Deal the enemy.

Only conservatism can defeat Communism. The liberals have tried and failed. Conservatives have a more positive program, Frederick insisted. Then he repeated the Right-wing commonplaces of foreign policy. Limit foreign assistance to military aid. "Give Chiang Kai-shek almost anything he asks for." Sympathize with the colonial powers. Don't be afraid of precipitating World War III; we're in it. Tear down the Berlin wall. We must dare to win.

What about civil liberties in the United States? "I'm more concerned about slavery in Hungary," Mr. Walker replied. The subject of social equality did not especially interest him. Mr. Walker admitted that if he were a Negro, he would think differently; but he wasn't. The American Civil Liberties Union may be tolerated, but he could never support it. Library books written by Communists should be labeled to protect the unwary. He would write a sponsor to urge him to drop a Communist television entertainer, and he certainly would boycott the sponsor's product if he refused to take action. How about a professed Communist employed as a clerk in a store? "I would refuse to trade there."

Except for two years at a photographic institute, Mr. Walker has had no formal college training. Equipped with considerable native intelligence and an active curiosity, he has read in all directions and acquired the easy confidence of the self-educated. He has a quick conservative opinion for every issue and is impatient with those who cannot see the obvious futility of the liberal position.

However, it is important to Mr. Walker to feel that he is

arriving at his opinions independently. During the confusion over the Syrian revolution, Mr. Walker discovered that he was eagerly awaiting the next issue of *National Review* to find out the editorial line. He became alarmed at how dependent he was becoming and allowed his subscription to lapse. He also believed that *National Review* was lending its mailing list to organizations of a questionable nature, such as the American Committee on France and Algeria. When he first stumbled upon *National Review*, he thought it was a Left-wing publication because it seemed so literate. Generally, he feels the Right-wing press is limited by the low caliber of its journalism. "Human Events" is typical. It is too long-winded, especially the articles it turns out as special supplements. "I am for it but not with it."

The *New York Times* has an intolerable bias, says Walker. It is forever lumping together people like Buckley and Rockwell. Their "hate campaign" against Doctor Fred Schwarz is a sore point. First the *Times* tried silence and then distortion to discredit one of America's most effective anti-Communists. Also the *New York Times* never admits an error. Their silence on correspondent Matthews being so wrong about Castro is an example of this. The *New York Times* has taken the lead in the liberal distortion of the American Right.

Religion does not play a part in Mr. Walker's conservatism. He comes from a mixed religious background and considers himself a nominal Protestant who has not yet worked out an acceptable religious viewpoint. Communism is not feared because of its atheism but because of its political tyranny. He regards the religious anti-Communism of someone like Reverend Billy James Hargis as pathetic and a great disservice to the entire Right wing. At the same time Walker condemns the National Council of Churches for its excessive liberalism and was outraged when the National Council welcomed the Moscow Metropolitan when he visited the United States. This is the prelate who had signed a statement alleging that the United States was using germ warfare in Korea.

In politics Mr. Walker prefers to work through the Young Republicans. He has no particular objection to the new Conservative party in New York State, but Pennsylvania has no need of one. It does not have New York's problem with liberal Republicans. The Young Americans for Freedom are doing a commendable job, but they have not been careful enough in checking the connections of their board members with extremist groups.

The government's primary function, Mr. Walker thinks, is national defense. Its domestic functions should be confined pretty much to internal security. Offhand, he could not think of anything of the New Deal that he would like to retain. Although Mr. Walker himself is relatively sophisticated aesthetically, he can not see that the government has any responsibility in this field. If Seagrams wants to build expensive architecturally beautiful buildings, let them. The government does not have to compete here. This comes from a young man who drives a Saab and likes classical music.

As can be seen from his views on the *National Review* and Hargis, Walker adheres to a critical conservatism which demands clean hands of those who would be effective anti-Communists. Economic individualism is a dormant part of Frederick Walker's conservatism. It is overshadowed by the political warfare against Communism as personified in his latest hero, Doctor Fred Schwarz. The primacy of anti-Communism as an issue gives Walker's conservatism its urgency. Walker's dilettantish reading gives him an assurance which can easily edge urgency into militancy.

JOHN D. KELLY,
WORCESTER, MASSACHUSETTS

By the time of the 1956 election, John Kelly was convinced that Eisenhower's major objective was to refashion the GOP in the image of F.D.R. Any differences that had existed between the two parties could now only be the subject of stale jokes. Both parties were leading the country straight to you know where. John entered a political limbo. Although he had never been an active participant in politics, even such interest as he had was now deadened by despair. It didn't look as if anything could help.

Two of John's brothers first became interested in the John

Birch Society. One of them ended up working in the Belmont home office. John waded in with more caution. His wife is partly responsible for this hesitation. When the *Blue Book* first appeared in the living room, she raised the question of Robert Welch's reliability. But John became convinced that no program gets anywhere without an ambitious man and that you did not have to fear Welch's kind of ambition. "Welch might not be the best available man, but no one else has proved to be any better." He signed up.

How about the strong accusations of the "Black Book"? John admitted that few members of the society were permitted to read the book and that it would be much better if Welch would publish the thing. As for the charges against Eisenhower, well, he was a very naïve man and certainly was used. Is the United States 40 to 60 percent Communist? "I would say that socialist and collectivist control is that high," and, he added, socialism always leads to Communism and a police state. Socialism can never remain democratic.

John's chapter of the society is less than a year old. Another Worcester chapter is composed of professional people. His has more small businessmen. John himself is starting a chamois importing business but is of very modest means and lives in a typical Worcester tenement. There are no life members ($1,000.00) in his chapter. A couple of priests do attend regularly. Aside from letter-writing and promoting "Operation Abolition," the group has confined itself to planning a reading room for Worcester. John Kelly at thirty-three is the youngest member of his chapter.

Not all the chapter members subscribe to *American Opinion.* John has only recently subscribed. His older brother keeps him supplied with copies of "Human Events." He has canceled his subscription to *Time* but still takes *United States News & World Report.* When asked which liberal magazine he felt had the fairest presentation, he replied, *Newsweek. The Nation* was casually referred to as a Communist magazine. Despite the blast the Birch Society received from the *National Review,* John still reads it, but he has some interesting objections.

"The *National Review* is anti-Labor, and I am not, although I don't like Big Unions." Then he went on to make the remarkable statement that Buckley and his group represent nineteenth century economic liberalism "which I don't like." Back in the early nineteenth century, he said, conservatism could have oriented itself around labor instead of capital. By becoming too exclusively concerned with capital, conservatism became too materialistic. "It did not have enough Christian concern for those who can not make the grade economically because of mental or other limitations." Slackers are one thing. Those who try and fail are another.

This was an unexpected admission of agrarian conservatism, and Mr. Kelly did not shy away from the phrase. "Yes, I guess it is." This criticism of economic conservatism seems to be prompted by religious feeling. As a sincere Catholic, John feels that social ethics should be determined more by religious influences. This could have made John a dedicated social reformer. But this road was blockaded by the conservative preconceptions of his time. The family had always been Republican and anti-New Deal. This precluded any "collective" or government-organized remedy to social injustice. So limited, a conscience pricked by religious impulse had to confine itself to exhortations to private charity. The meager response can be frustrating.

This residual respect for labor and distrust of finance capitalism recalls Peter Viereck's contention that McCarthyism can be explained in terms of populism. "McCarthy first convinced me of the dangers of the liberal position," said Mr. Kelly. The Senator showed the extent of collectivist control of our national policy.

There is a belligerent nationalism. "We can take on both China and Russia. We are strong enough." All foreign aid should be limited to military assistance to our proved allies. We should get out of the United Nations and limit all international organizations to trade and travel. Nuclear testing should never have been interrupted. Mr. Kelly spoke of the demonstrated health hazard of fluoridation of the water supply but feared nothing from nuclear fallout in the atmosphere. "Most conservatives," concluded Mr. Kelly, "think the same about foreign policy."

"There is a high sense of conspiracy. Chancellor Adenauer was willing to allow Spanish forces to use German bases in aiding the Hungarian Freedom Fighters, until our State Department objected. Franklin Roosevelt deliberately broke the country up into conflicting classes and groups. Grafting bureaucrats connive to extend their power. The press maliciously distorts our activities," says Mr. Kelly.

Yet at the same time, there is a strong regard for democratic observances. Fred Schwarz is condemned as too extreme a demagogue for the Birch Society. Mr. Kelly takes a dim view of boycotts and censorship. He condones sit-ins. William Buckley is felt to be "way out" in his implicit defense of segregation. However, John does admit that he does not consider the Supreme Court decision as law. "How can nine men we don't even elect make a law?" Peter Viereck has heard a good many populists ask this question.

Probably the unique feature of John Kelly's social thinking is the extent to which religion has played a role. This has given him a rare view of capitalism. As he puts it, "It makes my conservatism less cut and dried."

CHAPTER 15

The Young Intellectual Decides

CONSERVATISM can be taken at two levels. One may be called "common-sense" conservatism. This is a visceral, unreflective, highly intuitive variety which is perfectly content with what has been called a "theory of the first look." It has immense confidence, if not conceit, and tends to be impatient with those who do not accept the simple and obvious conclusions to which their own hasty glances have led them. Their constitutions cannot stand too rich a diet of theory, which they prefer in packaged, condensed, and digested form, when it is absolutely necessary.

Reflective conservatism, on the other hand, is more theoretical, rational, and likes to push issues back to first principles. It is more temperate, prudent, and aware of complexity. These are two moods which will vary with the temperament and intellectuality of each conservative.

The libertarian or what I have called "propertarian" school of conservatism is more apt to exhibit the common-sense mood,

almost overwhelmingly so. The traditionalist school is more reflective although it frequently relies heavily upon intuition.
Within each school there may well be a different emphasis of
mood depending on the issue at hand. The libertarian, however,
generally prefers the common-sense mood, if only because so
many of his problems can be reduced to considerations of
property, about which there must be no nonsense.

Most young conservative men in business and politics reflect
this common-sense mood and are libertarian by preference. With
the possible exceptions of Congressman Goodell and Frederick
Walker, this was true of all the young congressmen and businessmen interviewed. Congressman Dorn's libertarianism is moder-
ated in places by traditionalism, and Derwood Chase's common-
sense mood is relieved by considerable reflection, but all remain
essentially common-sense libertarian conservatives.

If conservatism is to maintain a healthy balance, it needs
more of an infusion of reflective traditionalism. This requires the
efforts of conservative intellectuals who must be recruited mainly
from the universities. The Intercollegiate Society of Individualists would be in a position to help, but its literature is pre-
dominantly economic libertarian, as are virtually all of the
publications read by young conservatives.

The well edited student efforts such as *Gentlemen of the
Right, Insight and Outlook*, and *New Individualist Review* reflect
more of the traditionalist emphasis, but they are still outread by
YAF's *New Guard. Modern Age*, formerly edited by Russell
Kirk, comes the nearest to a traditionalist emphasis, but it has
a very limited circle among young conservatives.

The new libertarian conservatism offers the young conservative a parody of traditionalism. Tradition itself is replaced
by vindictive iconoclasm. Phariseeism bows as Christianity. The
non sequitur parades as reason. Voluntaryism atrophies as indifference (especially in civil liberties). Prudence is traduced as
jingoism. Harmony is slandered as conformity, and community
emerges as States' rights.

Even if the young conservative should concentrate on a
traditionalist defense of his position, he faces formidable obstacles. First of all, he would not encounter a systematic political

theorist until he went back to Hobbes. If the conservatives are serious about fabricating something akin to a Tory attitude toward politics, Hobbes would be more substantial and productive fare than Burke, who is merely an impresario by comparison. From another tack, much could be done with Christian political theory which avoids the tired conclusions of laissez-faire economics and politics (for example, civil rights).

Then there is the problem of communication, not just with liberals, but with his fellow conservatives. In many ways, the new libertarian conservatives could be grounded more quickly by an honest application of traditionalism than by the most formidable liberal arguments. They apparently realize this and seldom take traditionalist critics seriously. Peter Viereck is a typical prophet without honor within the conservative camp, so is Rossiter— both of whom are here classified as moderate traditionalists.

As long as the young intellectual prefers Buckley to Viereck, the conservative insurrection is never going to get in off the streets.

A popular confusion which should not mislead the young intellectual is the tendency to equate conservatism and anti-Communism. Without the cloak of anti-Communism, the surly nationalism of the Right wing would be an embarrassment. It would pay the young intellectual to examine some of the sources of anti-Communism to see what and whom he is incidentally supporting. The organizations briefly examined in this book suggest some of the possibilities.

It must be remembered that the much-advertised YAF rally in Madison Square Garden was staged as an anti-Communist rally which solicited support beyond the conservative camp. Crowds of course are deceiving. For example, the rally delegation from Princeton numbered ninety, but only fifteen were members of YAF. Ben Davis at the University of Oregon demonstrated that he could match the turnouts of Senator Goldwater. Everyone loves a circus.

The conservative movement cannot feed upon anti-Communism indefinitely. As things are, an enterprising young conservative probably couldn't find a Communist on a scavenger hunt. It is just as well that the domestic menace has receded. The "libertarian's" indifference to the niceties of civil liberties was not winning many converts, and it is probable that his foreign policy will have the same effect.

An erosion of student idealism in foreign affairs is called realism. What promising reality will emerge from reducing conservative support of the United Nations to 20 percent, as has been done? W. D. Ross insists that "Idealism is the power of seeing ideal elements in the actual, in preference to destroying the actual in the hope of finding it elsewhere." Just who is the moral vandal?

Tocsin is a liberal group of students organized by Peter Goldmark at Harvard. Twenty students were recruited to spend a summer working in Tanganyika and they even learned Swahili. Meanwhile *National Review* ridicules the Peace Corps. An army of 5,000 students descended on Washington in February, 1962, to protest resumption of nuclear testing. The conservatives claim we should never have stopped. The NSA by unanimous vote acclaims the Algerian rebels. YAF supports the French. In each case the conservatives tried to buck the tide of student idealism.

This is something like saying let's try to take over the GOP by promising to abolish free enterprise. The conservative activists seem determined to explode idealism in the student's face. All this balloon busting makes a lot of noise but not many friends. If the conservative continues to find student idealism an obstacle, he is indeed playing a losing game.

Conservatist "realism" may have some unfortunate consequences democratically. The Opinion Research Corporation put the following proposition to conservatives in eighteen colleges: "What this country needs most, more than laws or political programs, is a few courageous, tireless, devoted leaders, in whom the people can put their faith." Forty-nine percent of the club officers agreed while 53 percent of the nonofficers agreed.

It may be that the conservative's emphasis on individual moral regeneration gives him a stronger theory of leadership than the liberal. Studies cited in this book indicate the conservative is more prone toward authority. However, we have no liberal reaction to the above proposition. On the author's poll, liberals and conservatives were evenly split on giving more votes to people with more education, although no liberals and 20 percent of the conservatives wanted to do the same for property.

Also, conservatives were more distrustful generally of public opinion (70 percent versus 58 percent of liberals). What these figures do suggest is that the conservatives may be more tempted to jump the rules of the game, and their extremely low concern for civil liberties (8 percent support of ACLU) sustains the doubt.

Once again anti-Communism has intruded to obscure the conservative's sensitivity to civil liberties. His militant defense of loyalty oaths, HUAC, "Operation Abolition," his indulgence of extremists and his nonchalance toward the Negro's plight make his loud talk about natural rights sound hollow. As Father John Kelly of Dayton University formulated it " '. . . all men are created with certain inalienable rights,' among them the right to a good name."

All of which seems to suggest that the word "propertarian" is an appropriate description of this libertarian conservative. Even when he champions free association, he means "right to work" laws. He refuses to heed H. S. Commager's wisdom that the only free enterprise is intellectual enterprise.

The libertarian conservative must stop this nonsense about being the only champion of individualism, since neither he nor the liberal can agree on what "self-realization" or "freedom" means. Let's propose a test: Which side leaves more freedom around unused? The young intellectual will decide. As he does, perhaps he should be reminded of the counsel of Bernard Bosanquet: "Truth must be many-sided; and what is many-sided is always liable to be wrongly grasped, and is quite easy to caricature."

At the risk of caricature, I would conclude that the present rise of conservatism among the young is in part the result of an ambivalent attitude the American middle class has harbored toward the New Deal. Never completely sold on its ethic of social justice, but receiving its benefits, the middle class has always been susceptible to arguments that the New Deal somehow represents a betrayal of moral individualism.

No one touches this sensitive nerve more effectively than

Senator Barry Goldwater, a regular guy with a conscience many middle-class citizens feel they should have. William Buckley's rise to prominence was nurtured by this same uneasy conscience. This young man from Yale was also able to keep alive the Mc-Carthyist legacy of suspicion in a very nice sort of way.

Being checkmated in a cold war, feeling your strength and yet not being able to use it, contributed a mood of exasperation which is not difficult to manipulate. Meanwhile, as the teachers say, the American public is "doing a unit" on anti-Communism.

Finally, there is the factor of giving the conservative underdog a hearing. This is still going on, and it is well financed, organized, and publicized by people who realize the unique confluence of events and opportunity.

Consequently, many of the conservative-prone young are receiving overtures and encouragement they never had before. The New Conservatism has given a backbone and voice to those who were already right of center and there are still many more to be aroused here. They are consolidating the ranks of the liberals (if that is possible) and getting virtually nowhere with the uncommitted. It is not fashionable to be a conservative on campus. Political apathy is still the fashion with an occasional response to an idealistic cause. In the vast majority of schools the faculty, deans, chaplains, and ethos are still predominently liberal, and with very few exceptions, the New Conservative is regarded as a little odd. His economic liberalism is considered discredited and his foreign policy cuts across the grain of student idealism.

The young New Conservatives may yet ride the heights of a bullish market, but eventually they will be seeking the cool comfort of debenture holders in the Liberty League.

Index

307